The Winner's Way

*A Proven Method for
Achieving Your Personal Best
in Any Situation*

Dr. Pam Brill

McGraw-Hill

*New York   Chicago   San Francisco
Lisbon   London   Madrid   Mexico City
Milan   New Delhi   San Juan   Seoul
Singapore   Sydney   Toronto*

Praise for *The Winner's Way*

"If you think that *The Winner's Way* sounds like pop psychology, you are in for a wonderful surprise. Pam Brill's work and writing is authentic, insightful, original, and grounded in solid research. The bonus is that she writes from both her head and heart. If you want to change the way you relate, collaborate, or lead, this volume should be one of your primers."

—Terry Pearce, University of California, Berkeley;
London Business School, Author of *Leading Out Loud*

"Pam Brill uncovers the secret formula for achieving new levels of personal best. An adaptable, intuitive model, architected from years of research and clinical experience, *The Winner's Way* is the 'prescription' for anyone eager to live life in their peak performance Zone."

—Susan Underhill, Vice President, Global Channel
Programs, Hewlett-Packard Company

"As a business leader, sports coach, and athlete, I read reams of books on achieving peak results in competitive business and sport. Dr. Brill has succeeded in writing the first business book I've encountered that can help business professionals, athletes, and families reach their full potential. Everyone should read this book! Whether you are involved in a business or not, this is a must-read if you want to achieve greater heights."

—Tom Raffio, CEO, Northeast Delta Dental;
Fellow, Life Management Institute

"How can you focus your mental and emotional energy so that you actually can live the life of a winner—whatever 'winning' means to you? Just put yourself in Dr. Pam Brill's special care and you'll enter—and stay in—the Zone, and live the life you've imagined."

—Gail Blanke, President, Lifedesigns; author of
*Between Trapezes, Flying Through Life's
Transitions with the Greatest of Ease*

"*The Winner's Way* provides practical techniques and strategies that everyone can use to get into the peak performance zone at work, in sports, and for all the extraordinary and mundane daily challenges that life throws us. This is a terrific book for any individual, team, or organization that aspires to give their all to be a high performer."

—Robert Kriegel, Ph.D., author of *How to Succeed in Business without Working so Damn Hard* and *Sacred Cows Make the Best Burgers: Developing Change-ready People and Organizations*

1 2 3 4 5 6 7 8 9 0   AGM/AGM   0 1 0 9 8 7 6 5 4

ISBN 0-07-142363-X

This publication is designed to provide accurate and authoritative information in regard to the subject matter covered. It is sold with the understanding that neither the author nor the publisher is engaged in rendering legal, accounting, or other professional service. If legal advice or other expert assistance is required, the services of a competent professional person should be sought.

> —*From a Declaration of Principles jointly adopted by Committee of the American Bar Association and a Committee of Publishers.*

McGraw-Hill books are available at special quantity discounts to use as premiums and sales promotions, or for use in corporate training programs. For more information, please write to the Director of Special Sales, McGraw-Hill Professional, Two Penn Plaza, New York, NY 10121-2298. Or contact your local bookstore.

Library of Congress Cataloging-in-Publication Data

Brill, Pamela.
    The winner's way : a proven method for achieving your personal best in any situation / Pamela Brill.—1st ed.
        p. cm.
    Includes bibliographical references.
    ISBN 0-07-142363-X (hardcover : alk. paper)
    1. Achievement motivation.   2. Success—Psychological aspects.   3. Self-actualization (Psychology)   4. Motivation (Psychology)   I. Title.
  BF503.B74   2004
  158.1—dc22

                                                                  2004000785

Contents

Acknowledgments

First, this book is dedicated to my parents, Stan and Rita Brill, and to their parents, Justin and Katrina Brill, Louise and Phillip DeDominicis.

Then there is the wonderful family of mine that has held down the fort during the decade-long evolution of ideas into a book—my husband, Bill Voorhees, and our daughters—Katrina, Julia, Maggie, and Sophie, student-athletes and young women of whom I am unboundedly proud.

My support team of readers deserves applause: Dan Bloom, industrial designer credited for the book's figures; Eric Haas; Nat Niles, M.D.; Barbara Tellerman, M.D.; Sue Bee; Floranne Hammond; Susan Suffes; Mark Griffith.

I have learned from amazing people: Mr. Galloway, Diedrick Snoek, Ph.D.; Doctors Bill and Irene Mehnert; Stan Rosenberg, Ph.D., and Harriet Rosenberg, M.A.; Gary Tucker, M.D.; Nick Verven, Ph.D., and Carol Verven, M.A; Josie Harper, Dartmouth Athletic Director; Dartmouth coaches including: Jim Wilson, Julie Dayton, Amy Patton; Weems Westfeldt and Hans Hohl at Aspen-Snowmass Ski School; Terry Pearce. Thank you to friends and business associates: Susan Duprey; Pam Patenaude; Susan Underhill; Joel Goldstein, Ph.D; Susan Aaronson; Brian Johnson; Tom Raffio, Connie Roy-Czyzowski, Northeast Delta Dental; "Mrs. Brown," Linda, who tended the home front.

Thank you to my literary agent, Jim Levine and assistant Melynda Bissmeyer, and McGraw-Hill's editor extraordinaire, Nancy Hancock, and assistant, Meg Leder.

I extend a huge thank you to the researchers whose work grounds my ideas, including Bob Nideffer and Dave Givens.

I am grateful to all of the people with whom I have consulted—individuals, teams, and organizations who opened their hearts and minds to seeing and doing things differently. To those who venture into these pages, I say—Go for it—look forward, move ahead, get in the Zone. Life's too short to live it anywhere else.

Introduction

From Surviving to Thriving in Times of High Stress

There is no getting around it. We live in a time of extreme stress.

While it might feel strange to us, rugged times like these are nothing new. Throughout the ages, people have been confronted by disasters, natural and manmade, economic downturns, and the horrific damage we human beings can inflict on each other and on ourselves. Our turn has dawned.

Now, more than ever, we long to move beyond merely surviving, with background stress that will not quit, to thriving. We yearn to be free to fully commit to living purposefully. We want to get into "the Zone," where we *willfully* engage each moment, even in the face of daunting danger. *The Winner's Way* provides a simple, proven system to engage your own heart and mind and commit the resources of your body to best meet the challenges of life.

The quest for the competitive edge that has enabled people to prevail over extraordinary circumstances is a basic human instinct that crosses cultures and millennia. Our natural thirst for answers took ancient Greeks as far as Delphi on once-in-a-lifetime pilgrimages to consult with the Oracle, whose gaseous fumes imbued knowledge of self and inner harmony. Today's pilgrims venture to Buddhist meditation grounds, where the power of being present, here and now, is far removed from the fast pace of modern living. Modern wayfarers take daily virtual treks to *Amazon.com*, trying to ferret out the one correct way, of 1001 possibilities, that can provide the ticket to excellence.

The cure, however, has never been external. Just as the Oracle suggested, it is within. The solution to turning even life-threatening events around is in knowing yourself and accessing the power of will to purposefully connect with any challenge that life might present. In *The Winner's Way*, I will teach you a unique, research-grounded, and field-tested system to genuinely connect with each moment in order to achieve your personal bests in any situation, no matter how ordinary or extraordinary your life might be.

I'm not suggesting that you will always win. But you will be tuned in to the three critical processes within you that, when aligned at personally correct levels, lead to personal bests. Whatever the circumstances, you will know how to access the correct level of energy, tune in to the essentials, and examine assumptions and beliefs that might be outdated and getting in your way. You will be in the Zone of engagement for living life willfully.

It's as Simple as 3 A's

I've traversed varied terrain during the past 20-some years as a psychologist—from street corners with juvenile offenders to corner offices with Fortune 500 executives, from ski slopes with elite athletes and others just wanting to enjoy the ride, to manufacturing plants with hardworking people doing a good day's work. My clients and seminar participants have confronted life-altering and life-threatening challenges as well as the grinding daily hassles at work, home, and on the roadways, events that are capable of throwing any of us off our best game. They needed a reliable way to solve their problems on the run, a simple system for achieving their personal bests at will, consistently, anywhere, and anytime. And so did I.

So I developed the system I call *The Winner's Way*, based on my consulting in clinical, sports, and business settings and teaching during 14 years as an adjunct faculty member at Dartmouth Medical School. This system is supported by research in peak performance in business, sports, stress, and the neurosciences. I concluded that there are three elements that exist within each of us at all times, and that are within your control. *Activation, attention,* and *attitude*—"the 3 A's" of *The Winner's Way*—are the three omnipresent factors that determine how you feel and how you do.

Activation is the physical and physiological part of your experience; attention includes those things that you choose from your internal and external world that become your personal reality, and attitude consists of your guiding values and your beliefs and assumptions. Existing between the things that happen to you and how you respond, these three elements are the result of the unique way your brain is formed and the distinctive chemical balance resulting from the "things that happen" to you. The 3 A's are what you feel when your brain and body collaborate to produce thousands of natural chemical reactions in response to the multitude of things you encounter, including the thoughts you generate.

The 3 A's collaborate to determine what you perceive and how you view it—good, bad, neutral, or marvelous. When all three are aligned to the situation in a good personal fit, people connect to the real deal to achieve their best outcomes and feel their best, even when they are coping with circumstances that really are frightening, events that legitimately engender anger, or losses that warrant sadness. When any one of the three is mismatched to the situation, poorer outcomes are accompanied by miserable feelings, ranging from mild irritability to full fury, from feeling blue to apathy or depression. But it doesn't have to be that way.

Why Now? Timing Is Almost Everything and the Time Is Now

You're either in the Zone, totally engaged, or you're not. Living a rewarding life in the Zone is no longer merely a choice. Now, with expanding demands, shrinking resources, and a desire to make the most of life's time, it's a responsibility. Learning how to get into and stay in the Zone for every circumstance is a true necessity. With the 3 A's, the choice is yours.

That's why *The Winner's Way* is more timely than ever. Every one of us wants to rise to meet and triumph over the challenges ahead—whatever they might be. At the same time, each of us must deal with dozens of daily tests and obstacles. These can range from unexpected downsizing that shakes up your life and rattles your self-esteem, to news-generated visions of destruction and doom, to everyday routines like driving your kids to school in the rain. Some of them, like a diagnosis of a serious illness, can instantly alter your life.

I know that being in the Zone is imperative in order to overcome setbacks, big and small. Living in the Zone is a way of life. You can live there too with "the 3 A's" of *The Winner's Way.*

Chapter 1

A Zone for All Seasons—
And an O-Zone Too

GAME PLAN

At any moment, you're either "in the Zone" or you're not. What is the Zone and what is the o-Zone?

The Zone isn't about competing, winning, or sports—there is a Zone for all seasons.

Three critical elements distinguish the Zone from the o-Zone—"the 3 A's" of *The Winner's Way*.

In the Zone for Living Willfully

What do the following have in common?

- Managing a team of 20 who used to be your peers
- Frosty cold sales calls
- Connecting with your kids in genuine conversation

- Battling it out to represent your clients in the courtroom
- Navigating a downhill ski racecourse at breakneck speeds
- Getting yourself out of the door on time in the morning
- Operating as part of a surgical team
- Choosing and undergoing state-of-the-art surgery and postsurgical treatments to confront cancer head-on
- Implementing an organizationwide, competitive strategy to maintain market share in the face of new competitors with innovative, low-cost ways of doing business that you never saw coming
- Commuting in traffic

They are all life challenges that had the potential to set my clients soaring to reach achievements beyond their wildest dreams. They have also been powerful enough to send them spinning toward results that were disappointing, disastrous, and sometimes even deadly. And those are just a few of the ordinary and extraordinary life challenges where my clients have learned to apply the 3 A's of *The Winner's Way* to engage fully to create personal bests. You can learn to get in the Zone for living fully too. It's as strategic as 3 A's.

The Competitive Courts

For Tom, *The Winner's Way* gave him the strategies for taking control of his racing pulse and for connecting with his heart to rebuild relationships with colleagues, employees, and family members. Plus, he rekindled his passion for his driving experiences.

A self-avowed doubting Thomas, Tom was a lawyer with more than 20 years of victorious courtroom experiences. He was good at it. Now Tom was struggling, not during his daytime competitions but in the privacy of his home where his racing heart, rising blood pressure, and fast-forward breathing alerted him that he was having a heart attack—

every night. But all of the diagnostic tests had ruled out any indication of heart problems. Aligning his 3 A's gave Tom the power to calm his heart on the road, at his office, in the courtroom, and even at home.

Once Tom took control of the three crucial elements of *The Winner's Way*, he recaptured his love for the game of life, even in heavy traffic. Tom developed a new outlook on life and realigned his heartbeat to match the actual situations facing him. He learned to review his situations and reevaluate his assumptions about how the world should be, whether it was how fellow commuters drove, the way his administrative assistant greeted him in the morning, or how his kids spoke to him at dinner.

Tom's relationships improved. His kids wanted to spend time with him again, and his newest administrative assistant continued to work with him past the average three-month stay of her predecessors. Tom's wife remembered why she had married him, and his colleagues renewed their confidence in his leadership abilities. Tom even got rid of the attacks on his heart. And his doctor, the physician who originally referred Tom to see me, got to see the World Series instead of spending his evening hours in the Emergency Room.

The Head of the Table

Then there was Mary, so talented at engineering that she was appointed to head a team of her former peers. But Mary, in her early thirties, had no experience at being a leader. And many of "the guys" on the team had been around the company and had more lifetime years under their belts than Mary did..

No wonder Mary was a self-proclaimed "nervous wreck" when it came time to sit at the head of the conference table. Compromised by the "stress makes you stupid" hormones surging through her system, Mary's palms sweat so much that they turned her feet cold and wet. Feeling tongue-tied in this new leadership role, Mary found it difficult to delegate work to the team members who used to be her peer group. So she ended up doing most of it herself, leaving no time for the managerial tasks that were her new job.

Luckily, Mary realized that she was sabotaging herself when she broke her lucky power pen. Believing that the pen was what supplied her with intelligent insights and the ability to express them, Mary had vice-gripped this pen like she was holding on for dear life. When the pen cracked, Mary knew she was near her own breaking point. It was time to follow up on her boss's suggestion. She came in for leadership coaching and developed her Winner's Way.

Winner's Way strategies provided Mary with a road map to chart her way through this undesirable territory. She was able to choose routes that were effective and long lasting. First she learned to keep her energy in bounds for listening actively and responding thoughtfully—without strangling a pen. In the comfort of our consultations, Mary took a time-out to look realistically at the strengths that she brought to the leader's seat. And she worked on ditching the skills and mindsets that were compromising her, including her own self-doubt. All these changes went a long way towards helping her get in, and stay in, the Zone of engagement for effective leadership. Ultimately, Mary earned the respect of her team and reestablished her own self-esteem in the process.

A New Lease

Jim, a successful middle-aged businessman who had been diagnosed with a slow-growing cancer, presented his own set of challenges. With the right treatment, Jim's chances of eliminating the cancer and living a long life were good. But, tuning in to hear only a portion of what his doctor told him and overlaying his skeptical attitudes about modern medicine, Jim didn't see that. Convinced that he was destined to die soon, Jim was referred by his physician, who was concerned that Jim was not seeking the treatments that could help him.

As a preteen, Jim's best friend had lost his mother to cancer. This was a woman who had been like a mother to Jim. That was an era when people did not talk about cancer and would not consider discussing such things with kids, even their own. So Jim and his friend assumed that this lovely woman had died within weeks of being diagnosed when really it had been years. Jim layered an attitude that cancer was an immediate death sentence on top of his diagnosis, even though his cancer was highly treatable and treatments had improved dramatically during the previous 30 years. Focused on the grim picture that he had painted for himself, Jim was unmotivated, lethargic, and depressed because he was responding to his own personal vision of loss as if the losses were real! Jim needed to get himself refocused, energized, and confident for healing. So we redirected his attention from perceived losses to probable cures.

Jim took the challenge and ran with it, which reawakened his energy, his competitive drive, and his confidence that he could prevail. Jim's physician was pleasantly surprised when Jim became a committed advocate for his surgical and postoperative procedures. They were cutting edge. They were grueling. And they worked.

After applying his 3 A's to make it through intense treatments, Jim migrated this method and retooled his career. He actively chose to relinquish a high-level management position for a job he had dreamed of for years. Jim went back to school to get his teacher's certificate and transferred his knowledge of technology and his skills at managing people from the high-tech boardroom to the high school classroom. According to Jim, "I've learned to live in the Zone, and I'm determined to live there for a long time." Tom, Mary, and Jim are just a few of the clients I've consulted with during the past 30 years. Their experiences—and thousands of others like them—have proven to me that there is a Zone for personal bests for everything we do. When we bring the full force of will to connect with our experiences with body, heart, spirit and mind, we access the "Zone." Getting there is as basic as 3 A's.

The Extreme Challenges of Everyday Living

I work with people who face extreme challenges. I'm not talking about the optional thrill-seeking adventures when you trust your fate to a bungee cord to leap from high bridges. My clients have confronted the truly extraordinary situations of life: critical diagnoses that threatened their longevity, life-altering disabilities that prohibited them from enjoying former pastimes, accidents that swept them off the pavement of weekend road warrior sports events or ousted them from elite athletic competition, and abusive trauma that profoundly affected their ability to function fully. And those were just the early years.

For the past 15 years, I have consulted in the wide worlds of competitive sports and business with individuals, teams, and entire organizations facing their own brands of extreme forces and ordinary foes. No matter what the setting, street corners with less fortunate teens trying to make their mark on the world or corner offices with Fortune 500 competitors vying for market share, I have constantly seen people confronted with similar challenges producing dramatically different outcomes. I wanted to know why. The answer was much less complex than "1001 ways..." It was as simple as three words. They were "In the Zone," where peak achievements and pride abound. Except "The Zone" had nothing to do with competing. "The Zone" was about connecting.

In the Zone—You've Already Been There

Think of a time when everything was clicking, when you were so intensely involved in the moment that everything else slipped away to a dull background. You might have been perched bolt upright at your desk or sprinting for the finish line on a report with your thoughts and fingers furiously pounding at staccato pace on the keyboard. At home it could have been a heart-to-heart dialogue or a heated debate with a partner, parent, child, brother, sister, or friend that captured your heart and your mind. You might have been carting a daypack for a leisurely destination-unknown stroll in the woods with your loyal Golden Retriever. Or perhaps you were schlepping a heavy briefcase or bulging backpack through crowded walkways for a briskly paced commute to the office or your next class. Maybe you were traveling at a more moderate pace in a meeting where participants, including yourself, needed to keep their cool to address and resolve underlying conflicts. Then again, it could have been as simple as kicking back with the remote after a long day of blazing daily trails and trials. No matter what the setting, no obstacle could get in your way.

Whether you were pumped up or mellowed out, your energy was fully engaged. You were optimally activated, *summoning just the right pace for the task at hand. Totally immersed, you* attended *only to the essentials and tuned everything else to a dull background roar. Your* attitude *was proactive and confident. No matter how daunting the challenge, you played to win with total commitment of body, spirit, and the logical and emotional sides of your brain.*

The Power of Will—It's as Simple as 3 A's

Based on my years of practice, backed by decades of research into peak performance in sports, work, life, and supported by discoveries from the neurosciences, I concluded that there are three core elements that, when aligned at optimal levels, hold the power to boost you into and keep you in the Zone. Activation, attention, and attitude—I call them "the 3 A's" of *The Winner's Way*. Activation, attention, and attitude are the effects that you feel of the thousands of natural chemical interactions going on within your body and mind at any moment and that work together to create your thoughts, feelings, and behaviors. They are timeless and real.

Activation—Get with It

Activation is your physical and physiological experience at any moment.[1] For as long as you are breathing, you are activated. Activation signals reverberate throughout your body in your fingers and toes, in your heart, lungs, and gut.

Attention—Get into It

Attention is your focus, the things to which you give your concentration. You "attend" with all of your senses—what you see, hear, smell, touch, taste. Your sense of moving through space and your gut's intuition provide other attention-mediated insights. The way you direct your attention determines your selective reality.

Attitude—Get over It

Attitude is your psychological stance, which includes your outlook, beliefs, assumptions, and mindset about everything you deal with. It includes your beliefs and assumptions about "how things should be" for yourself, others, and the world. Attitude can be motivating, open-minded, purposeful, determined, and proactive to push you into the Zone, or it can be debilitating, judgmental, meaningless, apprehensive, and reactive to pull you down to o-Zonal depths.

A³ Willpower—It Takes Three

"Things" happen all the time. When they do, the body and mind respond with more than a thousand muscular, physiological, neurological, and chemical brain-body interactions.[2] The 3 A's are the real effects you feel of those reactions taking place. The power of your will is in committing to read, fine-tune, and adjust your activation, attention, and attitude to link and deal with the events that you face—the good, bad, and unsavory things that make up your life. *The Winner's Way* provides a route.

It's not "the things that happen" that make you act, think, or feel the way you do. In reality, it's the 3 A's. And it takes three.

The 3 A's co-labor in circular feedback loops. Spiraling simultaneously, they generate your thoughts, feelings, and behaviors, and therefore, your results. At times, they become the next thing to which you respond. When you're in the Zone, performing at your best, each of the three is aligned at a level that is personally optimal for you in the particular circumstances. By willfully aligning your focus, energy, and the value-laden beliefs that you rely on to assess a situation, you propel yourself into the Zone of total engagement where winning is a pleasant side effect.

The Zone—It's Not about Competing—It's about Committing

"In the zone"—these three simple words paint vivid images. We associate the zone with sports and with competition. But most of all we picture winning. The Zone isn't only about scoring the big client in business or slam-dunking the final basket that wins the game. The

Zone isn't about competing. And it isn't about winning. The shiny medals, home runs, and game-turning goals are just hard-won by-products of giving it your all. The Zone is about connecting with each opportunity life offers you.[3] Connecting brings the wins.

When you harness your 3 A's to create a personal best, you always get a megadose of pride. Sometimes you even get a medal.

The Zone extends to every field of life.[4] There's a Zone for thoughtfully crafting a state-of-the-art business plan with your team members. And there's a different Zone for implementing it. No matter what zone you are in, you are immersed in the experience.

There's a high-energy Zone for ferocious competition, whether you're giving it your all to win a customer in business, earn a top grade in school, or reclaim parts of your life stolen by disability. On the opposite end lie recouping Zones. These are moments when relaxing with the television and a bag of chips, flying on your Harley, shoe shopping, or running solo are just what you need to refuel for the demands of life's curve balls. Perhaps it's just ordinary days when navigating the nine to seven can try even the most resilient.

There's also a grieving Zone, the place to acknowledge real losses, focus on the new reality, and feel sadness. Here strength can be gathered and physical and mental resources mobilized so you can progress into the healing Zone. My efforts with athletes grappling with serious injuries, people like Jim diagnosed with life-threatening illnesses, and entire organizations facing possible extinction demonstrated the value of this healing Zone. In the healing Zone you're focused on determining and implementing solutions, whether it's to seek necessary medical treatments like Jim or to rebuild twin towers.

There's a Zone to heal, another to wheel and deal—and one for everything in between. But no matter what Zone you are in, your 3 A's are aligned for the challenge facing you. And when they're not, you'll find yourself disconnected from the real deal that faces you, floundering in the o-Zone.

An O-Zone for All Seasons

At any moment, you're either in the Zone for the card that's been dealt you or you're not. Instead, you're in that opposite unsavory state that I fondly named "the o-Zone" where everything feels out of synch and you feel out of sorts. We've all been there. When you're mired in the o-Zone, the 3 A's are mismatched for the challenge afoot. They might be lined up for another situation, but they're not quite right for the current moment.

The sensations of the o-Zone are nasty. The results are substandard, and the experience itself feels awful, often erasing any confidence that existed. When we're in the o-Zone, we end up feeling disappointed with ourselves and others. Demoralized, we often disengage to never try again, reassuring ourselves that we're simply "not good at that…" Or we get carried away with rage in response to things that we've blown out of proportion, overshooting the goal or erupting in angry outbursts on the roadways of life.

The memories of the o-Zone are unsavory. We'd rather forget them, but instead they linger on, returning to haunt us when they become the stories that our opponents revisit as if they're some desirable destination. With a life of their own, the recollections of the o-Zone occupy lots of mindshare as the nightmarish daydreams that we replay, rewind, and review as if we are film critics bestowing the two thumbs down. As powerful stimulants that trigger the 3 A's, o-Zonal memories can launch us back into the lulls or the high-frequency states of the o-Zone.

When you're in the o-Zone, you feel like things are spinning out of control. This tailspin can start when any one of the three A's isn't a good fit. Once it's started, because of their circular self-feeding relationship, it takes just a nanosecond for the other two to jump on board for the downhill slide to disengaged disenchantment or the ride over the edge to irritation and rage.

It could be activation that launches the o-Zonal spiral. Your energy might be too low to step up to the table and take a leadership role like Mary. Energy can be too low for extraordinary challenges too, like it was for Jim and other clients who found it difficult to connect with a devastating piece of news—a life-threatening diagnosis, a personal trauma, a collective disaster. In other instances, activation is just too high for dealing effectively. Some people feel the urge to run away. They channel their ramped-up activation to other endeavors, choosing the zones for working obsessively like Mary, driving furiously and yelling at their kids like Tom, cleaning closets, building stone walls, or escaping in shopping and feeding frenzies. Others throw words around, lashing out in angry retorts in response to things that they have blown out of proportion. Consider Tom, who perceived questions from his kids, wife, assistants, and law partners as attacks on his billable time. But it was exactly the wrong lineup of the 3 A's for engaging with the moment and creating a positive result.

The trip to the o-Zone can also start with attention. One CFO focused on the detailed analyses that suggested that the company needed to cut expenses if they wanted to maintain the business. The CEO, who was also the owner, ignored everything but the vision, which was unrealistic for their new, competitive market, dismissing the CFO's concerns as irrelevant until he couldn't make payroll. A preoccupation with only one focus to the exclusion of others frequently pushes people over the edge.

Just as attitude can bolster you in the Zone, it also can drag you down into the o-Zone when you live with chronic disbelief in self and others, leading you to play not to lose. *Mary's unrelenting self-criticism initially drove her activation to depressive lows. When she convinced herself that she didn't deserve the nod for the leadership seat and that no one would listen to her anyway, Mary's harsh, judgmental attitude jacked up her energy to high-activation peaks where she did almost all of the work herself, nearly burning out. Tom's nonstop scathing reviews started his late-night o-Zonal spins. His attention narrowed to focus internally on the signs of rising acti-*

vation that spiraled higher until they drove him to call 911 each night to get a lift to the Emergency Room. Attitude, attention, and activation were all working together. In this case, they were working against him!

When any one of the three A's is off, they all go and you land in the o-Zone. You feel discombobulated, out of control, and out of sorts. You generate results and feelings that you often regret and would rather forget.

An undesirable destination, the disconnection of the o-Zone is a miserable way to start or end a day. We've all been there. Sometimes, we're simply in the zone for something other than the moment. At home, when you're in the Zone for planning the dash to work, it's the o-Zone for connecting with your kids. Caught up in your agenda for the day, you have no recollection of what you promised them on the ride to school or if you even got them to school. In other instances, we're only half-involved.

Ensconced in the zone for daydreaming or for screaming at fellow commuters rather than for maneuvering through crowded lanes of traffic, Tom reported more than a few instances of missing his exit for appointments. Driving off the wrong exit drove Tom deeper into the o-Zone of enragement. At work, wandering concentration often lead Mary astray from really listening at afternoon team meetings where, powered by high activation, she raced forward to mentally prepare her retort based on a colleague's first few comments. Checking out for the rest of what was said, her seemingly smart response, based on half of the previous information, left her team members wondering if she had lost her brain. Mary started to believe that they might be right.

When you check into the o-Zone, confidence, performance, and mood suffer. You feel intellectually and emotionally inept. No wonder we pine for the Zone and want to avoid the o-Zone where we feel disenchanted, disengaged, disjointed, rageful, fearful, foolish, and downright stupid. And it can get worse for those who don't know how to access the power of their 3 A's. The feelings and results that we create in the o-Zone can become the next stimulus that we react to with another round of inappropriate activation, attention, and attitude, holding us hostage in the o-Zone, where stress makes us intellectually and emotionally stupid.

Activation, attention, and attitude are powerful, simultaneously occurring internal processes that work in a circular system and generate long-lasting effects. The three co-labor to create your thoughts, feelings, and behaviors in response to the things that seem to happen to you and those difficult people who seem to clamor for your attention. With the personal power of your will, you can match them to the situation to engage and do your best. Or you can let them determine the quality of your life. It is still as straightforward as 3 A's.

Postoperative Debriefing

- There is a Zone for all seasons and an o-Zone too.
- The Zone and o-Zone are about connecting with the challenge facing you from the daunting to the daily. Winning, golden coins, and medals are nice side effects.

It's as simple as 3 A's.

Chapter 2

The Power of Will

The Power of Disengagement

Life can stress you out. Or so it seems. When we look at life as the "things that happen to us" or "all of those other difficult people" and blame those "things" and those "other people" for the stress, emotions, and pressures that we feel, we relinquish our individual power of *will* to choose how we perceive things and how we react to them.

If you're feeling stressed out, you're in good company. The rates of depression, stress-induced illness, and chronic pain and their costs in the workplace and at home have recently soared.[1] At the same time, it is estimated that a mere 30 percent of the workforce is genuinely engaged with their work.[2] The costs of bringing only a portion of your self to your job, to sports, to genuine dialogue, and to personal and work relationships exert a downward spin on bottom-line results. It makes sense that disconnection on life's fields can spawn a negative impact on the health and morale of a team, a family, or an entire organization.[3]

Engagement, on the other hand, in sports, work, and life, enhances productivity and pride. Things get done, and they get done well. Issues get resolved. People feel content, sometimes jubilant. Even competitors want to work and do business with teams and organizations where engagement is the norm—in sports, work, personal, and family interactions.[4]

Even with all of the technological wonders that we have created for managing our time, making it through the nine-to-five can seem overwhelming, especially on those mornings when you could easily convince yourself that this is it—you really do have mono and crawling back under the covers for a few days is the only reasonable response. Rather than seize the day, we flee the moment. Still, we hold to the belief that the *things* that have happened are the causes of our distress. While this might take us off the hook and offer some relief in the short term, it also puts the solution out of reach, well beyond our personal control.

But it doesn't have to be that way. By learning to connect with the "things" and "those people" that are, after all, your life, you can get into the Zone for living fully during good and bad times. It goes back to those 3 A's.

For as long as we are alive, we are *activated*, we are *attending* to something through our personal filters (even in our dreams), and we harbor *attitudes*—assumptive beliefs that allow us to put a context and give meaning to the things that we take in through the selective lens of *attention*. Your baseline constellation of the 3 A's contributes to those things that you select from the universe. This same baseline triad of the threesome provides the framework that you use for interpreting their valence—are they good, bad, ugly, or absolutely ravishing?[5] That same commuter who looked like an obstructionist intent on making you late when you were traveling at high-activation intensity will look like another beleaguered fellow traveler on mornings when you have a more moderate energy level and the right beat in your heart or on your sound system.

Fortunately, the 3 A's can be harnessed.

When you *willfully* align *activation, attention,* and *attitude* to levels that are individually right for you for the particular moment, you access the *Zone of engagement.* You might be connected to step up to the plate to swing at a ball, or you might be engaged in a genuine dialogue with a prospective client, or you might be fully focused on implementing the strategic maneuvers for building your business. When you are immersed in any experience, all three A's are aligned at the level that is right for you. At any other levels, the three conspire to plummet you into the *o-Zone,* where disconnection and discontent reign. In such instances, you might be connected to a subjective version of reality that might not be an accurate picture of what is going on in front of your eyes.

What You See Is What You Get

Tom, Mary, and Jim each had their own challenges that exerted pressures on their hearts and in their mind's eye. When I first met them, they had relinquished their individual power of will, reacting as though on autopilot. By looking at their respective events through a limited lens, they had created a view of reality that prevented them from genuinely connecting with the actual challenges and real people in their lives. Instead they responded to the personalized version and the attributions that they had attached to that image just like an athlete who turns a competition into a defense of valor rather than a simple point or putt or another lap of the race. This triple-A alignment did not allow for generating solutions, and it led them to miss out on some great experiences and relationships.

*Tom believed that most people were out to get him with their questions, driving demeanors, or demands on his time. His outlook, as well as his mental and physical stances toward life, resembled those of athletes who turn every point into an attempt to beat the competitor. Tom had turned every aspect of life into a combat zone. Constantly fending off the enemy— whether it was fellow commuters, colleagues, his wife and kids, or the revolving door of executive assistants— was exhausting. This defensiveness relegated him to left field, out of position for fully engaging with the opportunities all around him. When he was confronted with the genuine stress generated by his own two-thumbs-down nightly reviews of his day, he was too depleted to be able to realistically evaluate it and offer himself constructive counsel. So he spun into heart-wrenching acti*vation, *with its characteristic companions of narrowed* attention *and a narrow, rigid mind. Throughout his day, Tom was fighting battles of his own making.*

Mary designed her own truth as well and choreographed her responses to fit it. Mary had convinced herself that her team members did not respect her and that she was an inept leader. With this attitude, *she narrowed her focus to find evidence that supported her conclusion. On the defensive, like athletes who "play-not-to-lose," Mary kept her* activation *high to keep her guard up. Mary's team members thought they were at a meeting. Mary responded as if she was being tried in a courtroom where her former colleagues were the jury. So she did what anyone in that situation would do. She aligned her 3 A's to defend herself. At times, Mary turned the table and became as harsh a judge of her team members as she was of herself. With these countermeasures, she felt safe, at least for a few minutes, from the glared daggers that she believed that they were hurling her way. But it did nothing to forward her as a leader in their eyes and instead created a self-fulfilling prophecy of her worst beliefs.*

All Jim could visualize was his demise. Cueing in on the word cancer, Jim had not heard the details of his diagnosis. Instead he recalled himself as a 12-year-old when his best friend's mother died. This was a period when people did not talk about cancer—especially to their own children. No one had disclosed that this kind woman had developed a cancer that had, in fact, been growing for years. Within weeks of the disclosure, she was suddenly gone. Naturally, Jim and his friend determined that once a person was diagnosed with cancer, the end was in sight. Generalizing from this dramatically different scenario to his own situation, Jim convinced himself that he would live no longer than six months. This vision had become Jim's reality. It kept him sidelined from life, not unlike athletes who believe that they do not have the skills to launch an effective offense or defense.

Stuck in a personal reality, all three were much like athletes who lose their focus or their confidence or get so agitated physically that they choke. Choking is merely the ultimate in disconnection, turning a point or a shift on the ice into something beyond a point or a shift on the ice. With your three A's lined up for defensive countermeasures, you play not to lose. In such a stance, you rarely do your best. When your three A's are lined up to connect, you play to win, in the Zone reserved for personal bests.

The Lens of Accountability

Tom, Mary, and Jim chose to harness their *willpower*. Once each of them tuned in and realized that there was at least one other way to see the predicament, and acknowledged that the perspective and path they had chosen thus far was not working, they made a proactive change in their three A's. At that crucial point, each one directed the power of *will* to choose the energy, focus, and beliefs that would connect them to a deeper, broader and more realistic view of the situation.

Once they tuned in, with their three A's aligned to connect with the real deal, they were able to master their struggles and move on.

Finally Tom was freed to take fewer cases and to commit time to building relationships with his family and colleagues at work. With a new perspective on the invaluable role of his assistants, Tom engaged in genuine dialogue with them, and even learned a new assistant's name in less than three weeks (the prior norm). When the turnover of assistants slowed, he had more time to breathe. Once he started to really listen to his clients, he was able to represent them more effectively as well, freeing even more time to get to know his family. Finally, he was able to return to the person he had been before his life had become one big billable hour.

Mary found herself sitting in productive team meetings, rather than some fabricated concoction in which team members were glaring daggers that she needed to fend off with verbal barbs out of her arsenal of defensive weaponry.

From his new vantage point and energy level, Jim's reality changed dramatically. Faced with a manageable cancer, Jim chose the treatments that would allow him to move to the next phase of his life. First he made a series of triple-A adjustments to align himself with the challenges of grieving his loss and then moving on to the necessary medical procedures for healing. During a brief recovery period on the beach with his wife, Jim downshifted and took the time to review his life choices and how he saw himself thus far. With this new perspective, he was able to choose to return to the classroom, first as a "very old student and teacher" in his words, which I reframed to a "seasoned learner" and "beloved teacher and wise coach."

The same processes apply to the circumstances that convene to make up *your* life. The power to turn them into manageable, magical opportunities resides within you. It is present in your *will* to choose to align your energy, focus, and assumptions to enable full connection and, therefore, optimal performance. It starts with ditching the blame—it's not "those things" and "those people"—and choosing to be accountable for how you perceive and respond to your draw. Your ability to choose and control your reactions and responses rests in your purposeful choice to tune in to and turn on those three strategic A's.

It's Not the Other Drivers, the Kids, or Those Difficult People

From the early morning circus of getting out the door to the midday crash of trying to juggle it all and into the late-night comedy of reality and TV, each of us is bombarded by thousands of "things that happen"—the internal and external stimuli that compete for your *attention*. On top of the "things" are all of "those people" who won't leave you alone—the kids, your partner, customers, and clients who shout your name. With all of them clamoring to occupy the majority of your mindshare, it starts to make sense that your pounding head feels like it is about to burst. It also explains the pains in your backside and your heavy heart.

For Tom, our attorney, the daytime "things" included what his adversaries, the opposing attorneys and judges, said or didn't say in court, other drivers, and his assistant's questions seeking clarification, and in the evening, the way his kids spoke to him along with his own self-evaluative thoughts. Traveling at fast forward where attention narrows and minds become cast in black-and-white granite, there was only one way—his. Because most folks refused to see it his way, they were, in Tom's eyes, just plain stupid.

For Mary it was the mere sight of her colleagues' faces that sent her three A's spinning to 0-Zonal pen-snapping highs. With her feet sweating and her tongue tied, Mary was unable to think or speak clearly. Flying at such activation *highs, her* attention *narrowed to ferret out signs in the looks and tones of former colleagues that confirmed her theories that they didn't want her as the leader because she didn't have the "right stuff."*

When Jim heard the word "cancer," his thoughts stole any attention *from his physician's words. He could hear nothing but his own fatalistic fast-forward, dire-and-hopeless predictions and the pounding of his heart. Jim's outdated* attitudes *about cancer, based on the days of less effective diagnostic and treatment procedures available when his best friend lost his mother to cancer, created a reality that was different from what Jim's physician and Jim's wife saw.*

Between the Things That Happen and What You Feel, Think, and Do

Activation, attention, and *attitude* lie between the things that happen and how you respond. It is not the things or people who create your thoughts and feelings and make you do foolish or superb things. It is the 3 A's. Enduring and real, *activation, attention,* and *attitude* are based on the thousands of biochemical dances going on within each of us at all times. These systemic interactions are the result of natural biochemicals, including stress hormones, which are released in predictable triple-A constellations that you will learn more about in Chapter 6.

These three-part constellations are the result of how you perceive your world. And those personal perceptions and evaluations of your world are determined by your baseline *activation-attention-attitude* configuration. It is a classic chicken-and-egg systems relationship. And it takes all three which, working as one unit, serve as both the cause and effect of how you perceive your world and how you respond to it. The effects of the three working together are synergistic. Rather than additive, they work in an A-cubed (A^3) fashion. (See Figure 2-1.)

Stressors—The Good, Bad, Ugly, and Absolutely Marvelous

In psychological jargon, the "things that happen" are called "stressors," "stimuli," or "activating events."[6] Some stressors are acute, one-time only events. Others are chronic or recurrent. Stressors range from mild

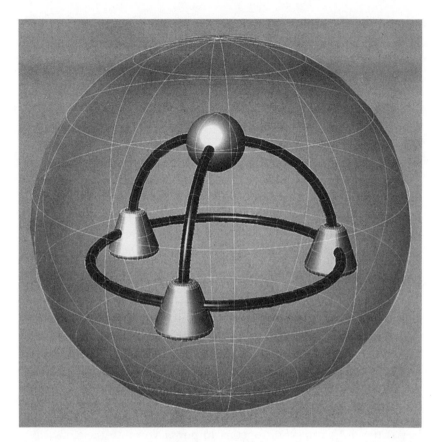

Figure 2-1 Triple-A Attribution. The 3 A's co-labor to form your world view that becomes your reality. The larger globe-shaped circle of weblike filaments represents the entire world. Instead of global, attention is selective. At any moment, we choose what we let in and what we tune out, creating the smaller circle that represents our personal view of reality. Each cone represents one of the 3 A's, connected in a circular system and always impacting each other and generating our reality, our perspective, and point of view. The 3 A's work together to generate our picture of the scene and our responses—the thoughts, feelings, and behaviors that then determine the quality of our results and our experiences. To change these, tune in to and align your 3 A's.

(sitting in traffic) to severe (being rear-ended in traffic). And some are traumatic, so severe that they really do threaten your sense of safety (the events of September 11, whether you witnessed them firsthand or through the media, and the continued threat of living as a world "on alert," could qualify here). But stressors aren't all external. Your own thoughts and sensations of activation can act as stressors with the power to set your 3 A's soaring.

It can seem like "the things that happen" or "those people" make us feel, say, and do things like Tom, who believed that his administrative assistants, law partners, and kids ate up all of his precious billable time. Tom blamed them, holding them responsible for the sieges on his heart. Really it was Tom's 3 A's lined up for constant combat that set his heart and blood boiling. Just like Tom, when we blame external things and people, we characteristically react to the events of the day with strong feelings, behaviors, and verbal as well as nonverbal language, both publicly spoken and privately held.

All Together Now—AAA Performance at Work in the O-Zone

Just as the 3 A's can work together to power you into the Zone, they can also align together to banish you into the o-Zone. That's what happened to Tom, Mary, and Jim at various times. With *activation* and *attention* mismatched for the current situation, *attitude* slides. Self-doubt creeps in, undermining confidence and making efforts that much more of a struggle.

Floundering in the o-Zone, whether you are standing on the service line of a tennis court or being served instructions for your next move by your supervisor, your energy and enthusiasm wane as your *attitude* plummets. Not surprisingly, performance follows suit.

Here's how it works:

If you perceive a threat—it could be your coworkers' faces gazing at you from around the conference table; the sight of the telephone beckoning you to make those daunting "cold calls;" the driver who just cut you off; a person who looks like or shares the same name with your tormentor from grammar school; or your own thoughts, as was the case with Tom—your body gets tipped off by your brain to respond in a certain way.

With your heart racing, your breathing becomes shallow and picks up the pace to match your pulse. Your gut seems to flutter butterflies. And your palms, smarting from the fingernails digging imprints into them, sweat so much that you wonder if puddles are forming on the floor beneath you. Your feet, suffering with their own perspiration problem, turn cold and wet. Muscle tightness is so pervasive that your whole body seems to cramp. The voice that squeaks out from your constricted throat sounds a helium-induced variation of your favorite mouse, whether it is Minnie or Mickey. You are *overactivated*, in the o-Zone.

That's not all. Because the three A's work in synchrony, excess *activation* has a characteristic effect on *attitude* and *attention*— it narrows them. With *activation* riding high, you experience that embarrassing and frustrating "stress-makes-you-stupid" effect, because of the stress hormones released in response to perceived threats even when you have no conscious sensation of feeling threatened. Our executive brain, which enables abstract thinking, also allows us to disguise things to ourselves with mental mechanisms of defense that include denial and blaming others or ourselves. Under this defensive veil, we often have no awareness of feeling threatened even while we are lashing out at others.

Threat comes in a variety of disguises in our modern-day competitions that can send us to defensive alignment of all three A's. For one client, it was a younger new employee, a graduate from a highly esteemed school, who made the seasoned manager question his ability and his longevity in the workforce. In response, he found himself being overly harsh in his judgments, betrayed in his bulging-veined eyeballs. Once the senior manager realized that the new hire was quite similar to himself when he first started out, he took the younger man under his wing and mentored him, creating a win-win-win for himself, the young hire, and the company.

For many of us, it is the other parents who always remember to bring the requisite 35 cupcakes for class parties and even make them from scratch while all you can muster is a bag of golden fish snacks that were stashed in your car for road trips. When we feel under attack, no matter how subtle, we often unconsciously lunge in to defensive overdrive or check out in halfhearted apathy.

Whether a perceived threat is conscious or not, a characteristic hormone bath is unleashed, which launches a hostile takeover of the brain's structures responsible for rational thoughts as well as the ability to *attend* through a wide-angle lens and shift *attention* flexibly. When these abilities are impaired by hormonal deluges, it is difficult, and sometimes impossible, to make reasonable assessments of whether something is good, bad, awful, awesome, benign, or a genuine threat because we are geared up to find fault and threat at high activation speeds. We also make mistakes. You end up stumbling over answers or fumbling for the ball. Of course, this confirms your self-limiting beliefs. Your *attitude* is humbled to new o-Zonal lows. *Attention* follows suit. The triple-A spiral takes on a life of its own.

Along with *overactivation* comes hypervigilance, a narrowing of *attention* and of *attitude* to a chronic stance of skepticism and literally being on alert for danger and potential attack. This is *activation* and *attention* working together, but in such cases, unfortunately, they're working against you. You focus on a single point, which works well if it's the right point or when you don't need a broader perspective for functioning at your peak. Athletes describe this as "visual narrowing" and, not surprisingly, it's at these moments when many of them get injured because they are literally blindsided.[7]

This concept extends well beyond sports. It's the same thing that happened to Tom in the courtroom when he lost his train of thought and at home when he lost sight of the television as he zoomed in on his beating heart. That's why I call it "*attentional narrowing.*" It too is based on that hostile takeover of the brain by the raging stress hormones that we will explore in greater detail in the chapter on your inner workings.

With *activation* elevated, *attention* narrowed, and *attitudes* cast in black-and-white granite, it is difficult, if not impossible, to realistically evaluate a person, thing, or event as good, bad, gruesome or attractive from such a defensive posture. Plus, it is hard to see what is coming at you. Companies get blindsided by economic trends or new competitors they never saw coming. Individuals might find themselves sidelined by symptoms they screened out for too long while they continued to travel at fast-forward *activation* levels pursuing career goals. Or they might arrive home to an empty house, unaware that their partner and kids had tired of competing for their *attention.*

If, on the other hand, the biochemical bath slows to a drip, *activation* is too low for the challenge at hand, you are *underactivated*— "asleep at the wheel"—no matter where you are: behind the steering wheel, a desk, a stove, or a computer screen. Slumps can occur when you perceive a threat that seems too overwhelming to even approach. Or it can happen when you perceive nothing with which you want to engage in the current situation. So you check out, leaving problems unsolved and joyous occasions unclaimed.

When you are *underactivated,* your *attention* wanders, either broadening to focus on extraneous elements or dwelling on unproductive thoughts and feelings. Extraneous stimuli might spur you to daydream or plan the future. Unfortunately, these "time outs" don't involve your doing your best at what you are supposed to be doing at the moment. At such low levels of *activation, attitude* nosedives. You feel bored or preoccupied or apathetic. You just don't care. And it shows. People take note when your chin hits your chest to abruptly awaken you in the middle of an important meeting. When the three A's are mismatched to the situation, it can ruin a good day. Left unchecked, a poor fit can ruin your life.

The 3 A's—You Can Read Them and You Can Catch Them

The 3 A's create our feelings.[8] When they are aligned at levels matched to the situation, our feelings might range from wild elation to somber sadness. Remember, when we're in the Zone, we're connected to the present. That includes being engaged in moments when it is appropriate to feel sad and in celebratory times when joy and pride are the result of the just-right triple-A fit. Feelings will, therefore, vary widely and appropriately.

Aligning yourself to experience the moment and its feelings sets you free to deal and to move on in a way that is not possible when you live in the o-Zone. When we disengage in an attempt to shield ourselves from painful feelings, we end up prolonging the misery and, oftentimes, creating self-fulfilling prophecies more painful than the events that we were trying to escape. While Jim's cancer was highly treatable, without proactively attending to it, he was destined to cut his life short and to compromise the time that he did have.

Activation, attention, and *attitude* are always affecting you. Operating between the things that happen and how you respond, the threesome determines what you select and allow into your attention and how you perceive it—is it good, bad, ugly, or so beautiful that you will scale tall mountains in pursuit? Or is it merely neutral, barely a blip on the radar screen? You will interpret the same comment from a partner differently when you are idling at a calm to moderate speed than when you are in a fast-forward agitation. In a centered state, it is easier to examine assumptions that might be outdated so you can see things more realistically and respond to the real deal. That is harder when you are traveling at full throttle at a speed that is too fast for the moment with a body and mind that are suffering from a hostile takeover by stress hormones.

Activation, attention, and *attitude* are your constant companions. The good news is that you don't have to be held hostage by these three elements—they're real and within your control with *The Winner's Way*. You can choose to work with them or you can allow them to work against you. When they are matched for the situation, you are connected and immersed in the moment with the energy of your body, mind, and heart.

Learning to Adjust Your 3 A's Gives You the Resilience to Live *Willfully*

There's a universal appeal to quotes that inspire us to live fully. Some advise that peace cannot be found by avoiding life while others warn against the regrets of a life half-lived. And others, from favorite musicals like Kander and Ebb's *Chicago* choreographed by Fosse, profess that you really can live a life that you love! [9] The risks of never straying beyond comfort zones range from illness to depression to living with resentment and misery. They are a sharp contrast to the health, joy, and mastery that are the fruits of leaping into life.

In their saddest extreme, I have worked with clients who, when it appeared to be too late to turn back, reviewed their lives with enormous regret. Still, when you sense that you are being bombarded with negative events, the vision of living fully can seem too risky or out of reach or just too time-consuming. It takes a leap of courage along with awareness of your own 3 A's.

Top athletes call it "the zone" or "the cocoon" or "flow." [10] No matter what you call it, the state of engagement is a prerequisite for creating personal bests and offers the best payoff of your life. It comes at a small cost. You have to be willing to stop looking to others for answers. It means ditching the beliefs that "those people" and "those things" are to blame. Taking back the personal accountability that is at the heart of free will is the starting point.

Then you have to be willing to fall down, knowing that you can pick yourself up again and get back into the game. That entails taking the risk to immerse yourself— to replace hypercritical self-consciousness, that can keep you paralyzed on thresholds, with the self-awareness of *activation, attention,* and *attitudes.* Such awareness facilitates total engagement and enables you to create and implement solutions. True engagement in life is characterized by the right fit of energy and physical tensions, a focus on the essentials and the moment, a personal accountability and building a purpose for engagement with even the painful life experiences that will cross your path. The unwavering belief that you can prevail even when the score is against you is a necessary item to carry on when you get on board. You have to be willing to commit to jumping in with both feet.[11] Once you have made the commitment, aligning your 3 A's with the strategies of *The Winner's Way* is the easy part.

Stuck in the Weeds on the Bank

Each day we are faced with situations and people offering opportunities for connection. Often we get stuck on the riverbank, refusing to reach out and leap on to life's rope swings that can take us over glistening waterways and offer the cool, refreshing plunge of a lifetime. This is usually because we don't believe we can do it. Or we focus our *attention* to create a scenario that is different from the rope swing, turning it into a threatening noose.

For Mary, the mere sight of coworkers' faces could send her activation *to highs. To Mary, they were no longer friends but were instead a discerning jury of her peers who wielded hangman's nooses of their own. In her mind's eye, she was under their scrutiny. And Mary believed that she did not have what it would take to adequately propel and direct the swing and navigate the leadership role. So she mucked around in the weeds, doing most of the work herself.*

The telephone on his desk was what set Al's heart racing and doused his self-confidence in icy water. A sales pro in the financial services industry, Al had lost his edge and his love for the game. The same telephone had previously looked like an appealing tool for connecting with prospective customers, but now his beliefs about his ability to perform launched a triple-A plunge into self-doubt. Al had convinced himself that he could not risk the rejection implicit in the cold calls that were a tool of his trade. So now the phone turned his feet cold, paralyzed his fingers, and froze his brain. Al, an athlete, would have gladly traded the phone for any rope.

Looking only at what she did not have time to accomplish drove Steph, an editor with three school-age children, to agitated highs and apathetic lows. "When I'm at work, I feel guilty for not being a good mother. When I'm at home, I feel anxious about not being a devoted employee." Steph had fabricated a belief that the mothers of her first-grade daughter's peers perceived Steph to be inadequate. Approaching them for a conversation had grown to river-leaping proportions.

"It started with the cupcakes. Ever since that day that I forgot to bring two dozen cupcakes in for a classroom celebration, I have seen them look at me like I am the deadbeat mother of the year." Since that day, Steph had been very defensive around the other mothers, retreating from her previous level of engagement in conversations at after-school pickup time.

We create our own life plots. The scenery might vary but the monologue is often the same—a wishful "I don't think I can. It's not going to come to me. I've seen others do it, but I don't think I have what it takes." Oftentimes this belief is based on a personal view of the situation that is not realistic—the rope looks like dental floss too flimsy to offer support, former colleagues look like fearsome foes, and cupcakes look like a death sentence from the "good parenting" court. Or an inanimate telephone appears to be sculpted from ice and shouting your name along with your inadequacies.

With these beliefs come crippling visualizations of failure that emblazon themselves on the brain. They feed self-doubt. They freeze our feet, curl our toes for fight, or propel us to flee. We create a different reality than what is actually in front of us. Instead of a swing that could provide refreshing delight, we see a life-threatening free fall from a thick cord that looks like a string too slender to support our insecurities.

Stepping Up to Swing

Engaging with the moment takes a conscious commitment. It helps to practice in your mind's eye to create a vision of something toward which you want to strive. That visualization might be all that you need to alert you that you have been generating a personal scene that is radically different from the real deal that others around you are living. Then, with your 3 A's lined up in such a way that you can see things from different angles and entertain realistic views with eyes and mind open, you can proactively make your choice—to get on the bus or off the bus, to grab the rope or sit on the shore. This decision is the breakthrough. Aligning *activation, attention,* and *attitude* ensures your success on the upswing and for the magical dive.

Your first dives and the fiery falls from which you learned to walk and ride a bike are seared into your mind. They are the leaps of faith that each one of us has taken, with our senses alive and our 3 A's aligned. The soaring sensation generated from purposefully lining up our 3 A's to move beyond limiting beliefs—our own and others'—is the reward of living *willfully.* Take a moment to relish some of your swings when your 3 A's set you up to soar beyond your own beliefs and well beyond the beliefs of others.

Using Your Mind to Come to Your Senses

The same processes apply to all of life's leaps. First you consider making a change. You wonder, "Could I just grab the rope and jump? If I do, will I know how to do it so that I get the desired results? Or will I freeze, crash, and burn?"

You picture what it would be like for you to make the leap. Merely considering this requires that you open your mind and heart. It requires being open to immersing yourself in the process, letting go of outdated images of yourself, of old ways of doing things, of the dusty mental models that have kept you grounded on shore. You have to be willing to risk the hits and falls that might be part of the journey, just as you did when you learned to read or to ride a bike, to cook, or to pick a winning stock. You have to even be willing, in some cases, to skin your knees, shed some sweat and even some tears.

Then you work through the layers of *attitudinal* blocks that have painted the pictures of doom and gloom—the "what ifs" that inevitably, at first, predict crashes, falls, and dire consequences that you believe are your fate. You refocus from your internal beliefs to real-world observations. After all, you have seen 50 people jump off of the bank, and they all lived. In fact, they enjoyed it so much that they chose to do it again. You replace the mental pictures of crashes with images of progressive success in which your grip is just right, your focus is right on, a healthy dose of skepticism allows taking smart risks, and your confidence is realistically high. The new and improved visions in your mind feed a newfound purpose and the courage in your heart. Proactively propelling yourself toward the stair-step goals that will bring you closer to your vision, you shift your *activation* to the appropriate level for moving yourself toward the rope.

Inspired by your *will*, summoning up the courage of your heart, you can see, feel, and taste the air and the water. You feel the success and pride that await you. Now you know you are ready. You stride to the rope, take hold of it firmly, and make the leap. And with that spring into the air, self-consciousness slips away, replaced by the self-aware, pure-power surge of *really* doing it.

Swinging from ropes, stepping up to bat, leading a meeting, investing wisely, connecting in genuine dialogue with a teenager, acknowledging a diagnosis of cancer, learning to accept the traffic jams and accidental injuries in life—these are all life challenges. Each offers an opportunity to connect with the opportunity and do your best. Each challenge, just like the rope swing, provides a forum to *willfully* engage or to hide under the leaves, run from nooselike images, or turn the scene into a battleground that gives you an excuse for not engaging.

Instead, you get to blame others. When you *willfully* choose to connect to your life's events on a macro and micro level, you capture the love for the rope-swing rides that are life's journey. Genuine connection is as simple as aligning your 3 A's to reach out, grab on, hold tight, and eventually release the rope to soar.

You Want to Come Out from Under the Covers

Much like the rope swing, frosty phone calls, and unbaked cupcakes, the good, bad, horrific, not-so-great-looking, and awesomely attractive stressors are the ingredients of life. Merely managing them doesn't make for satisfaction or joy—it's nothing more than holding on. What you turn them into is where your power lies. By learning to harness your *will* to read and adjust the 3 A's, you'll take control of the things that you can influence. You'll improve your stress resilience—your ability to confront stress head-on, deal with it, and bounce back—rather than overreacting to it or avoiding it, pretending it's not there while your stress hormones rise with the heavy burden of carting resentment wherever you go. Resentment and apathy are just too burdensome to carry onto all of your flights.

You can choose to direct your *will* to harness the power of the 3 A's to live purposefully. In doing so, you can change your life and the lives of those around you. Plus you will get rid of those pressures that feel like a Sumo wrestler is sitting on your chest or perched atop your skull, generating aches in your head and pains in your neck. Or you can choose to keep looking for those bothersome things and people. It is all in the power of your inner *will*, that force that is uniquely you. You can create astounding results beyond belief when you purposefully choose the energy you access, your beliefs, and how you will direct your *attention*. While each of the three essential elements is powerful, it takes all three to live willfully.

It Takes Three

The things that happen to you and other people don't have the power to generate your thoughts, feelings, the results you achieve, or the quality of your experiences. While breathing helps, it's not the be all and end all. Turning your head the other way and screaming at yourself to "listen up!" or "pay attention!" won't get you far unless, of course, you're tuning into the whole truth that confronts you. It takes more than thoughts in the form of mantras like "I like myself" or assuring yourself that getting it done is a matter of "just" doing anything. It takes all three A's to be fully present so you can respond to the actual situation to get the results you want. The effects of the three working together are synergistic—more than you would expect from simply adding them together. Rather than additive, they work exponentially in an A-cubed (A^3) fashion. With purposeful effort, you can read and adjust them at any moment. It is possible to read and adjust each and all of the 3 A's with the power of your will. It doesn't even require expensive and weighty biofeedback machinery. It's this mighty trio and your will.

For doing and feeling your best, being present is generally a good approach. And that takes all three A's of *The Winner's Way*. With *The Winner's Way,* the way you live is within your control. Choosing a life you love and loving that life that you choose, as they promise in *Chicago*, is within your reach. It really is as basic as the number three.

Postoperative Debriefing

- It's not "the things that happen" or "those difficult people" who make you feel, think, or do things: it's the 3 A's teaming together.
- The 3 A's generate your thoughts and feelings, and thereby lead you to take that next step forward and leap—or to retreat to the sidelines.

- *Activation, attention,* and *attitude* are the real processes occurring within you at every moment that work as a collaborative system to cause your aches and pains as well as your smiles and sensations of pride. They are based in your physiology, in your brain, and in your body, and they occur in predictable constellations.
- The good news is that the 3 A's are within your control, once you choose to harness the power of your *will* to turn your A's around and move from a stance of blaming to one of accountability. The quality of your life rests in your hands—in your mind, body, and in your *winner's will.*

Chapter 3

Activation—Keep Breathing and Sweat the Big Stuff

GAME PLAN

Activation is both physical and physiological. It has a significant impact on your ability to engage with challenges and do your best. The best-fit activation for any moment is not one-size-fits-all. Instead it is both situational and personal and affected by your activation style.

From the Top of Your Head to the Tips of Your Toes

Activation—you feel it in your fingers and in your toes and everywhere in between. For as long as you are breathing, you are activated. *Activation* is your physical and physiological experience at any moment.[1] Activation ranges along a continuum from restful levels for

37

recuperation and restoration to heightened levels for circumstances requiring high physical, emotional, or mental energy.

Activation signals reverberate from the top of your skull to the bottoms of your feet. Your muscle tensions provide a marker of activation. The pains in your jaw, stomach, back, neck, backside, and other body parts are giveaways. So is your grip, whether it's a white-knuckled grasp on the steering wheel or the burrowing of your toes into the soles of your shoes or ski boots. You also feel activation in your pacing, your physical energy level, stance, and gait. The way you stride, shuffle, or saunter into a room, along with the tone and the bellow of your voice are easy clues to activation.

The pumping of your heart, the pace and depth of your breathing, your red-hot head, the butterflies beating in your gut can all alert you to activation. Then there are the moisture signals—your dry tightened throat that emits a voice unfamiliar to you even though it's your own, the sweat quotient put out by your palms, the puddles in your shoes that turn your feet cold—these, and other markers, are all physiological signs that inform you about your level of activation. You can see it in others too. Bulging veins in the neck and eyeballs, nonverbal hand gestures, and a beet red face that looks close to gasket-bursting suggest activation is soaring. Deep sighs accompanied by eyelids that need to be propped up by toothpicks and dragging feet are giveaways of activation on the wane.

Activation resides throughout the body. Each person and group has a characteristic spot where activation is carried from the top of the head (including the heads of organizations) to the hands (who do the work) and anywhere in between, including the backbone, the operations that support the rest of the structure. That's why some people experience pains in the lower back and further down when they feel the agitation and irritability of carting excess activation around. Others feel butterflies that can metamorphasize into ulcers. And for some it's the tension in the jaw that is the giveaway leading them to bite people's heads off, chew their own nails, or engage in feeding frenzies to burn off tension.

For Tom, thinking on his feet and being wired up for quick mental maneuvers were decisive skills for success in the courtroom. It was little wonder that Tom carried most of his activation in his wingtips. When Tom realized his own power to tone his activation up or down, he learned to wiggle his toes. "When you tense your fist in the courtroom to blow off steam, everyone thinks you're getting ready to pounce on the witness. But when you tense your toes in your wingtips, nobody knows." Once Tom learned to wiggle his toes in his running shoes at home, he knew he was getting it.

For Mary, it was the hands that carried or released activation. Mary had snapped a pen in half at one of her earliest leadership meetings. By monitoring the grip on her pen and learning to release pressure when it started to head over the hill to agitation, Mary learned to adjust and realign her activation during meetings. This in turn opened up her field of vision and her mind to consider things from alternate perspectives. For Mary, getting a grip usually meant loosening up.

Jim's jaw was his activation vehicle. When we first met, his jaw was hanging down to his knees. After he got powered up to become an active participant in his cancer treatments, his jaw squared a bit more. He was ready to go to the mat to defend the treatments that he wanted in his battle against cancer. Other clients who have carried their activation in their jaws have often complained of jaw pain and an urge to chew gum or to chew people out.

What about you? Where do you carry your activation? Do you feel it in your fingers or in your toes or somewhere in between?

Groups—teams, families, and entire organizations—also experience activation. You can feel it in the grip of management, a word derived from hand—the white-knuckled grasp of micromanagement or microparenting, or the laissez-faire touch that lets people slip through the cracks. In the middle lies the human touch that holds and values people and releases them to test their wings.

The tensions between the parts, the breathing spaces, and the sweat quotient signal group activation as well. An organization's heartbeat, the pulse of the people, the pacing of the environment, and the stance that an organization takes in relationship to employees, shareholders, customers, clients, vendors, and contractors are all clues to its activation.

You can feel the effects of a group's activation in the energy level from your very first contact in the voice over the phone or answering system that greets you. Activation signs are also apparent in the sweatshop quotient and the breathing room. You can sense it in the time spent on restoration, whether it's coffee breaks full of congenial chatter or chronic complaints, offsite retreats, lunchtime group cycling treks, afternoon reenergizing walks, or the frenetic pacing or slouching gaits of people in the hallways. You can see the bottom-line results of organizational activation in the turnover, the quality and quantity of achievements, the return on investment of human resources, and productivity and financial results.

Where does activation live in your groups—work groups, teams, family—when it is high, low, and right in the middle? Is it too high, too low, or generally just right for achieving the group's goals, including development of team members and building a positive morale and team culture?

The Feeling of Activation

Activation is an informative giveaway to your emotions. For many of my clients, admitting to feelings let alone naming them has been a challenge. Few athletes wanted to talk about fear for fear of causing it. But they were willing to discuss their activation. To them, after all, that was real. Better yet, activation, attention, and attitude were within their control and offered a proven methodology to improve performance and recapture their love for the game.

The same holds true in the workplace. Even with the recent interest in emotional intelligence and its significant impact on productivity and morale for individuals and organizations, talking about feelings with colleagues is still a rare phenomenon, especially when it comes to discussing feelings associated with vulnerability or weakness. Many people in the business world have told me tales of putting their hearts on the table, so to speak, in a negotiation only to find that they had set themselves up for an arrow to the heart. And it felt nothing like Cupid's desirable dart. Putting energy, focus, and attitudes on the table made them less of a target.

In the behavioral sciences, there is a debate over whether emotions are separate from thought. In fact, the origin, care, and feeding of emotions has occupied much of psychological investigation. For those who believe that they are separate phenomena, the next point of contention is which came first? It is the chicken-and-egg battle. I am proposing that thoughts and feelings are indeed separate from each other and that both are impacted by activation, attitude, and attention. Still, it happens in such a split nanosecond that it all jumbles together as part of your experience. The good news is that it is considerably easier to read and adapt your 3 A's to fit a situation than it can be with feelings.

Activation might be one of the best clues that you have for reading feelings—your own and those of the people around you. Though we rarely consider this, we each experience feelings differently, in a unique manner. That's why one person's adrenaline rush that feels like an ecstatic thrill might be experienced as another person's fear factor. In part, this is a result of attention—what we look at. It is also due to attitude—the beliefs we layer on top. These attitudes include beliefs about the feelings that we will allow as part of our self-image. The activation sensations that one young man, who is cautious of anger, labels anxiety might be experienced by another, who refuses to see himself as anxious, as rage or as nothing more than an inconvenience caused by all of those stupid people.

Derek was living at the juvenile state prison, when we met. Flailing his arms as he described his view on what had landed him behind bars, Derek's activation went haywire.

As Derek described a brutal attack on an elderly retired man, his face got red, his squared jaw pulsated, he flexed his arms, and he sat forward, ready to pounce. When he was finished with his tale, he looked exhausted, as if he had relived every moment. Derek also appeared furious. From his tone and his words, he sounded mad. When he had calmed and I asked judiciously if he had any feelings about the matter, Derek was quick to deny that he felt angry. In fact, in his desire to set me straight, he announced in a booming voice, that he really didn't have many feelings. He just felt agitated and worked up all the time by how stupid other people were. At that moment, I think he considered me to be one of those people.

Activation is a personal matter. When activation is matched for the situation, you know when it feels right. The accompanying feelings might range from intense despair to unbridled rage and everything in between. When you are engaged with the moment, the feelings seem appropriate to the "objective" reality—in other words, what most other people would agree was really going on. Tuning in to read activation—your own and others'—and matching it to the situation at hand can make you emotionally smarter.

It's Personal and Situational

Imagine a world in which everyone traveled at the same activation speed. While it might sound like an intriguing alternative, if we were all wired the same way, we would have self-destructed long ago. Activation comes in a range of styles.

To understand the variety of activation styles, all you need to do is look around you. Each individual and group has a distinctive activation style that can be flexibly adapted with the power of will. While some of us run at the high-octane velocity of Robin Williams and that powerhouse leader Governor Ann Richards, others stroll at the energy-efficient stride of the subtle yet powerful Senator Elizabeth Dole and the extraordinarily steady Vice President Dick Cheney, who doesn't seem to skip a beat even during emergency situations that could set others' hearts afire. And many travel at moderate levels exemplified by Senator Bob Dole and the highly achieved Barbara Walters. There is no right or wrong—a difference is a difference. We each have a unique tolerance for different levels and ranges of activation based on personal or organizational style. Think of your upper and lower limits as your thresholds and your characteristic velocity as your set point.

Your activation style will make it easier to connect with certain people or situations where it feels like a natural fit and more of a reach with others whose style seems to drive you up the wall or put you to sleep. You might have people in your life that you see as "hot reactors," similar to wired Weimaraner puppies with frenetic energy that seems out of control. And there might be others that look more like steady golden retrievers, powered by low-voltage elevator music, whose energy can fall to levels below your personal bounds, making it difficult for you to connect.

When we experience extreme mismatches, we often label the people or situations as "difficult." In reality they are simply different. Whether it is hardwired at birth or a learned phenomenon, variety in activation creates strengths that we can leverage to live together in team, family, and community settings. Identifying activation style—your own and that of others—and willfully shifting up or down will enable you to join in with a wider variety of your life experiences and people.

Tom's style was characteristically high velocity with a limited range. Fearful of losing his edge and believing that only the fastest speeds ensured his success, Tom insisted on spinning his wheels at high rpms. Tom's physician was concerned that Tom was headed for serious health problems if he could not adapt to thrive at lower speeds. Once Tom learned to gradually let his edge inch down and realized that he could still achieve his desired outcomes, he experimented with more judicious levels of activation. He learned that he could achieve the same and sometimes even better results with more moderate velocity.

Mary hovered near the middle ground of activation, vacillating to either extreme when she assumed that she could not meet the perceived leadership challenges that she encountered throughout the day. Mary was dealing with a large group. When her activation headed to highs in response to her own fabrications about the looks and comments from team members, they could see her fuming. But she held it in and denied feeling frustrated. This was exhausting and eventually her activation plunged. Learning to identify her activation style and her team members' styles enabled her to more accurately read others' looks and to check in and check concerns out with them rather than jumping to conclusions.

Jim typically rode the low-velocity end of the activation curve. Still, his activation had dropped even below his personal threshold for functioning at his best when he was diagnosed with cancer. I provided Jim with an opportunity to refocus. By focusing Jim on making field trips to the medical center library to learn more about treatments with a high probability of improving his health, Jim's activation rose to pursue the hunt for material. His threshold rose inch by inch, though he was certainly of a different activation nature than fast-paced Tom.

Living mindfully and with enhanced awareness can be confusing. I am suggesting that you direct your mindfulness to activation along with its constant companions of attention and attitude. Once you start to recognize your activation levels during the day, you will understand why finding the right balance of tension—your optimal "Zonal" activation— depends on the situation. Some events, like those when you are genuinely threatened, call for very high activation while others require lower levels. For activities of recuperation and restoration, extremely low levels of activation will serve you well. These are the same levels that ensured our survival as a species during times when rest-and-digest periods provided the respite from fierce battles and fast flights from barbarians at the village gate. A lower range of activation has worked well for clients recovering from surgery or injury or participating in chemo and radiation treatments. I can assure you that lower levels also facilitate total immersion for reading a bedtime tale to a small child; comforting another person; accompanying and supporting the parent you love through intense and frightening medical treatments; slowing down to access creative, strategic thinking; and reevaluating the assumptive attitudes that continue to keep you on the overdrive, fast-forward track.

Extremely high activation levels are a good match in times of extraordinary danger when success depends on your ability to fight or run. In typical daily situations, where we are no longer stalked by furry mammoths, and fighting, running away, or hiding under your desk are not options, such high levels of activation are excessive. In fact, they can be disastrous, leading to deadly confrontations that we see too often in outbursts of rage on the road, at work, at kids' hockey games, and in schoolyards.

Jim's steady-state activation style was a sharp contrast to Tom's fast-forward fashion. Each style brought strengths to different types of tasks. Jim's style was a natural fit for resonating with students in his new career, while Tom's was a match for the intensity of courtroom battle that was his daily fare. But relying primarily on their individual strong suits did them no favors when it came time to link with circumstances or people where a different style was the secret to authentic connection and success.

Once Jim learned to accurately read the activation requirements of different situations and developed personalized triple-A strategies for adapting his activation to a broader range, he was able to power up for taking control of his cancer treatments and his healing. Tom's activation adaptation enabled him to enjoy the satisfaction and emotional sustenance of deeper relationships with his wife and children. It also gave him more time because he no longer had to interview administrative assistants every two months.

O-Zonal Activation Can Ruin Your Day and More

Chronically excessive or inadequate levels of activation and even one-time mismatches have a negative impact on performance, mood, and health.[2] Performance is compromised. It extends beyond lost points and matches. That is why it is so important to design and practice a personal game plan for getting yourself out from underneath the covers on those mornings when you really do feel like you have been afflicted with chronic fatigue syndrome and to have a well-rehearsed plan for decompressing from over-the-edge activation with its accompanying resentment and rage.

Errors rise in acts of commission and omission when you function at excessively high or low levels of activation. Anxiety and agitation, sometimes bordering on rage, are the characteristic feelings of the high end. Berating others in explosive outbursts—unsuspecting motorists, coworkers, fellow students, or family members—is too often the result when overactivation is not reigned in. At its worst, we see crimes of the heart on the road and in sports arenas. It is apathy and boredom, which can destroy motivation or create low-level depression that can pull you down at the low end. At either extreme, people often resort to abusing themselves with substances intended to take the edge off or to bolster them up.

Oftentimes we do not realize that activation is too much or too little for the current scene. When we travel at high activation speeds, attention narrows in and thinking becomes rigid because of the stress hormones that accompany such high velocity, which you will read about in The Inner Circles chapter. This leads us to hold tight to our beliefs that high activation is the needed edge for getting the job done.

At chronically high levels, we often create a personalized view of reality that is different from what others around us are seeing. A match point is no longer a mere match point and is instead a statement of our personal worth. From this high speed, it is natural to become self-righteously judgmental and overinvested in defending our turf on the freeway, in the workplace, on sports fields, or at the dining table. Carting excess activation around is exhausting. And it is confusing to those around you, who see a different view of the world. They wonder, as did Tom's family, clients and workplace contacts, sometimes aloud, what on earth you are doing and why you can't get a grip. Really what you need to do is loosen that grip.

Tom's wife and kids were often baffled by his angry outbursts. Once Tom learned to keep his activation within appropriate bounds matched for the current challenge, he realized that he had been seeing each day as a series of turf battles. And it had been draining. Lowering his activation threshold provided Tom with a new lens to view his experience and new flexible attitudes about what he wanted to do versus what he should do. Now Tom didn't have to go to such extremes to blow off built-up tension. He didn't need to yell and scream.

Mary described activation swings that seemed to drive others away. Quite frankly, Mary often wished that she could crawl out of her own skin and get away from the jaw-tensing high ends when her thoughts swirled in judgmental criticism of herself and coworkers. For Mary the key was in learning to adjust her activation to appropriate highs for enlisting the hearts, minds, and efforts of different team members and to tone it down for genuinely listening to team members who wanted to discuss workplace processes that interfered with efficiency.

The excess stress chemicals released during high activation that pump up your heart and send energy from your gut to your arms and legs to ready you for a speedy getaway or a victorious battle can work to power you through a sprint. But, when harbored for long periods of time, they can make you sick. The health hazards associated with excessive and inadequate activation include strokes, heart illness, gastrointestinal problems including ulcers, cancer, stress-related disorders, a compromised immune system, and poor recovery from illness and injury.[3]

There are emotional side effects too. In addition to rage, disengagement, and disillusionment, there are a number of emotional effects associated with extended excess and inadequate activation, including sleep disorders, burnout, depression, apathy and amotivational syndrome, attentional difficulties, impulse control disorders, anxiety disorders including panic attacks, and chronic hostility and rage. [4]

Even in the genuinely dangerous situations that we face in our modern-day world, very high activation can get you into more trouble than not. When your heart is pumping, it is difficult to remember the moves that you practiced whether you're skiing gates, defending your client in a court battle like Tom, watching your physician mouth words that terrify you like Jim, or delivering an inspiring speech to team members like Mary.

That is because the same stress hormones that pick up the pace of your heart also shut down the outer layers of the cortical portion of the brain that provides abstract thinking and flexibility of thought. The prefrontal cortex enables you to shift attention so that you can consider alternative plans b through z and assess the utility of attitudes and options in a particular situation. At low activation levels where you check out, the natural chemicals configure to allow attention to expand in such a way that your focus becomes broad. Sometimes this makes it difficult for you to discriminate what is important or valid. This includes beliefs and attitudes that you might accept as truths though they have no grounding in reality.

Overactivation and underactivation are hallmarks of disconnection in the o-Zone. In our modern world, optimal "Zonal" activation usually lies somewhere in the middle of the activation continuum.

A Perfect Match

Whether you're pumped up in fast-forward Springsteen rock-and-roll mode or traveling at a slower Norah Jones smooth jazz pace, your activation is a personal fit, matched precisely to the situation at hand when you're "in the Zone." Even with extraordinary effort, there's an element of ease when activation is in step for the scene. And when it isn't, you will feel the uneasy feelings of lethargy or tension that alert you that you are in the wrong zone for the scene in which you find yourself.

In the face of genuinely life-threatening forces, when my clients got themselves activated for dealing effectively, they kept their respiration, perspiration, and heartbeat within a range that empowered them to keep going. The activation of clients when they were stuck in the o-Zone was significantly different, either too much or too little, landing them in the zone for other situations like road rage or depressive ruminating or, like Mary, for doing all of the work themselves. But, unless they were race car drivers or immersed in grieving a genuine loss or operating a one-person startup, this was not the right energy level, focus, or mindset for successfully mastering or enjoying the reality facing them.

When you are in the Zone, you are connected fully to the experience at hand, allowing you to use your body and your mind the way you optimally desire. With your energy adjusted precisely for the challenge that confronts you, you do your best given any internal or external constraints.

"Really Do It!"—Where Your Activation Lives

Where do you feel activation at this moment? Is it in your fingers or is it in your toes? Is it in the slope or tension of your shoulders or lower back? How's your breathing? Is your activation matched to the situation for reading with an open mind— to assimilate and understand the material, to make it your own? Drop your jaw. Center your shoulders. Take three deep breaths. Wiggle your fingers and your toes. *Zoom* back in to the words on the page.

Postoperative Debriefing

- Activation is physical and physiological.
- Learning to flexibly adjust activation has a significant impact on the quality of your experience as well as your results, your mood, and your feelings.
- Activation ranges from bleary-eyed asleep-at-the-wheel relaxation to wild-eyed spinning-your-wheels agitation.
- The extremes are generally too much or too little for today's common challenges, even the extraordinary ones.
- Optimal activation is not OSFA (one-size-fits-all). It is personal and situational. And it is within reach with your winner's will.

Chapter 4

Attention—What You See Is What You Get

GAME PLAN

Attention is multidimensional. Attention plays a significant role in determining your ability to see, hear, and engage with the real deal to maximize your experience and improve your results.

A Sliver of the Pie

If you could attend to everything that is going on inside of you as well as all of the stimuli circulating outside of you, you would drive yourself crazy with sensory overload! With so much going on around us, it is a good thing that attention is always selective, a human capability that continues to ensure individual and group survival. Because of the way our brains and nervous systems are wired, we can attend to only a sliver of what is happening around or within us. Selective attention assures your survival. Willfully choosing the right sliver ensures success, longevity, and happiness. When you are connected to the situation at hand, you are focused on the requisites of the moment.

Attention includes every element that you select from the wide world and from inside of you—the things you see, hear, touch, smell, your thoughts, your physical sensations, and your gut reactions. This unique perceptual field is *your* reality—your personal construction of what is real that might or might not match up with a more "objective" view.

At any given time your attention is either directed inward or out. Within each of these dimensions, attention can be narrow or broad.[1] When you are focused on your thoughts, feelings, or bodily sensations, your attention is internal. When you attend to competitors, the work environment, the weather, drivers crammed in next to you on the morning commute, indeed anything happening around you, your attention is external. There is also a time dimension to attention, ranging from a focus on the moment, which is generally the right place to be, on the past, which works well for reviewing previous performance or reminiscing, or on the future, a good spotlight for strategic planning and visioning.

Each individual or group relies on a particular sense for processing information. Some are good at seeing things while others rely on hearing and hearsay. The gut provides a good source of information for some. And still others are great at sniffing out the truth from things that smell fishy. Here again, a difference is a difference. Knowing yourself and adaptability are the keys to opening your aperture to get the whole truth, or at least as close to it as our human nature will allow.

Tom relied on his ears for most of what he took in from his internal and external worlds. He spent a good portion of his time tuned to internal stimuli, including the beat of his racing heart, his scathing reviews of himself and the rest of the world, and his strategic plots to defeat other road warriors. Tom's reliance on the auditory channel made it more of a challenge to accurately see and read the nonverbal cues of other people, which he often misread or ignored altogether.

Mary, on the other hand, looked externally to the visual world for most of her cues about what was going on. That's why she had such a strong response to the looks from former colleagues who were now the members of her team. Just seeing her team members' faces could propel her to new highs much like sales pros I have worked with who have described a bone-chilling response to the mere sight of the telephone beckoning them to make what they saw as calls that were dreadfully cold.

Jim's primary sense was his gut. Jim was a hands-on learner who thrived in his management-by-connecting-with-the-people. So it was no surprise when he experienced his diagnosis as a gut-wrenching experience that immobilized him until he enlisted the power of his eyes and ears to hear the whole truth and to look into the future to see a bigger picture.

Whether you have thought about it or not, you have your own strong suit for coming to your senses. When you want a fix of news, do you update yourself on trends from newspaper or magazines or alerts on the Internet? If so, your visual sense might be the one that carries you. If, on the other hand, you prefer the radio, the auditory channel is probably your strong suit. If you absorb most of what you know watching the television while you are on the treadmill or your favorite piece of stationary exercise equipment, your gut and physical sensations provide a vast amount of information that others might miss. Because we each tend to regress to our strong suit when we are under pressure, it is vital to know yourself and know how to open your mind's lens with the power of your will.

Groups, teams, and entire organizations are always attending to something too. Sometimes they're focused on winning factors (including core values) that position them to claim larger market share than their competitors. At other times they attend to o-Zonal distractions that can lead to small mistakes or to their demise. They miss competitors who seem to blindside them or opportunities that could create business growth. Names like Woolworth's and Digital spring to mind. Or companies shoot themselves in the foot by not paying heed to what is going on in the heads. Enron, TYCO, and other smaller companies who have met a similar demise fell prey to such internal distraction.

That's why it's crucial that organizations, just like individuals, realize that the same focus that might have been a good fit yesterday might be a poor match today. A focus on core organizational values is internal and narrow and works well for organizational development sessions and as a daily enduring guide for behaviors throughout an organization. But in and of itself, it will not guarantee success. Concentrating only on the corporation's stock value is narrow too. However, this time it's external and might be the ticket to organizational downfall when it becomes the force that occupies the mindshare of the executive team and Board, and if it leaves no room for attending to doing business with ethical values.

Is your family or work team tuned in through the eyes, ears, or the gut? Hints abound. When appearances rule and marketing is done through visual media, the eyes have it. When attention is paid to how things are said and what people are saying about you, it's the ears. And when it is how people feel when they are working in or doing business with an organization, the heart and gut are at work. In some organizations that are already practicing attentional flexibility to capitalize on differences, it might be all of the above.

The Feel of the Wavelength

When you are genuinely engaged and focused on the appropriate elements of a situation, it feels like you are on the right wavelength. You can sense a similar vibe with others who are hanging in there with you even when there are differences in attentional style. While your feelings might range from sadness to joy to anger, they are a good fit for what is going on around and inside of you.

When your attention is captivated by extraneous factors, thoughts, or feelings, it feels unsettling. Feeling dumbfounded and disoriented, like everyone else might be on a different page than your own or frustrated that no one else sees things the way you do are common sensations of the o-Zone.

Sometimes you simply check out. It's not that you're not attending. You're just tuned in to things that are irrelevant to the moment. Captivated by extraneous thoughts at the dinner table or in a meeting, you suddenly realize that people are focused on you. The silence suggests that they are waiting for your response. Embarrassed, you find yourself speechless, asking for the question to be repeated and fumbling to fudge a response. At other times, you essentially insert yourself in left field when you choose a sliver of the reality to which you respond that is not a very good picture of the real deal.

When you're not quite connected or entirely checked out, feelings can cover the gamut. When your focus is off, you feel uneasy, out of step, and disoriented. It's a sensation that you are missing something and that you're in a zone that is different from the people around you. And that is exactly the truth.

It's Personal and Situational

Then there's the matter of personal style.[2] Each individual and group tends to have a strong suit when it comes to attention that slants perspective. Some focus on people, others on things, some on the big picture, and others on the microimage. For some, like Jim, the process looms in the forefront, while for others it is the bottom-line outcome that captures all mindshare. For some, it is the big-picture vision. Looking far and externally, these individuals and groups see the world in a very different way than those who rely on the nitty-gritty details and analysis, searching narrowly and within, to provide validation of what is real.

Attention also extends along a dimension from feelings to data. A sole focus on feelings to the total exclusion of data or vice versa can create the misunderstandings and miscommunication that lead to conflict. For some people like Tom, bottom–line, data-driven results rule. Facts and objective data captivate their attention to the exclusion of the impact on people or the broader emotional climate that their colleagues are tuned to. A focus that ignores recognizing people can inadvertently drive employees and customers out the door to do business with your biggest competitor, just as Tom's assistants fled through a revolving door. Worse yet, you might find yourself with your children grown and realize that you missed out on their childhood. On the other hand, inadequate attention to data and details are a blueprint for error and can land you in the o-Zone, where people submit the wrong information to the wrong customer or send data to a project team that isn't adequate.

Think of attentional style like a lens. Differences in attentional style play a significant role in misunderstandings and communication difficulties in every walk of life when we assume that everyone is seeing the same picture, having the same conversation, sitting in the same meeting, or watching the same movie. Even with similar styles, each individual or group has a unique way of seeing things. We run ourselves into trouble when we don't communicate the elements of our attention that have painted the unique view of reality that is our own. Misunderstandings blossom when we don't check in to ask people what they are seeing or hearing.

Tom was a master at selecting narrow portions of his reality that focused in on behaviors that he interpreted with a negative spin. When Tom learned that not everyone heard what he heard or saw the world from his perspective, he was amazed. When he stepped back, took a breath, and looked at the bigger picture, he realized that there were a number of ways to see his life's scenery. Tom saw that some of the scenes were high-return-on-time-investment for building results, relationships, and satisfaction.

Mary's attention style was dramatically different from Tom's. She gathered most of her information from the world of people and feelings. Once Mary learned to check in and check things out with people when she was interpreting a look or other visual indicator of their opinions, she realized that she often overinterpreted "looks" and "stares." Learning to field-test her conclusions and branch out to use other senses, including her own gut, provided Mary with a richer picture of the world around her.

When Jim asked how you were doing, he actually wanted to know. But his concern with others got in his way when it came time to deal with his cancer. Jim was so worried about how others would feel that he was reluctant to disclose his condition to anyone but his wife. Ignoring the factual information communicated by his physician, Jim was unable to seek out the real data that could lead to state-of-art treatments and that could draw him in to true investment in his healing. Once Jim focused on this real deal, his activation powered up and his attitude turned around to get him in the healing zone.

There Is No Time Like the Right Time. The Right Time Is Now

When athletes are performing at their top game, they are focused on the here and now, and it has nothing to do with meditation. This is a focus on the moment even while traveling in fast forward breakaway speeds with your eyes cued in to your goal. The same holds true for life on other fields. When you focus on the moment, on the process rather than the outcome, you will connect completely and therefore do your best. It is embodied by the *Field of Dreams* approach. When you focus on building the baseball field, people really do show up to see the game.

The time dimension plays in here. We all know people who struggle to extricate themselves from the past, singing *The Way We Were* as the soundtrack for their lives while others, who long for a new future, are carried away by any song about dreaming. Immersing yourself in the sequential processes that make up the journey toward your vision is generally the best focus for reaching your outcomes. A soundtrack for your life that focuses on being the champion of today's world is a better bet.

When we focus on the outcome, we distract ourselves from the moment, and that bit of energy that is spent considering the "what ifs," even if they consist of pictures of beating out the competition, is not available for pursuing the current goal. That does not mean that it is never appropriate to contemplate future dreams and formulate goals and outcomes. In that case, you would be in the planning and visioning zone, where being in the moment would consist of dreaming, crafting goals choreographed to get you to your destination on time, and developing Plans B through Z for those just-in-case curve balls. Still, remember that once you put aside the outcome during the action and immerse yourself in the process, you will get to the finish line often ahead of your expectations.

When you are in the Zone, your attention is matched to the demands of the task. Common nonessential distractions take a back seat as you zoom in on the essentials and block everything else out. Whether your attention is directed internally or externally, it is unwavering, in the present, when you're in the Zone. You focus on the fundamental elements for engaging fully while you dismiss imagined enemies, including your own overblown scathing reviews of yourself, as unrealistic or simply irrelevant. It's an unconscious concentration that delivers the presence of being here now, from meditation retreats to real life. This total immersion is fulfilling in and of itself and contributes to improved relationships and stellar results.

When my clients tuned in to give the moment their all, they created personal bests. Even when they knew they were losing ground to cancer or when the score was against them and the truth was not always pleasant to face, they were able to determine and tune into the internal and external facets of a situation that were critical for success. They were in the moment, focused on the elements of their situation that were within their control and essential to forging a solution. At the same time, they were able to tune out the factors that could lead them astray, especially those things over which they had little control. They saw the situation anew and "as is," with full awareness of the real predators in their world—a foreboding industrial trend, an illness or injury, a brewing conflict, or their own inner thoughts that could undermine them.

Just as important, my clients who engaged willfully with the actual situation learned how to turn away from imagined or overblown dangers, including the looks and tones that they had previously interpreted and perceived as threats—the hairy eyeball from a boss, the tone of a partner's voice, the moves by a fellow commuter, the mere thought of a competitor, preoccupation with physical sensations of a racing heart, or the dangers that newscasters would have you believe are outside your door. These are the daily things that happen that can draw any of us into the o-Zone of helpless depression and fear or prime us for retaliatory frustration and rage, whether it's on the road or at a hockey rink. When we get sidetracked from the Zone by such looks, along with our own thoughts that can distort reality or disconnect us from it, we land in a different zone but not the one for doing our best in the moment.

Tom's internal, narrow focus on his signs of increasing activation powered his activation to new highs throughout the day. Spiraling in a circle, his internal focus on rising activation then drove his attitude down to a level where he doubted his ability to get back in control, and he convinced himself that the end was in sight.

By shifting his focus externally, Tom saw things anew and changed the quality of his feedback during the day. Now he could see and hear positive aspects of people's behaviors at the office, and he even tuned into the things he had done well in the Courtroom. With his new focus, Tom was able to keep his administrative assistants for more than a few months. This shift also changed the quality of his evening debriefs. With a different focus, Tom was able to lower the activation associated with his reconstruction of the day so he didn't have to take his nightly ride to the E.R. When he learned to limit these reviews and to refocus on his family and, later, on watching his favorite sports teams on television, Tom's relationship with his family improved significantly and so did his energy during the day. He was fueled by nighttime "R&R" respite from surging stress hormones.

Out of Focus in the O-Zone

If your focus is too narrow or too broad, if your focus is weighted too heavily toward the internal or the external, or if you direct some of your energy to concerns with the outcome, removing yourself from the process, you will find yourself out in left field in the disconnected o-Zone.[3]

O-Zonal attention carries its own set of dangers. Mistakes, misunderstandings, miscalculations, missed deadlines, intercepted passes, off-center shots on goal, belated birthdays and forgotten anniversaries, and missed appointments are the norm when attention is focused on the wrong things. It's easy to be caught off guard. Like a camera that's out of focus, your judgment is blurred.

If you attend too narrowly, you might miss the big picture or neglect significant competitors who can blindside you or catch up from the rear. Suffering from information deprivation from the marketplace, you continue to do business as usual while your competitors claim a bigger portion of market share. Hyperfocus is one form of narrow attention. Like the Johnny-one-note song that you can't banish from your mind, hyperfocus consists of worrisome thinking, replaying the same thoughts in endless circles. It can be worse than any song that you can't eject from the virtual music player in your head.

If you are thinking that Tom was hyperfocused, you have it right. Whether he was weaving in and out of traffic or mercilessly reviewing the events of his day, Tom's wheels were always spinning. And they often spun around and around on the same track. That is because hyperfocus is characteristic of the high levels of activation and self-righteous blaming attitude that were Tom's constant companion.

Succumbing to the spiraling thoughts of her poor leadership and reviewing the looks of all of the faces at the table could occupy the better part of a morning for Mary if she let it. Those thoughts just kept spinning with no release until she learned to pack them into her thought balloon and heave them into the hallway outside of her office. Then, steeled by a new focus on the work and leadership goals that she had proactively chosen, Mary could get back to business.

The information overload of too broad a focus, in contrast, can lead you astray if you miss fine details that are crucial to performance, like an internal symptom that alerts you to organizational discontent brewing or an illness. Captivated by the panoramic view from 30,000 feet, you might have trouble turning your visions into action. And you might fail to recognize what's going on in time when there are problems brewing at the ground level. Missed opportunities, failed dreams, and unmet deadlines abound.

Once Jim was on the healing curve, he admitted that he had felt lousy for quite a while before he consulted his physician and learned that he had cancer. A master at putting small pains under the rug and looking up to the sky, Jim had felt so guilty for causing his cancer that he initially retreated to focus on the subterranean dark side. When we are confronted with a serious challenge, our first tendency is to rely heavily on our strong attentional suit. Then, though it might seem strange, we commonly bolt to exactly an opposite vantage point. That's where Jim was when I met him.

On-the-lookout hypervigilance is common in athletes who have been injured. When they return to the field, they are alert for anything that is reminiscent of the conditions of their accident. In sports psychology, it is called "guarding." It extends beyond sports to all of life's venues. When we have been hurt or have experienced a loss, we try to delineate the factors that led to the poor results. It could be as random as the weather or the shoes we were wearing or a not-so-lucky pen. This is the negative side of superstitious beliefs.

We end up guarding ourselves, shielding ourselves from new ideas or novel ways of doing things because, after all, the last time a new technology was introduced, the whole place shut down. Or we hold tight—to ideas, ways of doing things, or our wallets. Witness the pull back in the market fondly named market jitters. At high levels of activation with narrow vision, investors and their advisors might overinterpret current events and market trends. By holding back, they cause the very thing that they most feared. Guarding diverts some of the precious attention that is necessary to staying on your feet and staying in the game. It removes part of you from the moment. In the end, guarding can result in causing an injury or loss by virtue of its drain on all three A's.

The Match Point

We really do see what we want to see and hear what we want to hear—nothing more and nothing less. Any two people or groups might select out different aspects of an experience. This becomes their reality.[4] What you attend to affects your performance as well as your behavior, thoughts, and feelings.

When we actively choose the correct elements for our focus, we are able to engage with the situation to solve the problem at hand. Wrong choices land us in the o-Zone, which might be the zone for solving a different dilemma or an overblown interpretation of the situation at hand or for escaping from a harsh reality. But it is not the right spot for doing your best at what faces you.

When you are in the Zone, you are tuned in to the bare essentials to connect you to the moment. It feels just right.

"Really Do It!"—Attend to Your Reading Zone

Focused reading requires a narrow, external focus that is intertwined with your internal ruminations where you process the information and personalize it. Here's a way to identify and get rid of all those internal and external distractions now.

Drop your jaw slightly. Take three deep breaths. If you can, inhale through your nose and exhale through your mouth. Try counting to three on the way in and on the way out.

Notice the sounds all around you—the loud noises that clamor for attention, like the conversations in the next room, as well as the subtle ones, like your breathing.

Picture filling a balloon hovering over your head with these o-Zonal stimuli. Make the balloon look like one of those big black trash bags. Actively load it full. Take a breath in, drop your jaw slightly. As you exhale slowly, release the balloon, your *TRASH*, into the air—hurl that bag and shout to yourself *TRASHIT!*

Enjoy the image of this trash floating upward and your power to choose your focus.

Zoom in to focus your eyes on the words on the page. *PACK* a vision of learning to connect authentically with more of the people and challenges in your life and of knowing when to fold or walk away. *PACK* a vision of living with awareness of your 3 A's and the inner strength of knowing that you know how to read and control them to live willfully.

Postoperative Debriefing

- Attention is selective and determines the reality that each one of us creates.
- Attention can be directed inward or outward in a macro or micro breadth.
- Adapting attention to join the now is fundamental to success and satisfaction.

Chapter 5

Attitude—Say It When You Believe It and Believe It When You Say It

---

GAME PLAN

Attitude is much more than self-affirmations. It is your mental stance, the mindset with which you approach life. Attitude includes your value-riddled assumptions and mental models about yourself, others, and how the world "should" be.

Unearthing the attitudes that drive you and determining which attitudes you want to bring on your life journey (and which ones you can leave on the shore) can make the difference between a life survived in the wings or a life *willfully* engaged on stages of your own choosing.

Attitude Is Everything—or Is It?

Attitude is everything, or so they say. Attitude is on everyone's lips and everyone's minds. We even have shorthand cues to spur ourselves and others on. "Get over it!" "What's your problem?" "What do you mean you just can't do it?"

Ask any kid playing on a sports field or competing in the classroom. They will tell you that attitude is key. And they will probably tell you that you just have to get over yourself and do it. Still, in their hearts, they know it isn't quite so simple. Pick up any book on improving your life. Whether it's in the personal or business realm, you will find more than a thousand and one ideas on how to change your attitude. Many of them say the same things—recite positive mantras and tell yourself you can do it. They include everything from looking in the mirror and mindlessly repeating that you like yourself to firing yourself up to scurry over hot rocks with hundreds of people that you will never see again. There are instances in which these equations might work—especially if you're already feeling good when you catch a glimpse of yourself in the looking glass, or if your work or home life involves scrambling over steamy boulders—not the metaphorical rocky shores. But there are other circumstances when I have seen affirmations create false expectations and disappointing results. It takes more than words and just striving for a positive attitude to get you where you want to go.

A realistic view of your attributes as well as your areas for development is a start. (Some call them weaknesses; I choose to reframe them.) An honest appraisal of your walk—what you really do—as well as your talk—what you claim to do and believe—provides a real picture of your attitudes—the beliefs and values that you carry in your lifetime carry-on luggage.

Everyone Has "An Attitude"

Attitude is your mental stance toward life. It includes your beliefs, assumptions, judgments, values, and mindsets about everything—

including your self, the world, others, and "how it should be." These are your mental models[1] with which you approach and evaluate reality. Attitude also includes the core values, including a respect for life, that guide you. These are not just values that are mouthed with empty words. They are the values that you walk as well as talk—the values that your family, friends, colleagues, and strangers would identify as yours if they were asked to surmise your values from your behaviors, including the way you treat yourself and others in the workplace, on the home front, and on the roadways of life.[2]

Attitude can be open-minded, proactive, and purposeful to build confidence and motivate you to connect with the real deal, including the mundane and even the most daunting circumstances. In other instances, a mind can be so open that every option is considered. Or it can be close-minded, judgmental, grounded in outdated beliefs that remain unexamined, reactive, propelled by "shoulds" and "musts" rather than meaningful desire. In the first instance, attitude, working in conjunction with activation and attention, can enable you to engage with the real deal to resolve it and move on. In the second case, attitude can debilitate you and pull you down to an apathetic, checked-out state where everything feels like just too much, and victimized "learned helplessness" is the result.[3] In the third case, it can spin you into a desperate state where you turn every encounter into a battle as you attempt to fit the world into your prefabricated mold of how things "should" be. Resentment and blame live here.

Jim's attitudes about cancer were based on assumptions about the illness and treatments from an experience 30 years earlier. Medical treatment and the knowledge about cancer had improved drastically from when his childhood friend lost his mother to a different type of cancer. Such old, outdated beliefs were still powerful enough to keep Jim from even meandering to the starting line.

When Jim opened his eyes to his attitudes that were no longer valid, he saw that the effects of his beliefs were potentially more life-threatening than the disease itself. Once Jim was aware of how he was keeping himself grounded, he crafted a propelling, forward-looking vision, a personal mission and values that kept him moving forward first for treatment and then to rearrange his life.

There are characteristic outlooks associated with each attitudinal stance. With an open mind that examines alternative assumptions with genuine interest, you can view life's events as opportunities that you will approach with relish. Mastery, resolve, and personal victory enable you to roll with the punches and build personal meaning for the most mundane and the most severe serves that life has to offer. From the two versions of sieve-like open-mindedness and clamped-tight closed-mindedness, you will see everything as an oppression that you will endure with resignation or that you will battle with resentment. In the first underdog stance, misery, resignation, and victimization predominate. In the second bulldog stance, "mustery,"[4] resentment and domineering victimization of others is the fare for the day whether it is a shift on the ice, on the assembly line, on the floor of the stock exchange, or coaching your child's sports team.

Exchanging "If Only..." for "As Is"

Attitude ranges from the wistful "if only" to the dogmatic "this is the only way." In the middle is an "as is" acceptance of the real deal that is characteristic of genuine engagement.

From this stance, you accept the real deal with all of its blemishes and beauty marks. Then you proactively, *willfully* build meaning for joining with the circumstances that face you, even when the score is against you, resources, including time, are tight, or the diagnosis is really something you would rather trade for a rope swing.

Jim had to face a harsh "as is" medical diagnosis and rigorous treatments. Once he accepted the truth, he could grieve his losses and then move on to proactively participate in creating and implementing the solutions.

"As is"—I call this the Filene's Basement theory of attitude. If you have ever spent time in downtown Boston, you know about Filene's Basement. It was one of the first high-end discount shopping meccas and remains, to this day, a tourist attraction for fashion fanatics. You can find clothing for the whole family by the world's top designers for a fraction of its original price. But you need a healthy dose of skepticism buffered by the ability to create a realistic half-full, especially when the price tag reads "as is." And at Filene's Basement, much of the merchandise is "as is"—just like real life.

"As is" means there is a flaw. This could entail anything from a speck of dirt to a full-blown hole in the item of your choosing. With your mind and eyes wide open, you carefully evaluate the item. When you find the defect, you must make a determination. Can you live with this "as is," or do you want to fold on this one? If you decide that you can accept the "as is" and commit your hard-earned resources to it, you go for it. You accept that what you see is what you get. And you commit to *willfully* make the most of it. There is no room for wishing the "if only there wasn't a hole in it," and there is no benefit to strong-arming the item, stretching and pulling it to fit some predetermined mold that you have for how the world should be and what you deserve. It is just plain and simple "as is."

Somewhere in the middle of the "if only..." and "this is the only..." continuum lies a healthy acceptance of the "as is," the reality that faces you. Whether it is a suit jacket with a minor weaving flaw, a losing game score, a quirky customer, or a devastating diagnosis, your eyes are wide open to both the potential gains and the realistic risks associated with the real deal. With this thoughtful outlook, you accept things as they are. You consider alternative views and ways of approaching the challenge. And you proactively determine what you will do. In those instances in which you have the option to walk away or run, you make a conscious choice for which you hold yourself accountable. When folding is not an option, which is the case in most of the things we face in life, you proactively decide to deal—to connect and give it your all. You build desire.

With the power of words, you frame the situation in a way that builds meaning. Acknowledging that meaning is not something that you can find, despite what you might have read, you proactively draft a mission for why it is important to you to tackle this in the same way that Jim did to recover from his illness and discover facets of himself. You create a vision and goals for mastering the situation based on your real baseline even when it is compromised by factors such as fatigue, illness, or economic shifts. Then you make the courageous leaps of faith that allow you to commit to rope swings and other goals that require reaching out.

From this mental stance, you play to win. And you play for the love of the game. Lining up your sights and your energy, you go for it. It is from this stance that you can create a personal best. You might not always win. But you will achieve the best possible results given the resources that you have available to invest. You will also walk away with a heart full of pride and joy for a job well done.

Then there are the extremes that disconnect at least a part of you from the scene. On one end lies the wishful, sigh-punctuated "if only" and on the other is embedded the rigid "this is the only way and this is how it should be." Neither accepts the full picture or enables engagement of the heart and mind with the real deal.

When we operate from an "if only..." mental stance, we wait for the right moment and wish that things were different, a common companion of low activation. Here we search externally for meaning and motivation and a way to make sense of the nonsensical, especially the tragedies for which we do not have a framework. From this reactive waiting stance, when wishes are not fulfilled, we retreat to apathy. Too overwhelmed to connect with the real deal, we remain uninvolved in life. In small doses, we might engage halfheartedly and reluctantly, constantly concerned that we might lose. Claiming that we are in the scene because it just happened, we pretend that we do not care about the outcome. This keeps us safe—just in case things don't go as we would like. When we do achieve stellar results, we attribute them to some act of luck or being in the right place at the right time, wondering if we are imposters.

Avoiding risk of failure at all costs, we play not to lose. Fearful of making the wrong choice, we avoid decisions. We wait for others to go first, looking to the horizon for a better ship that might come in rather than jumping on board. We hold back on activation and divert some of our focus to holding tight to those things that we fear losing. Singing *Yesterday* and *The Way We Were* are the theme songs of this "if only" approach to life's challenges, including change.

Shielding ourselves from the real situation at hand, we resist change. We ignore an innovative way of doing business and dismiss the ideas of the new kid at work. Or we review a new piece of technology with the same fearful wariness that our ancestors used when they carefully examined a new cave to make sure no danger lurked within. Except in this new age, embracing change and putting novel technology to work is what will ensure our survival and put us at the front of our competitive packs.

I have seen people cling tight to old ways of doing things, radiologists who resisted new technology, engineers who scoffed at new systems for tracking materials, and financial pros who eyed new customer service initiatives with skepticism, only to find their customers fleeing across the street to competitors. Harboring an adamant, rigid belief that everything should fall into line, and there is no room for "as is," even at Filene's Basement, they tried to change things to fit rigid expectations. To stay in or get back in the game, they had to eventually open their minds and reevaluate that dogmatic belief, to view and do things anew. It's normal to migrate to the two extremes when we feel vulnerable. We believe we are being judged or we perceive that we do not have what it takes to succeed at the lot that has been cast us. We assume this attitudinal stance in response to a perceived threat—when the "as is" seems to be just too much. But, as you recall, the perception of threat is extraordinarily subtle and often unconscious.

It could be the way a person looks at you, as it was for Mary. For Tom, it was other drivers, especially drivers who were behind the wheel of the car of his dreams. Or it could be the associations that you have stored in your memory banks about cancer, as it was for Jim.

While these perceived threats are subtle, we respond to them with the full-court press, as if they were clear and present dangers. We retreat to the wishful "if only" or we lunge into the "my way" stance where we defend ourselves with the current-day version of spears and stones. We use words, which can wound a person's soul and heart even if they don't break bones. Either way, the experience and our performance is compromised because we are not aligned for joining with the actual circumstances. The substandard results do little for enhancing confidence.

Confidence—A Matter of the Heart

The attitude of the Zone is one of confidence. The word courage describes it well. Courage is derived from the word "*coeur*" meaning heart. When you're involved, you bring your whole self to the experience, including the passion of your heart. With an open mind, you build meaning even for the routine tasks of daily living as well as the extreme, fearsome challenges.

Committed, courageous, powered by an "I can" and "you can too" realistic belief in yourself, you craft a motivating vision and goals for reaching it. Then you proactively pursue them with a play-to-win passion. Playing not-to-lose is a surefire ticket to investing only half of your heart and only a portion of your 3 A's.

Still, attitude is far more complex than simply thinking that you can do something. It is multidimensional. Accepting the "as is" versus wishing for the "if only" is one aspect. Ditching judgment for enjoyment is another. Attitude includes framing "things" and "people" as opportunities rather than oppressions; approaching life with a mastery rather than a "mustery" mentality; and creating delightful moments that you can relish rather than resent, even from the most mundane chores like folding laundry. Attitude is about moving from a mental stance of blame to one of accountability.

Building meaning and making sense even out of the nonsensical enabled my clients to turn trauma into moments of growth and, sometimes, even into miracles. It took an open mind and a willingness to carefully consider the assumptive beliefs, including stereotypes and values, that they had relied on to make sense of life's events. Flexibility was key.

Confidence is a key to engaging with life's challenges, whether you are trying to win a point in a tennis match or in a negotiation or to connect in genuine dialogue with an open heart with a friend or loved one. Confidence has many meanings. I am not talking about an unflinching belief that you are better than others. And I am not referring to false confidence generated by repeating mantras that are not grounded on your realistic abilities. I am referring to a belief that you can approach and connect with any challenge, from those that appear demoralizing to those that look dull and even to those that initially intimidate you because they look like the opportunity of a lifetime. Your belief extends beyond your self, though. When your mind is open to possibilities and when you are willing to reconsider your assumptions and values, you believe in others as well.

Talk to Me

Attitude is more than generic affirmations that can often ring untrue and have an effect in direct opposition to what you want to achieve. Attitude is more than taking on an upbeat mood. Attitude is about beliefs, assumptions that lurk beneath the surface of all of our talk, whether it is in the running monologue that we all carry or in the dialogues with others, even with voice-mail machines. Attitude comes across in words and in tone.

Attitude, whether self-limiting or confidence-building, is reflected in the language you use, both to others and with yourself. Whether we admit it openly or not, we all talk to ourselves in that never-ending monologue encased in the thought balloon that hovers over our heads. If you've ever read a comic book, you know exactly what it looks like. Chock full of endless self-chatter, your thought balloon is the carry-on that never leaves you, transporting your attitude everywhere you go.

We've all had moments when we wish that we could dump the running monologue in our thought balloon on the side of the road or, better yet, leave it at home. When you use expressions like "I can't," "I have to," "I should have," "I must," and the ever-discouraging, "Yah-but...," you are speaking the "language of oppression"[5] that takes you out of the running for a personal best. You beat yourself up with critical, merciless, postevent reviews of what you've done wrong and what you should have done. This destructive feedback instant messages your three A's into the o-Zone for whatever lies next. The "language of oppression" can decimate any aspirations that we held when we got out of bed in the morning and can focus us on the negatives of even a beautiful day. This was the language that drove Tom's activation to new highs and Mary's to abysmal lows until each of them learned to attend to what they said and to reframe it—to use language to put a proactive spin on it.

When you're in the Zone, you talk in what I call the "language of opportunity"—"I can," "We can," "I will," and "We will do it." You express what you "want" to do and ditch the "have to's" and "need to's" of the o-Zone. And you don't use don't. "Don'ts" that keep you grounded at the starting line are replaced with the "do's" that tell you what to do and how to do it.

Try this—"Don't think about what time it is." Does a digital or analog clock pop into your mind's eye? Or did you look at your watch? The brain might not even process the word "don't" but might instead form images of the words that follow. And yet we all spend a portion of our time preparing for, or debriefing from, an event in the privacy of our thought balloons using language populated with plenty of "don'ts." When people are doing their best, even at reviewing or getting ready for a challenge, "don'ts" that can keep anyone grounded at the starting line are replaced with the "do's" that tell people what to do and how to do it. Language that tells you what to do is powerful enough to move yourself and others to assume a proactive stance and take steps that ensure reaching your strategic goals.

Tom was a master of the "shoulds" and the "don'ts." Once he realized the impact of changing his language on his own approach to life, he tried it out with his assistant at work. Remarkably, Tom found that she was doing the work the way he wanted her to do it and within the time frames that he needed. When Tom examined his attitudes about assistants, he realized that they had not been inept. They had simply been doing what he told them to do—in unclear language framed with "don'ts" that never provided a clear picture of what he wanted. With his new language, Tom's delegation at work and at home improved dramatically.

Mary's shoulders were weighted down with her arsenal of "shoulds"—how she should be as a leader, how her team members should respond to her and offer to chip in with project work, and how the projects themselves should go like clockwork despite the number of human factors that impacted them.

When Mary took a breath to review her assumptions, she realized that they were getting in her way of achieving her goals. It wasn't the team members or the workload. It was her inappropriate assumptions. By reassessing her assumptions and choosing new, more appropriate and userfriendly beliefs, Mary was able to set realistic goals and pursue her leadership development that contributed to her developing the team.

Really Do It!

Make a committed leap and try this. For the next 24 hours, listen to the running monologue in your own thought balloon. Each time you hear yourself say "I should..." picture hurling that balloon off into the sky. Now replace the "I should..." with "I want to..." Whether you decide that you "want" to go to the gym to

> play on the stair-climber to strengthen your heart and build your
> bones (a more appealing image than "having" to work out) or
> that you "want" to get home for family dinner, you will start to
> notice a *willful* component to your choices.

Igor

We each have a unique set of demons that, like an Achilles heel, seems
to get the better of us. Early on in my work, I knighted the larger-
than-life competitors with the name "Igor." I have seen Igors who could
send able-bodied athletes to choking states on sports fields and other
Igors who choked up well-prepared professionals taking licensing ex-
ams or making sales calls. Inevitably, Igor has a way of making it to
public speaking podiums even without an invitation. We all have some
version of Igor. Your personal Igors might include the things that happen, the people clamoring for your attention, or specific external conditions that seem to bring you down.

Igor isn't the problem. It is your underlying attitudes, the value-laden
assumptions and beliefs that you harbor about Igor and, more importantly, about yourself. When my clients learned to take a step back to
unearth and review the validity of their beliefs about Igor, Igor often
looked a lot smaller and less intimidating. And their own self-evalua-
tion, in relation to Igor, was usually much better than the fantasies that
had accompanied them for weeks, months, or years. At that point, they
were able to determine what they wanted to do about Igor, or, more
specifically, what they wanted to do about their beliefs about Igor. They
could maintain or ditch them. In most cases, they chose to ditch the
unrealistic beliefs and adopt new attitudes about themselves that prepared them to engage with a wider range of people and experiences.

What about you? What are your external Igors, the lifelong competitors or competitive forces that seem to knock you out of the ring and therefore out of the game? What are your top three "shoulds" that you say to yourself each day? How about your "have to's" or your "if only" musings? How do these help or hamper you from achieving your goals? Is there another way that you could reframe these messages to get the point across in a proactive way?

Attitude extends beyond individuals to groups and organizations. When organizations are in the Zone, they're confident, pursuing strategies, missions, visions, and goals that are clear and important to all. And they are powered by core values that are more than words on a plaque. These guiding attitudes are reflected in what people say, how they say it, and in what they do and don't do.

When groups are in the Zone, they use that same "language of opportunity," along with proactive visions, missions, and goals.[6] Communication is constructive and geared to helping others improve.[7] People tell themselves and others what to do rather than what not to do. Conflicts are seen as good and problems are addressed in a healthy manner. People walk the talk, choosing behaviors that are consistent with the values, holding themselves and each other accountable for acting in ways that are consistent with the values.[8]

When a group's attitude is matched to the challenge, they are engaged for doing their best, focused on what's important. Personally accountable, individuals proactively pursue organizational goals with their *willful* energy of body, mind, and heart. Engagement "In the Zone" is the ultimate in personal leadership at work and in life.

Feeling Good Even in Dire Times

When attitude is aligned for engagement, people feel confident and competent even when facing dire circumstances as well as ordinary situations that are beyond their control like clogged traffic arteries, bad weather, vendors who can't deliver on time. The feelings cover the gamut from the deep sadness of grieving a lost relationship or a former way of living to the joy of embracing a new relationship or celebrating a team triumph.

The attitude for true engagement isn't the unrealistic optimism of Pollyanna. And it isn't the judgmental Archie Bunker, suspecting that everyone is taking advantage of you. It is a realistic optimism based on carving out meaning even for events that seem senseless, overwhelming, and traumatic.

Viktor Frankl, a psychiatrist who was interred in Nazi concentration camps, wrote about the power of building an optimistic meaning even for dire circumstances that are seemingly beyond understanding. It was this ability to craft meaning that enabled Frankl himself and his fellow prisoners to psychologically and physically survive the brutal mental and physical trauma.[9] That same attitude of accepting the "as is" and crafting meaning and goals to keep you going has enabled prisoners of war, including the highly respected Senator John McCain, to prevail during captivity.[10] This same outlook positioned my clients to move beyond merely surviving the trauma of diagnoses and abuse that had been dealt them.

Powered by sheer will, you can proactively build meaning for ordinary and extraordinary events. You can consciously direct attention to what is good, what is meaningful, and what is within your control. This framing of the mind, augmented by the language that you choose, allows you to enjoy the spectrum of feelings even in extreme situations.

It's Personal and Situational

Each of us has a unique attitudinal style ranging from the mostly-empty skeptical mindset of Disney's Eeyore to the endless optimism of Pollyanna. It is partly due to your "shoulds"—your beliefs about yourself, others, the world, and the way it should be. And it is also based on the needs that are most important to you that might include achievement, accuracy, affiliation, acknowledgment, as well as others.[11]

Knowing yourself and others is the key. Learning to unearth and identify your characteristic attitudes and the situational factors that can drive you down to o-Zonal depths is the first step to getting a new attitude for yourself and others.

Some situations call for an amount of tough edge and assertiveness to get the job done. Negotiations at work and with your teenager or two-year-old are candidates for this category. The challenge in these instances is to bring enough healthy skepticism to get the point across but not so much that you become aggressive, closing down the other person's ears and mind. And you certainly do not want so little that you leave yourself vulnerable to a hostile takeover.

Scrutinizing data for errors, managing big- and small-ticket items for a project where saving money through the material can make all the difference to the bottom line, paying sharp heed to your small child's whereabouts in the grocery store and to your teenager's plans for the evening are situations in which a mild amount of skepticism will keep you in the Zone. On the other hand, it is an open mind that you will want to pack for introducing and embracing change and the new. The bottom line is to know yourself, your assumptions and beliefs that you harbor and whether they are still a good fit and worth packing to carry along on the journey.

When Mary started out, she believed that she was not a good leader, that she was not worthy of the promotion, and that she must take the slot to get on the career track. Once she opened her eyes to the outdated beliefs circulating around in her head about how it should be, Mary was able to pack more realistic expectations for herself, her role, and her team members. Seeing herself as a work in progress allowed her to take risks and to play to win in her own development as a leader.

O-Zonal Attitude Can Turn a Good Day into a Bad Week

When attitude is unrealistically negative and crippled by doubt, performance suffers. You proceed tentatively, constantly checking your work, accepting feedback as valid even from those you don't respect. Attention tunes out information that might reinforce confidence. Instead you focus narrowly on the information that reinforces your compromised image of yourself or others.

Living in disbelief and being ruled by chronically negative attitudes can severely limit the way you choose to spend your time and the quality of the experiences in which you do engage. At its extreme, it can lead to a life half-lived, unfulfilled relationships, and the stilted growth of children and others whose development is your responsibility. The results include a-motivational syndrome, a condition where it's difficult to even get out of bed, anxiety disorders, living under the influence of chronic resentment and anger, and depression, all of which might drive others away. This in turn might reinforce your o-Zonal attitudes, creating a lifelong o-Zonal spiral. But it doesn't have to be that way.

When we are risk-averse, we play not to lose, or, more often, we don't play at all. With only a portion of our self involved, we can only do a halfhearted job at best. We withhold affection, attention, recognition, and take no risks unless there is assurance of success. Because there is no such thing in life, we end up sitting it out on the sidelines.

While there might be instances when this is appropriate, it often keeps us grounded, victimized by an attitude of "learned helplessness," a term coined by psychologist Martin Seligman, characterized by a mindset that evaluates everything as too much and beyond reach. [12] From this attitudinal set, a person feels victimized. Low activation and low mood predominate. Even the small tasks that could bring pleasure seem just too much to handle. Life becomes an endurance event—you grit your teeth and bear it.

If one end of the disconnection continuum is about victimization, the other is about being the victor. At the other end of the continuum, rigid self-righteous beliefs rule as real. When you enter this terrain, your mind shuts down to alternative ways of seeing things. There is one truth and one way—"my way or the highway." It is punctuated with "shoulds" and "musts" that can drive you and others over the edge. At this end, you run the risk of playing so hard that you burn out. Taken as a lifelong stance, it can lead to criticizing or writing off others who refuse to see the world the way they "should" or at least the way you believe they should.

A Good Fit

When you are in the Zone, your attitude is proactive and confident. You play to win with total commitment of body, spirit, and both sides of the brain. By ditching worn-out assumptions along with self- and other-limiting beliefs, you exceed lifelong expectations to reach long-forgotten dreams and freshly forged visions. Destructive self-consciousness slips away, replaced by an accepting, constructive self-awareness. Challenges that had looked overwhelming, including the genuinely life-threatening ones, now seem within reach and feel satisfying.

When my clients thrived in extreme challenges and ordinary hassles, they proactively built meaning and confidence that they could prevail. By questioning their own attitudes—the judgmental beliefs about how they should be, how it should be, and how others should be—they evacuated the zone for self-righteous judging and accessed the open-minded zone for joining and enjoying. They convinced themselves to vacate their comfortable zones of anger, fear, apathy, safety, and depression where they were unable to confront current and looming challenges or to engage with their simple or their most amazing moments of joy.

Tom learned to ditch attitudes about how people should be and how he should be so that he could kick back and enjoy good music while sitting in traffic and connect with people at home and at work. Mary learned to build a meaningful vision for the step-up-to-the-plate challenges of effective leadership and team membership that initially felt awkward because she feared losing longstanding relationships with former peers. For Jim, that meant building meaning for becoming an active participant in and advocate for his medical treatments and later for how he chose to live the rest of his life. People, including myself, have built meaning for even the most repetitive wax-on-wax-off jobs like folding laundry or emptying the dishwasher or reviewing and summarizing long documents for a legal case, like Tom's assistants.

When you are connected deeply to yourself and to your experience, you allow yourself to engage completely, confident that you can do better than just endure the moment. With your attitude online and activation and attention aligned, you can learn to engage and thrive for both the mundane and the daunting.

"Really Do It!"—Listen Up to Hear Your Attitude

What does your self-talk reveal about your attitude?

Do you frequently (or constantly) beat yourself over the head with what you should or shouldn't be doing, eating, or feeling? Has this been an effective technique for changing your behavior or your feelings? How well does it work with others that you might advise in this manner?

Do you debrief conversations or segments of work projects or athletic training sessions by telling yourself what you did well? Or do you focus on what you didn't do so well or

what you didn't do at all? Does that provide you with the
guidance about what you will want to do next time around?
Does it inspire you to even consider a next time?
Do you live with relish or with resignation or with resentment?
Is that where you want to be?

Postoperative Debriefing

- More than affirmations, attitude consists of your value-laden
  assumptions and beliefs that color how you perceive the events
  and people in your life.
- Attitude is more than maintaining a Pollyannalike smile. It is
  about determining the assumptions and values that you want
  to adopt to live *willfully* and to turn oppressions into
  manageable opportunities to build strength and resilience.
- Proactively choosing your assumptive beliefs and the language
  with which you will frame challenges opens your mind for
  genuine connection to ordinary and extraordinary events.

Chapter 6

The Inner Circles
The Brain-Brawn Teamwork of the 3 A's

GAME PLAN

The 3 A's are not just fictitious psychological concepts. They are real. The things that happen, other people and stimuli, including our own thoughts, set off chain reactions in which naturally occurring chemicals send messages between brain and body that are both chicken and egg with the 3 A's. The biological and neuroscience fields are in a fast-growth, early stage of development. Therefore, the definitions and evidence put forward by scientific investigations can seem confusing, sometimes even contradictory. Thus far, the chemicals norepinephrine, epinephrine, cortisol, dopamine, and serotonin have been identified as significant players associated with pumping up or cooling down the nervous system, which includes the brain.

Working together in complex, intricate, and sometimes confusing interactions, these natural chemicals have an impact on activation, attention, and attitude. One dose of the chemical cocktail sets us up for apathetic stupor, another for emotional and intellectual stupidity. When the chemicals bathing the brain and body are a good fit for the situation, we're "In the Zone," where we can access all facets of intelligence for genuine engagement and success.

By purposefully enlisting the force of your will, you can determine, choose, and access optimal activation, attention, and attitude to lay the foundation for the correct balance in your system. This will enable you to see and connect with the real moment. Or you can let your stress chemicals carry you over the horizon to an o-Zonal triple-A-constellation where you are disengaged, disenchanted, or enraged. You have the ultimate personal power to choose your reality and to choose how you respond.

The Objects of Your Distress

In honor of consistency, I am going to refer to the things that seem to happen to you as "stressors." These are the difficult people you encounter as well as the welcome guests to your mindshare, the situations that seem innately stressful and others that appear to be thoroughly enjoyable pleasures. This would include the frantic merry-go-round of your thoughts and anything that becomes the object of your attention.

Beauty really is in the eye of the beholder, and so is perceived danger or threat. Stressors, in and of themselves, are not innately good, bad, full of beauty, or downright unattractive. Research on stress has demonstrated that the amount of stress chemicals secreted in response to a stressor that enters your field of attention is influenced by appraisal of the stressor.[1] This is a sterling example of activation, attention, and attitude at work.

The verdict is further impacted by the baseline levels of your 3 A's. At high levels of activation, you might interpret another driver who hovers within inches of your rear bumper as trying to steal your turf or make you late for work, in which case you might retaliate with nonverbal commentary of your own. When activation is more moderate or riding low, you might wonder if one of your brake lights is out and pay no more heed to the image in your rearview mirror. In this case, it will be easy to get back to learning Italian or rocking out with your favorite song.

When fight-flight-fright responses were lifesaving essentials, stressors were simple—new barbarians who looked different and therefore strange, wooly mammoths, poisonous plants, and anything untried. Things are not so very different today. In a world where tigers no longer stalk us, psychological stressors such as change, the unknown and the unusual, new strangers as well as potentially "toxic" people and novel things provide the saber teeth. Psychosocial interactions, including competition, have been demonstrated to be more powerful than the stressors that earlier versions of the human race faced.[2] Public speaking; performing; negotiating; managing people who seem difficult because they see or do things differently, including teenage children; not receiving a promotion or raise or an invitation to a party—these are our current versions of barbarians at the gate. In the mind's eye, they pose the threat of loss—loss of face, control, or even loss of life—in this case loss of lifestyle caused by losing a promotion or raise or social standing. Each has the power to launch an individual into the same fight-flight-fright rage or the opposite state of apathetic rest-and-digest modes that disconnect us from the state in which we could do our best. In the first instance, stress makes us stupid and angry. In the second, stress can lead us to a stupor where apathy reigns.

Bare Bones Basics

You have two nervous systems. The central nervous system consists of the brain and spinal cord. The peripheral system, commonly called the autonomic system, is made up of pairs of nerve fibers that monitor and adjust the organs and the internal processes that control almost all of your bodily functions—respiration, perspiration, swallowing, digesting, and others.

The autonomic system has two parts that collaborate to keep you in balance and prepared to deal with extreme circumstances.

On the "sympathetic" side of the house, key brain and body structures release natural chemicals, including neurotransmitters and stress hormones that instigate the "fight-flight-fright" response. This readies you to deal with clear and present or imagined danger or to engage wholeheartedly in raucous celebrations. It is the same state of readiness that ensured our survival as a species when our ancestors had to fend off those pesky barbarians at the village gate along with the saber-fanged tigers.

The parasympathetic branch initiates the opposite response—rest-and-digest—that sets you up for rest, recuperation, and refueling. You have felt its characteristic effects on your 3 A's on those evenings when, after a hearty dinner, you had only enough energy to retire with the remote.

There are characteristic activation, attentional, and attitudinal constellations associated with sympathetic dominance (high activation; narrow attention; rigid, skeptical attitudes) and a parasympathetic reign (low activation; wandering attention; and a mind that is so open that apathetic attitudes can leave you vulnerable to the opinions of others).

The Quintet

There are five chemicals circulating in your system that impact activation, attention, and attitude—epinephrine (known to the world as adrenaline), norepinephrine (or noradrenaline), serotonin, dopamine, and cortisol.

Neurotransmitters are most commonly defined as those chemicals released by nerve cells that communicate with other specific and nearby nerve cells or with organs and muscles to set off other chain reactions within the brain-body system. Hormones, specifically stress hormones, communicate via the bloodstream and can reach further to impact more distant, though specific, areas of the brain and body. The advances in biological sciences provide fast-paced enlightenment into the intricate interactions between the multitude of natural chemicals that impact our responses.

It would be easy if I could tell you that each of these natural chemicals originated from a specific part of the brain and traveled to a particular location to generate a one-to-one response. But the brain-body interactions are far more complex. Sometimes the research seems downright contradictory, and that makes sense. The technology that peers into the nooks and crannies of the human brain and body and into the inner workings of animal and human research subjects is still in an early and exciting high-growth stage.

I am going to tell you about brain areas that impact and are impacted by the 3 A's. To begin with, consider that when these natural chemicals are putting on a full-court press, in response to a *perceived* threat, they align your A's for the fight-flight-fright sympathetic-dominated mode. They impact the bodily processes that you feel as activation. And they compromise attitude and attention via the prefrontal cortex—the part of your brain located just below your forehead that enables critical and strategic thinking, judgment, empathy, seeing things from different perspectives, shifting attention and distributing attention for the modern-day essential of multitasking. When the prefrontal cortex, the seat of executive thinking functions, is compromised by the chemical concoction bathing it, you experience the sensation of stress making you stupid, both intellectually and emotionally. When the chemical cocktail is too strong or too diluted for the moment, you end up disconnected with your 3 A's out of line, either overenergized and angry or too tired to care.

The 3 A's are within your conscious control. Research and clinical results from biofeedback, neurofeedback, electromyography training in which muscle firings are recorded in response to visualizing performing specific moves of a sport, investigations into meditation, and "the relaxation response" have all demonstrated that this seemingly automatic system (and therefore its underlying chemical mixtures) is within our control.[3] With your *Winner's Way*, you can exert your power of will to turn around seemingly autopilot chemical reactions. Or, better yet, you can head unwelcome brain baths off at the pass without carting hefty biofeedback machinery around.

Grand Central

If you could feel the underworld of chemical messengers communicating throughout your brain and your body, you would be in awe. The chemical baths of your brain and body work in inexhaustible circular chains. Some of these chains fuel each other in positive feedback loops and others in negative feedback loops, which shut themselves down.

The brain lying beneath your skull is like no other and a far cry from earlier models. This three pounds of gray matter is a complex structure consisting of billions of nerve cells (neurons). Your brain is unique in its overall shape and the fibrous corpus callosum band that connects its two hemispheres as well as the distinct configuration of the folds of the outer cortex layer. This cortical layer is considered to be the most recent evolutionary addition, and its advantages are some of the last cognitive abilities to develop in individuals as well. You have seen their arrival when your preteens started to try to outwit you with their newly developed abstract reasoning skills. The prefrontal part of the cortex is the cornerstone of free will when it comes to choosing and adjusting your own 3 A's.

The brain is the control center for receiving and interpreting information from the external and internal world. It starts with attention. From the vast array of information swirling outside and in, you select, either consciously or as a passive passenger, items that become the objects of your attention.

At each moment, there are thousands of stressors swirling outside and inside of you, clamoring for your attention and mindshare. You select a sliver. Its breadth depends on baseline levels of the 3 A's. Because each of us is hardwired differently and operating with a different set of software (attitudes), each individual will be attracted to particular types of information, find others distracting or trivial, and be overwhelmed or underwhelmed at a different personal set point. That explains why large, crowded city streets swarming with festive folks during holiday seasons might be a source of beauty that sets your heart aflutter with joy. The same scene might be clocked in by your partner as overwhelming, a signal to hold fast to the wallet and head for the hills.

The Main Brain Players

Brain structures nested deep within your skull, beneath the brain's outer cortex layer, that impact the 3 A's include: the locus coeruleus, the cingulate gyrus, and other limbic structures including the amygdala and hypothalamus. These structures, along with the adrenal gland that emits stress hormones into the bloodstream and operates via a hypothalamus-pituitary-adrenal (HPA) circuit that you will read about later, are the primary origination sites for the chemicals that impact and are impacted by the 3 A's.

The prefrontal cortex, considered to be the seat of your executive higher-level thinking functions, is the recipient of the chemical drips or deluges. It is extraordinarily sensitive to such baths. While this sounds lovely, it can be dreadful and even deadly.

When the locus coeruleus along with the cingulate gyrus and other limbic structures are fired up in response to "perceived" threat, they go into fight-flight-fright mode and set your sympathetic nervous system on fire. They do this by releasing a stronger stress chemical cocktail that launches a hostile takeover of your prefrontal cortex, seriously compromising its abilities. There are characteristic effects on each of the 3 A's. Intravenous drips as well as floodlike chemical surges can nearly shut the outer cortical giant down. That is what is going on during those moments when you are either stuporous or tongue-tied, cannot see the forest for the trees, and are spinning out of control or diving for cover. This "stress-makes-you-stupid" phenomenon is what Rudyard Kipling was describing when he cautioned against losing your wits while those about you seem to be hanging on to theirs.[4]

Last In, First Out—The Cortex

Without conscious awareness, we are constantly responding to information from the outside and inside worlds. The outer cortical layers of the brain receive signals from the senses and from your thoughts. From this entry port, your brain instant messages the structures that make sense of the logged in information. The rational prefrontal cortex and the emotional inner limbic system colabor to generate the verdict of good, bad, awesome, or awful for the stressor under scrutiny. They are much like Felix and Oscar of *The Odd Couple* with dramatically different ways of seeing the world. The prefrontal cortex makes sense of information using its higher-order thinking processes, including rational, logical analysis. Its limbic colleagues rely on emotional valence.[5] Their mission is to collaborate on how the information is perceived—is it good, bad, ugly, marvelous, or merely a blip on the radar?

The dosage of chemicals produced and released is largely determined by this attribution process. The verdict, of course, will depend on your baseline attention, activation, and attitude. Stressors perceived to be good or attractive will be greeted with a different chemical cocktail than those perceived to be bad or unappealing.

This well-considered analysis occurs in a nanosecond. The rational cortical aspect enables us to think about things before we do or say them and to delay gratification. These abilities were not available to former precortex versions of our species. And therein lies our power of will to enlist our hearts and minds by purposefully choosing attention, activation, and attitudes that enable us to join with the real moment facing us rather than run for cover or flash our claws.

The Prefrontal Voice of Reason

Sitting just beneath your forehead is that part of the outer cortical layer known as the prefrontal cortex. This grand control station plays a central role in making sense of the information relayed to it. Strong enough to control impulses, this executive area communicates throughout the brain. The prefrontal cortex is your ally. With it, you can exercise your will to determine, choose, and access the optimal levels of the 3 A's to link with most situations.

Last in and first to go, the prefrontal cortex is the most recent addition in the evolution of our species. It is also the last part of the brain to solidify during the early teen years and, sadly, it often makes a premature departure as we age. It is extraordinarily sensitive to stress chemicals, which can impair its ability in subtle and serious ways depending on the intensity of the chemical siege.

The attitudinal and attentional advantages granted by this brain center include the *abstract thinking and judgment* that allow for thoughtful decision making, critical thinking, and postponing gratification. It enables you to generalize, make judgments, draw conclusions, and formulate assumptions whether it is with numbers or moral dilemmas.

The prefrontal cortex affects *"cognitive flexibility"*—your ability to shift attention from one thing to another and consider attitudes and beliefs from a different point of view, enabling you to open your mind to new ideas.[6] It is critical to your ability to thrive with the unknown—change, the new, and the uncertain—and to communicate and negotiate successfully. Cognitive flexibility allows you to reflect on your attitudes, to take a new view to determine if they are still a good fit for the current circumstances. When the prefrontal cortex is compromised by high dosages of natural chemicals emitted in response to a stimulus (another person, an event, your own thoughts, or your own signals of activation as was Tom's case), attention narrows and thinking becomes rigid. Jumping to conclusions and the blame game are two of the manifestations.

The prefrontal cortex is a major contributor to *attitude formation and attribution.* It determines if the things to which you attend are clocked in as good, bad, ugly, or so dangerous that other brain structures, which you will learn about shortly, are immediately activated and alerted to send out chemicals so you can run or fight or find an agreeable rock to hide under. Paradoxically, this decision interferes with prefrontal area efficiency and can virtually close it down, generating the "stress-makes-you-stupid" syndrome.

The prefrontal cortex plays a major role in attention.[7] When it is working well, you can *sustain your focus* and not fall prey to distractions. You can stay with it to the finish line on projects or lines of thought. In today's world, the prefrontal cortex provides a valuable ability to *multitask.* It enables you to do two or more things at once or hang tight to a *vision or goal* even while you focus on the current moment. For Jim, that meant holding tight to a vision of becoming a trusted advisor to teens as teacher and coach while focusing on painful treatments that would ensure his ability to stay in the journey for the long haul. This is a real advantage for navigating your way through traumatic experiences as well as loss and change.[8]

The prefrontal lobes also enable you to travel in time—to use *forward thinking* to strategize, plan, and organize time and to look back to *reflect* so you can learn from your experiences. (That is why young teens, just learning to flex these mental muscles, often seem oblivious to lessons learned). Whether you are mapping out your life, a tennis match, a surgical procedure in which you are physician or patient, or a competitive business plan, the prefrontal cortex provides the *strategic thinking* edge.

The prefrontal cortex contributes to more than rational intelligence. It is a major contributor to *emotional intelligence,*[9] providing the valuable ability to take the perspective of another individual or group—to *role take*—to move beyond your self-interests. This area enables you to engage in social interactions and see things from a variety of perspectives without hasty conclusion-jumping. When it is in working order, role-taking and mature moral reasoning facilitate the development of *empathy and a social conscience.* Both of these soft skills are associated with emotional intelligence, which is a significant contributor to success and satisfaction in every aspect of life, even the competitive ones like work.

Beauty really is in the eyes of the beholder, or at least in the prefrontal cortex. The prefrontal cortex makes many judgment calls during the day as to whether the stressors that you encounter, including "those things" and "those people," will be admitted and processed as opportunity or oppression, friend or foe, a thing of beauty or just plain ugly. Unless you want your sympathetic system primed for escape, attack, or stowing away under your desk, you will most likely want to have the full force of this area available to you. It will enable you to make the critical judgment calls that ensure survival against today's version of road warriors and corporate barbarians so you can enjoy life's gifts.

Curiously, as smart as it is, the prefrontal cortex can lead to its own demise. When the prefrontal cortex determines that something is dangerous, it alerts the biochemical-releasing structures, including the locus coeruleus, the cingulate gyrus, and the limbic structures that team together with your glandular endocrine system to flood the prefrontal cortex with stress hormones and neurotransmitters that short-circuit it.

The prefrontal cortex is extraordinarily vulnerable to these baths. When the prefrontal cortex is impaired by chemical deluges associated with fight-flight-fright, you lose many of the valuable abilities that this area provides. That is why you experience the dreaded "stress-makes you-stupid" phenomenon (intellectually and emotionally) when the prefrontal functions seem to slip away, replaced by impulsive responses and the sensation of being frazzled. With your A's out of line, you are literally short-circuited.

In those instances when the verdict of danger is not realistic and your chemicals are roaring, your view of what is real will be severely limited. Colleagues, family, and friends will find your responses to be curious as you battle it out for a freeway lane with a driver you assume to be brain-dead who, in fact, might be an undercover highway patroller or the prospective customer or employer you are rushing to meet. We can assume that this is the chemical siege that Tom's brain was under when he engaged in frequent yelling bouts at home and at work and when he regressed to ferocious road warrior battles on his daily commutes.

Alternately, the prefrontal cortex might determine that something is not worth the effort, releasing instead the chemical A-team characteristic of rest and relaxation. When this is a poor match for the real deal, it might leave you vulnerable or checked out in apathy. Worse yet, it can lead to your missing the opportunity of your lifetime—and you probably won't realize it until it's too late—when your prefrontal cortex gets back on line and is fully operable. In either case, when the chemical dosage is a poor fit for the real deal, the prefrontal cortex functions will be compromised at best, stripping your wit for sharp thinking or a hearty laugh.

Therein lies your power of will. The prefrontal cortex is smart, and it is powerful enough to fend off and even avoid the autopilot responses of the emotional brain and other centers that flood it with stress chemicals. There is a narrow window between the time that stressors are admitted to your consciousness and how you respond.[10] During this slender aperture of opportunity, you can adjust one or all three of the A's to enjoy the benefits of the *willful* strengths of your cortical mind and heart.

The real danger ahead is not the stressor. Instead it is in allowing yourself to be captivated by your 3 A's running amok. This leads you to triple-A levels where you chronically catalogue stressors in as bothersome dangers, pains in the neck worthy of the full-court chemical release, or as insignificant or benign and not worthy of more than a slow intravenous drip when they might in fact be wonderful opportunities or true dangers that require a faster heartbeat.

The prefrontal cortex does not work solo. It is part of an ensemble cast—the locus coeruleus along with the limbic system. They are well networked with each other and to the cortical areas. As chemical-releasing cast members, they collaborate to produce the physiological reactions, physical tensions and relaxation, attentional shifts, and attitudinal effects that you experience as activation, attention, and attitude.

The Locus Coeruleus and Cingulate Gyrus

The locus coeruleus and the cingulate gyrus can compromise your prefrontal cortex through the release and uptake of norepinephrine, epinephrine, and dopamine. When they are turned on in response to alerts sent from the prefrontal cortex as well as the limbic structures, they release chemicals that are shuttled back to the prefrontal cortex and other areas. The prefrontal cortex takes a serious hit in response to the cocktail that they send, ranging from mild compromise to shutdown, short-circuiting your intellectual and emotional intelligence and impacting the 3A's.

The *locus coeruleus*, a primitive brain stem area that sits atop the spinal cord, is well networked. It has strong connections to the areas of the brain, including the cortex, that acquire and process information from all of your senses. The locus coeruleus is one of the principal origination points for norepinephrine. The locus coeruleus is also networked into the limbic brain structures that release stress-related chemicals. When you attend to something that is logged in as stressful, the locus coeruleus receives the all-points-bulletin and releases heavy doses of norepinephrine that acts as a main primer in a series of chemical circuits that pump the 3 A's up. This series of circuitous relationships, which often seem contradictory and are influenced by an individual's brain structures and sensitivity to such chemical releases, are associated with high levels of norepinephrine as well as dopamine and low levels of serotonin. They deal a blow to the prefrontal cortex. This state is associated with depression, a narrowed focus of attention, thoughts that gravitate toward negative and half-empty rigid beliefs, and impulsive, aggressive behavior and poor judgment calls, including road rage.[11] High activation, narrow attention, and rigid attitude are the markers.

As a chemical-releasing structure, the locus coeruleus affects *attention— how wide you can cast your net, vigilance (being on the lookout), and focusing on anything or anyone that is new or different.*. When the locus coeruleus releases high levels of norepinephrine and sets off chemical releases from other parts of the brain and body in response to perceived threat, *attention narrows, becoming more selective; vigilance and sensitivity to novelty rises.* Think of it as shutting your aperture for viewing yourself and the world. This is great when monovision will get you where you want to go. But it puts you at a serious disadvantage if you are in a situation where you need to deal with uncertainty or you want to consider alternative plans of action or strategies. When the locus coeruleus is idling at low in response to low chemical dosage, attention broadens to a panoramic view. When it is moderately active, your window of attention becomes moderately selective.

The *cingulate gyrus* is one of many structures of the limbic system, fondly known as the emotional brain. Well-connected to the prefrontal cortex as well as other areas of the limbic system, the cingulate gyrus impacts attention and attitude formation.[12] It plays a role in motivation, that facet of attitude that contributes to building meaning to get you out from the covers every morning and provides the resilience to face challenges.

The cingulate gyrus works closely with the prefrontal cortex and impacts your ability to *shift attention flexibly from one modality* to another—from sounds to sights to sensations. It also impacts the *cognitive flexibility* that the prefrontal cortex facilitates and is, therefore, a player in the *cognitive appraisal* of a stressor—good, bad, friend, or foe.

But they work in contrary directions. When the cingulate gyrus is hot, the prefrontal cortex is not. Under the influence of perceived stress, the locus coeruleus and cingulate gyrus collaborate to unleash a chemical cocktail that turns down or turns off the sensitive prefrontal cortex.

The high dopamine-low serotonin-elevated epinephrine triad is associated with unsavory effects that can get in your way of connecting with the moment and achieving your best. They get in the way of simply seeing the whole truth and evaluating the real deal. And they jack you up to engage in aggressive acts originally intended to defend you against saber-toothed tigers. Their effects reflect the high activation-narrow attention-rigid prefab attitude A^3 constellation that is appropriate in situations where getting mad or fleeing a situation will save your hide. But when they are released in response to perceptions of danger that are either not accurate or blown out of proportion, they will assuredly land you in the o-Zone of disconnected rage.

The chemical bath unleashed by the locus coeruleus and cingulate gyrus has a narrowing effect on attention known as *hyperfocus*. Like Johnny-one-note, you can't seem to get that song or thought out of your head, which is okay if it's a great idea or a Springsteen tune. But it isn't so great if it is an unpleasant thought or a song that you can't stand (in which case it is time for some attentional adjustment—change the tune).

This chemical cocktail also contributes to a sensation of *hyperalertness*. This is the same *be-on-the-lookout* sensation that our ancestors experienced in response to new smells and sights. Today we use it to scrutinize or thwart new ways of doing things or people who might look different than we do, which is not adaptive in a time when learning to embrace differences is the key to our survival as a species.

With high levels of dopamine and norepinephrine, *thinking gets stuck.*[13] Reconsidering your attitudes is difficult at best. Instead you will feel your jaw lock and your mind close. Your attitude heads south to negative latitudes in the form of *negative and worrisome thoughts* that continue to recycle throughout your mind, a form of rumination associated with depression and anxiety. The attributions you make from this attitudinal mental space will be based on attitudes that are cast in black-and-white granite, from your personal arsenal of how things and people, including yourself, should be. That is why people might see you as hardheaded, hardhearted, or just plain difficult.

The chemical bath let loose by the locus coeruleus and cingulate gyrus *revs up your activation.* Whether your Achilles heel is to party, shop, eat, or drink, you will have trouble controlling your impulses and delaying gratification. Under the influence of this chemical surge, you might also find yourself yelling at perfect strangers, biting people's heads off, hurling snide comments toward yourself and others, and acting much like Oscar the Grouch.[14]

Without the voice of reason of your prefrontal cortex, you might find yourself taking extraordinary risks that would seem irrational to you under the lens of a different chemical balance. This is a real advantage when you are in an emergency and need to exert effort beyond your normal resources. This lineup of the 3 A's has been responsible for many acts of heroism. But there is a downside when risk-taking is not an adaptive response. Aggression, crimes of passion, and road rage are characteristic impulsive responses when the locus coeruleus and cingulate gyrus become overactive during times of stress. In these instances, the 3 A's are lined up way too high for the real deal.

The locus coeruleus and cingulate gyrus have other partners in crime that assist in the hostile takeover of the rational prefrontal cortex. Meet the amygdala and hypothalamus, prolific suppliers of stress-associated chemicals that attempt to turn your 3 A's around.

The Limbic Brain

The prefrontal cortex has strong two-way connections with the limbic system, a group of more primitive inner brain structures considered to be the major players in generating emotions. While the cortex relies on rational and abstract reasoning and an analytic process to evaluate the meaning of information forwarded by the senses, the limbic system looks for emotional worth in its assessment of a stressor. Teaming together, they determine what amount and balance of chemicals to release into your system. The prefrontal cortex holds the power to veto and rule. That is, of course, when we willfully put it to work.

The amygdala is a major limbic team player that unleashes an extreme chemical deluge that pumps your activation up for fight-flight-fright. The amygdala has two chains of command for working its magic. In the first, it makes a direct hit through the brainstem. Its second attack route passes through a series of chemical circuits via the hypothalamus, another limbic structure. [15]

The amygdala can be a powerful contender against the prefrontal cortex. The amygdala's primary workforce consists of the dynamic stress duo of epinephrine and norepinephrine. As you would expect, they compromise your focus and thinking by launching yet another attack upon your prefrontal cortex. Together they are powerful enough to essentially shut it down in what Goleman and colleagues have termed an "amygdala highjacking." [16] The amygdala's direct effects on the brainstem generate *physical tensions and posturing* that resemble activation levels originally adaptive during fight, flight, or freezing. You experience the tensions from the top of your head to your toes, including the white-knuckled grip on your steering wheel or ski poles that was formerly a display of the clawlike talons and fists of previous versions of our species.

The narrowing of slanted eyes accompanied by the flaring of nostrils and the tight-lipped grimace, originally intended to inspire fear in those relentless barbarians at the gate and send them running under siege of their own stress chemicals, are signals that you can spot today. You will see them in the faces of teens and two-year-olds when you utter the word "No." And you can see them in faces gathered around the negotiation table when things get heated. They are a common sight among frequent flyers, evident in the faces of weary travelers at every airline counter serving customers whose flights have been canceled or delayed.

Today, the burrowing of your toes that set our ancestors up for the dash for the door and the low crouch that positioned them to pounce on the enemy is a handy posturing that can ready you to receive a tennis serve. The same stance can position you to lunge forward at the dinner or board table during confrontation or dive down a ski slope.[17]

An expert at delegation, the amygdala has another network through which it exerts influence. It works through the hypothalamus, another limbic structure that is small but packs a real punch through chain reactions that release stress hormones, including epinephrine and norepinephrine throughout the body in proportions that either chill out the parasympathetic side or excite the sympathetic side. This is yet another affront to the prefrontal cortex.

After its split-second verdict about the emotional significance of a stressor, the amygdala passes its judgment on to the hypothalamus as to whether this stressor is worth getting worked up about or not. The hypothalamus then gives the nod to the autonomic nervous system, either chilling out the parasympathetic branch or heating up the sympathetic system. In describing these loops, I am going to stick with the fight-or-flight-or-fright extreme reactions that occur when the amygdala sends out a "danger ahead" warning to rev up the sympathetic side.

Your hypothalamus activates the sympathetic nervous system in three circular systemic reactions. Two act on the adrenal gland and a third affects the pituitary gland.

The first adrenal circuit works through the adrenal medulla, the middle part of the gland. Registering a warning from the hypothalamus that a threat is looming, the adrenal medulla secretes epinephrine and norepinephrine.

Think major adrenaline surge. A portion of these hormonal messengers journeys via the blood stream for direct deposit to body organs. The rest feeds back into the hypothalamus, alerting it, in another positive self-fueling feedback loop, to produce more. You feel activation soar in *muscular tension, the urge to run, fight, hide, lash out, drive someone off the road, throw sticks and stones, or hurl their modern-day equivalents in words that can hurt other people's bones and wound their hearts.*

In instances when it is appropriate to run, fight, or hide, it feels just right. But many of the reactions that were adaptive for effectively dealing with hairy predators—they were Zonal back then—are just too much for most of today's dangers. Running away from the hefty pile of work on your desk, engaging in hardcore boardroom battle, or hiding underneath the desk are not generally accepted at home, at the office, or at school. You end up in the o-Zone feeling tense, irritable, or furious and, like our friend Tom, alone, because everyone else took cover or flew the coop. In many instances, we do not even realize how out of touch we were until after the fact. In our mind's eye, when we are caught up in the chemically induced moment, we believe we are acting reasonably. Once the prefrontal cortex kicks back in, things often look different through a new wider-angle, flexible lens.

Then there is the heart and lung piece. There's that heartbeat that you feel throughout your body, whether it's a pounding headache or a sensation that your red-veined eyeballs are about to burst with the pulsating tempo. Your *heart pounds so hard* that you convince yourself that everyone else can see it beneath your suit jacket, scrubs, or much-loved tattered gray sweatshirt. At the same time, your breathing rate skyrockets. It is *hyperventilation* time.

Your *blood pressure rises* to send blood to your extremities, a hard-wired response that enabled previous models of our species to engage in a speedy getaway or a ferocious attack. You feel twitchy or warm in your hands and feet. Blood surges to your head and turns your face blistering scarlet. You feel *hotheaded.* The veins in your temples and even in your eyeballs throb.

Then there is the moisture issue. All of the moisture from your cotton *dry mouth* seems to migrate to your palms, armpits, and feet, all of which *sweat bullets that produce puddles and* turn your *feet cold.* These are the signs of activation on the rise or over the edge. And it's not over yet.

Our ancestors had to be ready for fight or flight at a moment's notice. When they were under attack, *digestion shut down* to divert energy from the stomach to the legs and arms to hasten their escape. After all, why waste energy eating in a situation when you might be eaten. The same thing happens today when you feel like *butterflies* with flailing wings have taken up residence in your stomach. Or you might feel *queasy,* sick to your stomach, or a *gnawing* that can grow to ulcer proportion. Attention kicks in too. In response to this hormonal siege, *attention gets sharper—narrow and acute.* Details and colors pop out. Our ancestors had to be astute and zoom in to new scents or sights that could alert them to poisonous enemies or vegetation. Your senses become more heightened, especially your sense of smell, which is associated with the limbic system. Things really do start to smell fishy!

For memories logged in under stress, you get smarter. Epinephrine, mediated by the amygdala, affects attention in a way that is particular to the amygdala. Attention gravitates to stimuli that appear to be emotionally loaded, especially negative aversive stimuli. Under the spell of epinephrine, your memory for what you hear and what you see improves. Attention heightens, zooming you in to sear internal and external stimuli into your brain, particularly negative and traumatic stressors. Logged in under the influence of epinephrine, memories are extraordinarily vivid and enduring.[18]

There is still another effect of the stress that might enable you to leap tall buildings in a single bound or to traverse hot rocks. When your sympathetic system is rolling, your sensitivity to pain dulls. This might be a result of the release of naturally occurring painkillers in your system called endorphins along with epinephrine rushes. It might explain the increased sense of confidence that can border on unrealistic invincibility or sheer stupidity when you are barreling toward a monovision goal, invincible in the fast forward activation lane.

Cortisol Pressure

The commandeering hypothalamus has a third offensive adrenal gland loop in which it enlists the pituitary gland to alert the adrenal cortex that a perceived threat is in the air.[19] On command, the pituitary sends out its own messenger, ACTH. That chemical instructs the adrenal cortex to send out another powerful hormone, cortisol, which is associated with A^3 sensations of the high-frequency o-Zone. Think pressure.

Cortisol surges exert powerful effects on our bodies. Feeling stressed, a heaviness on your chest, or a sense of urgency are a few of the common side effects. There are times when such urgency is right on—you're in the Zone. And there are other times when they are the wrong fit. You know that you are off base when people look at you curiously, giving you the classic kick-under-the-table to alert you that you are in a different scene than the rest of the group. To make sure our ancestors' wounds healed over quickly even during the mad dash, cortisol increases blood clotting, which is not such a great thing in this day and age of strokes and other cardiovascular disasters related to this phenomenon. Carting excess cortisol around for extended periods of time is associated with an ever-growing slate of physical and psychological disorders, including osteoporosis, cardiovascular disorders, and depression.[20]

Stress Really Can Make You Stupid

The amygdala exerts a significant effect on your brain—on how smart you are. When it is fired up, it can turn even the most astute into emotional and intellectual buffoons by impairing your best line of defense, the prefrontal cortex.

Under perceived stress, high levels of epinephrine and norepinephrine bathe the cortical surface of the brain, particularly the valuable prefrontal cortex. While it sounds soothing, it feels dreadful because the "-ephrine" duo seriously compromise the ability of the prefrontal cortex to provide you with all of those high-end executive abilities including abstract thinking and flexible attention. While the effects of the limbic releases are similar to those launched by the locus coeruleus and cingulate gyrus, they pack an additional and even stronger punch.[21]

"Cognitive dysfunction" is the terminology to describe the compromises of the prefrontal cortex, particularly those associated with attention and attitude. Cognitive dysfunction includes compromises of your ability to *make decisions* (good ones or any at all) and your *planning and organizing* skills. Your ability to formulate *well-informed judgments and ditch worn-out beliefs and take on some better-fitting new ones* might vanish. What you experience is an unsavory sensation of stress turning you into an intellectual and emotional imbecile.

When your brain is ramped up on epinephrine and norepinephrine, attention becomes *hyperfocused*—that unsavory *Johnny-one-note* phenomenon when the same negative thoughts recycle endlessly or a tune from the elevator gets stuck in your head. These chemicals also affect attitude, and it's not in a positive way. Whether it's acute or prolonged stress, harboring epinephrine and norepinephrine decreases activity in the prefrontal cortex, leaving *you pessimistic, and riddled with self-doubt.*

From this mental stance, we often *blame ourselves and others.* Pessimism is associated with feeling helpless and frightened, out of control. Sadly, this can become a habitual style that frequently alienates others, leading us to create our own prophecy regarding our low worth.

When helplessness becomes a habitual way of thinking and perceiving, depression and anxiety or aggression can result. [22] These chronic biopsychological states have associated long-term shifts in the chemical balance and structures of the brain and body, creating feedback loops in which stress-associated chemicals dominate, continuing to feed the *negative half-empty outlook and pessimistic thinking.*

When the stress hormones and neurotransmitters secreted match the challenge at hand, even when they are very high or very low, we are optimally aligned in the Zone. But a more habitual response is that the stress chemicals ride too high for the real deal and we spiral into the triple-A lineup of the o-Zone associated with poor performance, narrowed attention, and a narrow mind full of blaming, judgmental attitudes. The strategies of *The Winner's Way* are designed to provide you with the countermeasures to launch a defense against the attempted takeovers of your reason and wit.

Stress Makes You Sick

The brain-body responses brought on by intense biochemical surges are also associated with stress-induced disorders.[23] Their side effects can be deadly. The stress chemicals are associated with a compromised immune system and negative impacts on heart function and are thought to be related to cancer as well as other illnesses, including gastrointestinal illnesses like ulcers that can eat away at us. Carting excess cortisol for extended periods of time puts you on constant overdrive and is associated with health problems that include increases in blood pressure, high cholesterol, and hardening of the arteries. There is some speculation and initial research showing that harboring high cortisol for the long run has further-reaching effects that include decreased bone density and memory impairment. Exposure to stress chemicals for an extended run can deplete the brain's serotonin levels and raise dopamine. This leads to anxiety, depression, aggression, including that directed toward the self, and sleep and eating disorders.[24] The effects are not appealing and can be devastating on your physical health and emotional well-being. Left unbridled, they can be deadly.

We can, when we live without awareness of the 3 A's and when we choose to let them determine their own course, actually make ourselves stupid and sick.

Each day we encounter a variety of situations requiring different levels of activation, attention, and attitude for making the connection. In some instances, a stress-bathed brain and body will get the job done. And in others, a less "sympathetic" response will be a better fit. In most instances, your triple-A lineup will lie somewhere in between these two extremes. The power to choose is still as straightforward as strategic alignment of the 3 A's.

The Other Side—Rest-and-Digest

But what about the other side of the autonomic system, the parasympathetic side where rest and relaxation, sometimes bordering on couch potato apathy and lethargy, rule? Although our distant relatives did not possess the prefrontal cortex and other outer layers, they were, in some ways, smarter than we are. After successfully beating out or beating up the opposition, they did what made sense—they kicked back and rested. They made the rest-and-digest time to recoup from the exertion of running, competing, and covering their rears in the corner of the cave. From fight-flight-fright, they retired to the "rest-and-digest" mode.[25]

The parasympathetic and sympathetic sides of the autonomic nervous system operate essentially in opposition to each other. The emotional limbic coalition sets your system ablaze in a sympathetic-stimulating dance that short-circuits your reasonable prefrontal cortex in response to stressors registered as very good or very bad. This same system produces a different, slow jazz samba when stressors are logged in as neutral or benign or as items that warrant a relaxed response. On the parasympathetic side, the chemical release is associated with feelings of nurturing, love, and security that we experience when activation, attention, and attitude are aligned for rest-and-digest in a trusting setting. [26]

Trust Is Relative

Keep in mind that the prefrontal cortex and limbic structures make their attributions based on rational versus emotional valence. Not all settings for trust are equal.

When you are at low levels of activation, your attention is taking in the panoramic view and your attitude is one of an open, vulnerable mind. In this state, you might leave yourself open to hostile takeovers by other people or companies. Again, the balance is subtle for engaging and soaring.

In the rest-and-digest response, activation, attention, and attitude are impacted in an opposite manner by the same stress chemicals as well as others that ramped you up for fight-flight-fright, for the breakaways in life, including road rage.[27] In this instance, the diluted cocktail winds you down. The baseline whir of activation, attention, and attitude plays a significant role in the attribution process on this side too. When the 3 A's are aligned in such a manner that the brain evaluates an entering stimulus as neutral or good, processes are set in motion that ratchet down the stress cocktail that was in full glory for fight-or-flight. Your 3 A's subside. The edge comes off. You can feel it when your shoulders release your head from their vise grip and your toes can wiggle in your shoes.

Sometimes it feels like a welcome life-saving relief. People often report the sudden release into this more restful state after sprinting for the finish line on a work project. Often the release feels just right, a time to refuel for the next "sympathetic" sprint.

In other instances it feels like you are losing your edge. Tom, the high-speed attorney, was initially uneasy with letting his shoulders down. It felt too much like letting his guard down, and he feared opening himself up for attack. By identifying the daily situations in which he could regroup and refresh in this "R&D" state, he realized that these moments actually provided him with the sustenance for getting back up for the sprints and intense battles that were part of his courtroom role.

Attention shifts too on the parasympathetic state. It gets very flexible and very wide.[28] In fact, it might shift too much. You might find yourself distracted or randomly tuning from one modality to another or from one thought or stimulus to another. You might find it difficult to determine the really important elements of a situation.

The chemical mixture on the parasympathetic side lowers activation and enhances attentional and cognitive flexibility. Your focus travels far and wide, and you entertain doing new things and even doing old things in new ways. This is a great place to be for planning a vacation, designing and implementing change on the home front or in the workplace, or for opening yourself up to embrace changes, even those that include loss. But too much can be too much.

With so many choices, it can be difficult to make a decision, so you put it off until tomorrow. But then tomorrow doesn't look so good either. Playing not to lose, you refuse to let go of options. They slip between your fingers or someone else scarfs them up right before your eyes. Lost opportunities abound—lost jobs, apartments, and outings with friends and family. Under the influence of mild disconnection or full-blown apathy and lethargy, committing to relationships is difficult at best. Your aperture for viewing the world gets very wide. The panoramic lens is great for scanning the environment for competitive trends but not so good for honing in on the most threatening competitors on the horizon, for reading to comprehend, for unearthing and resolving the differences of opinion that have been left growing under the rug for years, or for truly listening to another person.

This mix also impacts attribution. With the chemical dosage of the parasympathetic side and its characteristic triple-A lineup, your mind is unsuspecting, to the point of naïve gullibility. This nonjudgmental stance will do you well in secure, comfortable settings where being open and vulnerable connects you to the experience and to people. Taken to extremes and without the healthy scrutiny that has kept our species going, this might render you susceptible to victimization and hostile takeover.

During rest-and-digest modes where activation is low, there is a general sensation of calm relaxation. You can feel this in your fingers and in your toes, in your heart and lungs. When you remember to breathe, your breathing slows, sometimes to a relaxed deep sigh. Your heartbeat subsides and your blood pressure decreases. Sometimes you wonder if your heart is beating at all. Instead of dry mouth, you salivate, ready for digestion. Wet palms and toes are replaced with warm, dry hands and feet.

While you adamantly pointed your finger at others and your hands jutted forward in a menacing thrust on the "sympathetic" side of the curve, you let it all hang out on this end, displaying your hands with their palms facing upward in what could, in some settings, be interpreted as surrendering. Here you assume a more relaxed stance, leaning forward or back, lounging rather than lunging. Eye contact is different too. While your pupils dilated to saucer diameter to stare down the enemy on high doses of stress chemicals, they contract here. Rather than drilling into the eyes of another or looking aghast at something new, you gaze with genuine curiosity (or with the glazed daze of apathy, depending on the situation), nodding your head and grinning rather than grimacing.[29] When taken in correct, controlled doses and in the appropriate setting, this is relaxation at its finest. It feels wonderful when it is a good fit that does not sink beneath your personal threshold. In those instances, the restful groove can power you back up again and enable you to protect yourself from any perceived dangers. Meditation and "the relaxation response"[30] are two examples of parasympathetic-dominant states associated with lower readings of heart rate, blood pressure, oxygen consumption, and cortisol production. And it is not just a temporary thing.

Meditation and strategic relaxation techniques have a longer-term impact on keeping cortisol levels at a more moderate level than the momentary effects. The positive impacts on physical and emotional health have been documented in the mind-body research and anecdotal reports. [31] Willfully achieving such states supports the ability and power of the human will to purposefully align the 3 A's.

But can you be too relaxed? Surprisingly, the answer is yes. Too little might be too much. On a one-time basis, you might forget the moves you had planned, landing you on your backside or blindsided, just as one Ivy League diver did. When people idle at such low speeds on a chronic basis, it is difficult for them to rally and get into the game. Chronic low activation accompanied by a focus that is not adequately selective and an attitude that does not include a dose of healthy skepticism can be symptomatic of low motivation and apathy that will get in your way of enjoying life's small pleasures and its supersized challenges.

Taken to an extreme, chronic parasympathetic dominance is associated with apathy, lethargy, depression, and amotivational syndrome in which people have little interest or desire to engage with even the basic tasks of daily living and certainly do not push themselves beyond the comfort zone. It takes energy to reach out and grab life's rope swings. For those who insist on idling at a mere simmer, there may be regrets for swings left unswung and songs left unsung.

It Was Just Right

Somewhere in the middle of the two extremes is a state where the natural chemicals surging through you create a harmonious balance between the parasympathetic and sympathetic nervous systems, a just-right fit. In the middle ground, activation rides at a moderate speed, attention is focused to select only the essentials and tune out the rest, and attitude is both wondrous and beneficially, as well as healthfully, skeptical. That is the triple-A lineup that is well matched for most experiences of our daily lives.

Remember though, it is not one-size-fits-all. For every activity that you encounter, there will be constant, subtle fluctuations in circumstances that require precise shifts in activation, attention, and attitude for total *willful* engagement of the body, mind, and heart. Once you start tuning in to read your activation, attention, and attitude and make a conscious commitment to choose and align them to the moment, you will become more aware of the subtleties and better able to shift them with ease. Soon you will be soaring on autopilot with your prefrontal cortex providing judicious guidance that enables serious moments and raucous celebrations.

Coalition Building

The cortex is your ally. Build a coalition with it. The prefrontal cortex can help you to review stressors in a new light or from a new angle. And it can aid you in reframing stressors. With the prefrontal cortex, you can reason your way out of stress and summon up the resources of your memory banks to make a more informed decision rather than a snapshot judgment characteristic of high activation, narrow attention, and a stress-chemical brain bath.

You can harness the power of your will. You can take advantage of the prefrontal area to choose levels of activation, attention, and attitudes that are associated with a more moderate chemical release, which allows for a more even-tempered evaluation by the limbic structures. That is unless, of course, you are being chased down by a predator, in which case you can choose to talk your way out of the scene at a moderate activation pace or you can fire up to hightail it out of there.

The prefrontal cortex is smart and strong. It is powerful enough to intervene to circumvent the autopilot responses of the emotional brain and other centers that flood you with stress chemicals that might not be the right balance for the moment. The 3 A's provide the route for change. But only if you choose to get on the bus, grab the wheel, and drive.

Therein lies the power of will. By harnessing the power of will that is granted by your magnificent brain and nervous system and by the unique constellation that is you, you can live a life that you really do love. It is still as basic as 3 A's.

Postoperative Debriefing

- In response to perceived stress, which is a relative thing for each of us, natural chemicals, principally norepinephrine, epinephrine, dopamine, serotonin, and cortisol are released by different areas of your brain and body that are associated with heating up or cooling down your nervous system.
- These chemicals turn on the "fight-flight-freeze" response that has powerful effects on activation, attention, and attitude. Working in an opposite manner, in response to stressors that you perceive as benign or nonthreatening, they create the "rest-and-digest" response.
- The dilution and lineup of the stress chemicals impact activation, attention, and attitude. They generate the characteristic constellations—high activation/narrow hyperfocus/rigid attitude with its characteristic feelings of resentment and agitation and, on the rest side–low activation/broadband focus/open attitude associated with apathetic retreat.
- The prefrontal cortex grants many powers including abstract thinking, impulse control, cognitive and attentional flexibility. The chemical cocktail that bathes your body and brain during

high-frequency activation launches a hostile takeover of the prefrontal cortex. You experience "cognitive dysfunction"—the stress makes you stupid, intellectually and emotionally.

- The chemicals surging within you can ratchet up or down depending on what you tune into and select as your reality, the physical tensions that you carry on or ditch at the gate, and the attitudes that you pack in your carry-on.

- Too little or too much stress-related hormones and neurotransmitters can make you stupid, stuporous, depressed, and sick.

- The power of will is in learning to tune in to determine, and take control of the 3 A's to match them to the situation. That way, you can keep your wits about you and engage your prefrontal cortex when everyone else might be losing theirs.

Chapter 7

All Together Now—The Arc of Engagement

Activation, attention, and attitude are not stand-alone processes. They are interdependent. Their effects are synergistic—they team up to generate results that exceed what you could ever expect from merely adding them together. Collaborating in spiraling, self-fueling feedback loops, their effects are logarithmic—A^3 (A-cubed).

There are characteristic patterns between these three critical processes. They are mediated by the chemical cocktail circulating through you at any moment and have been documented in research in the behavioral sciences, including sports psychology, and confirmed in anecdotal reports in sports, business, and real-world challenges.[1] The predictable results of typical A^3 constellations can range from stellar to disastrous, depending on the fit of the three to the moment. The relationship between the 3 A's and the quality of your experiences is not linear, and it isn't black and white.

The Harder You Try

Many of us have been trained to believe that there is a direct relationship between how hard you try and the how well you do. The more

activated, the more focused, and the more confident we are, the better we'll do. That is what early psychology researchers predicted in
"Drive Theory."[2] Except they didn't talk about *activation, attention,* or
attitude. They talked about "drive" and "arousal."

Drive was the generic term for internal motivation, a burning need
that could be based on something as basic as hunger for food. When
the concept was extended to two-legged animals, the drive could be as
complex as hunger for a goal, whether it was a quest for knowledge,
recognition, or bottom-line results.[3] Drive was reflected in physiological arousal, also known as "activation." The exhausted mice and rats
running mazes under conditions of high drive, as well as two-legged
rat-racers in overdrive, proved this theory to be wrong. The relationship between drive and performance wasn't a straight line after all.

Drive Theory fell apart at higher levels of drive where performance,
rather than improving, took a nosedive. Many who have sprinted
through their precious life's time, based on this theory, have ended up
burning out. In sports, when athletes abide by the "harder you play"
rule, they often get injured or lose sight of the goal in that overactivated "visual narrowing" state where stress makes you stupid and you
can't see straight.[4]

The straight-line theory was abandoned. In its stead, researchers
dusted off the Yerkes-Dodson Law dating back to early 1900s. Also
known as the "Inverted-U Hypothesis"[5] this model proposes that performance improves as drive or activation rises into an arc-shaped top of
the curve where performance is at its peak. The band at the top of the
curve is where mice, rats, and humans achieve their personal bests. This
range of optimal functioning has been called the "Optimal Performance
State" or the "Individual Zone of Optimal Functioning."[6] I call it the
arc of engagement. At levels of the 3 A's that are below or in excess of
that ideal range, engagement, along with performance, deteriorates.

The inverted-U extends beyond basic drives such as hunger, the need
to avoid electrical shock, and the physiological arousal and muscle tensions that comprise activation. The inverted-U includes the "soft

side"—anxiety and drives such as the need to achieve, the desire for recognition, control, accuracy, the desire for close relationships and for self-actualization.[7] Recently, several such "soft" needs have been correlated with peak performance. They are major contributors to bottom-line results and significant improvements in returns on financial and human resources in the workplace.[8]

The inverted-U isn't one-size-fits-all. It is both situational and personal.[9] Your own curve, and that of the packs with which you are affiliated, will vary depending on your baseline health, your fatigue, and other factors. Hardy and colleagues, in their "Catastrophe Model" have proposed that the fall from the cusp of the curve is not a graceful slide.[10] Instead it resembles a straight-line tumble that depicts our disastrous outcomes that remain singed vividly in our memory banks.[11]

The Arc of Engagement

The inverted-U shape describes the relationship between *activation, attention, attitude,* engagement, and performance. In some instances, the farthest tail resembles a steep plunge characteristic of a catastrophe waiting to happen.

Each day we are confronted with a variety of situations that clamor for our *attention* and demand different levels of *activation* and *attitude.* Because they interact in a feedback loop, *activation, attention,* and *attitude* have characteristic effects on each other and on performance, thought, and feelings. The Zone and the o-Zone are not, in fact, discrete bands. Instead they span a curve that looks like an upside-down U with tails; because for as long as we are living, we are activated, focused on one thing or another, and we always have an attitude in our lifetime carry-on.

For each situation that you face, there is a unique, bell-shaped curve that represents the levels of *activation, attention,* and *attitude* that are too little, too much, or just right for doing and feeling your best and thinking at the top of your game. At the top of the curve is the "arc of engagement," the Zone where *activation, attention,* and *attitude* are a perfect personal fit for connecting to the moment. The extremes or ends of the curve, the "tails," represent the *o-Zones of disenchantment and enragement.*

The tails represent the two alternative experiences that are characteristic of o-Zonal disconnection—apathy and anger. On the left is the *tail of disengagement,* where disenchantment, apathy, despair, and possibly depression, along with regret and guilt, are the norm. On the far right lies the *tail of enragement,* characterized by mild irritability and feeling edgy to frustration, agitation, anger, and possibly rage and resentment along with blame. The two tails represent your experiences when you check out from the real circumstances facing you. For example Jim retreated to the tail on the left and Tom bolted for the far right. Alignment of the 3 A's at either tail assures you of a disconnected, subpar result.

In the middle, at the top of the curve, lies a personal range where your *activation, attention,* and *attitude* are a perfect fit for connecting to the challenge-at-hand. While some would consider it the arch of triumph, and it is true that your highest probability of victory occurs here, I have termed it the *arc of engagement.* Within this arc, connection, desire, and justified pride rule. This predictable inverted-U-shaped relationship can provide guidance when it is time to line your A's up to connect with the fast-beat challenges and the easy-listening experiences that are your life.

The curve highlights the characteristic relationships between activation, attention and attitude and their predictable effects on each other, on performance, thoughts, feelings, and behaviors. (See Figure 7-1.)

The curve highlights the characteristic A-cubed triads generated by the chemical baths surging within. On the lower left side of the curve lies the *underactivated/broadband-focus/open-mind triad.* On the upper right end, attention narrows, screening out important information critical to performance and well-being, contributing to the opposite *overactivated/narrowband-focus/rigidly narrow mind triad.*

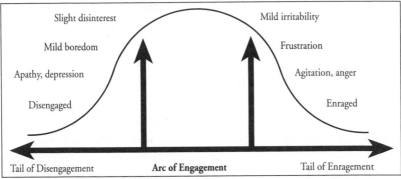

Tail of Disengagement	Arc of Engagement	Tail of Enragement
	ACTIVATION	
Asleep at the wheel	Just right	High alert
Too tired	Charged	Frazzled
Weary	Pumped up	Agitated
Halfhearted	Calm and centered	Edgy, tense
	ATTENTION	
Out of focus	Focused on the essentials	Out of focus
Generally broad or	Data people, micro or macro,	Very narrow on
On irrelevant factors	directed inward or out	self or others as targets
	ATTITUDE	
Harshly judgmental, especially toward self	Open Mind	Harshly judgmental, especially toward others
Oppressed victim	Opportunity	Oppressed oppressor
Language of despair: *"I/you/we can't…"*	Language of determination: *"I can… You can… We can…"*	Language of decimation: *"You/they can't do that to me…"*
Self-doubt, other-doubt	Confidence	Blame and other doubt
Unimportant, beyond reach	Important, meaningful	Urgent and a pain in the backside
	BEHAVIORS	
Retreat	Really do it — real deal	Retaliate
Check out passively	Active participation	Active and passive aggression
Do it yourself	Delegate realistically	Boss people around
Silence	Effective communication	Yell, sarcastic jabs, spread rumors
Complain to self	Effective feedback and conflict resolution	Talk about others, rant and rave
Rare recognition of others	Recognize and reward others	Recent recognition of others
Suspicious of differences	Accept and leverage differences	Resent differences, seen as affront
	FEELINGS	
Apathy	Realistic emotions based on the situation from depression to joy	Rage
Depression, despair		Impatience, irritability
Impotent	Reality-based sphere of power	Omnipotent
Indifference	Pride, joy	Resentment
	THOUGHTS	
Nobody cares.	I'm competent and lovable.	Who cares? They're to blame.
I don't deserve it.	I have worked hard for this.	They deserved my wrath.
I have no control — I give up.	I have control over myself. and a realistic sphere of influence.	I'm taking back control at any expense or cost.
I'll show them how they hurt me.	I'll communicate with them.	I'll show them — I'll beat them.
I'll do it myself because they don't listen to me.	I'll delegate it based on strengths and interests.	I'm the boss. They should do it. But they're inept.

Figure 7-1   Arc of Engagement

Performance improves as activation rises until you reach a critical level just over the crest of the curve. At this point, an increase in activation or a shift in attention or attitude can send you plunging over the edge into the o-Zone. For each situation, you have an optimal range of the 3 A's at the top of the inverted-U that is characteristic of ultimate immersion and peak performance. Picture the tails as red—you don't want to go there—and the arch as green. The personalized markers that alert you to the upper and lower limits of your arc are yellow to signify "danger ahead."

At levels of activation below or above the green zone, you're stuck in the o-Zone. On the left, performance lags and is usually accompanied by o-Zonal feelings of apathy or depression and debilitated motivation. Once your activation has crested the inverted-U and soared above the upper Zonal limits, performance and satisfaction plummet. Anxiety and fear or anger and agitation are the most common emotions associated with this extreme.

Where You Ride Affects What You See and How You Frame It

At each moment, we are making attributions about the value of things to us—are they good, bad, ugly, beautiful, burdensome oppressions to resent or boundless opportunities to relish? There is a characteristic style of attribution at each tail. At the far left, we tend to see things through the lens of helpless victimization. Passive resignation rules. Or, when the triad of this end is a good fit for the situation, we entertain an open mind that is well suited for strategic, creative thinking. On the fast-breakaway right, there is a tendency to see danger looming and to assume a defensive or offensive countermeasures stance. Reactive resentment reigns. In instances when there truly is a clear and present danger, this attribution style could save your life. But when people ride this end of the continuum and chronically attribute threat to benign, and even to positive, stressors, they run into trouble, just like Tom, the attorney who lived on this end of the curve when I first met him.

When you perceive a situation for which you believe you have the right stuff—the mental or physical skills to prevail—you'll release the correct stress hormone dilution to land you in the top of the curve. There activation, attention, and attitude are aligned at levels that are personally optimal for the situation.[12] Within this arc, attributions are realistic. You accept things with the Filene's Basement "as is" attitude. Then you bring meaning to it, enabling you to approach the situation from a proactive stance.

The tails are characterized by surviving or managing. In the arc, you move beyond this to thrive and to exert the personal leadership that enables you to prevail over whatever pitches life throws you, including the spitballs. By learning to adjust your 3 A's to match the situation at hand, you can turn your own perceptions around to turn oppressions into opportunities and depression into desire to live a life of personal bests.

Remember, attribution is both chicken and egg to the 3 A's. Attribution is determined by the baseline lineup of the 3 A's. And it impacts them as well. That's why two different people might experience the same stressor—a new job, moving to a new house, starting or ending a relationship, a winning score for the Red Sox or the Yankees—as positive or negative based on baseline activation along with selective attention and preconceived attitudes. It also explains why you might experience the same event as stressful one day and manageable on another day. It depends on your baseline A's. As always, attention, attitude, and activation co-labor synergistically as a circular system. And these are within your control.

Here's how it works. When you perceive a stressor as negative—as a threat of loss (like Tom with other drivers), as overwhelming or oppressive, it is either because of:

- **Attention**—where you focus (e.g., the half empty—"We were going to miss the delivery date." or "The new job is longer hours and I have to manage other people." or "My heart is pounding so fast that I'm having a heart attack.").
- **Attitude**—the beliefs and assumptions you hold about the situation or yourself or other people (e.g., "My team screwed up. There aren't any options for us." "I don't do the management thing well because I hate coming down on employees who aren't working hard." or "I'm a terrible speaker.").
- Natural **Activation** levels along with the baseline **Activation** that you harbor at the time of the event (e.g., running on high octane like Tom –"My pounding heart took so much blood that I could barely lift my feet or see straight to get to the phone to call the ambulance service." Or coasting on empty like Mary—"I just didn't' have what it takes to confront that employee.").
- **All of the Above—Triple A synergy** propels you into the o-Zone.

Your attribution—is this good, bad, ugly, or beautiful?—will determine the next round of activation, attention, and attitude.

The Feel of What Happens

When we are out of alignment for the moment, we end up feeling sad or mad in the tails of the curve. Feelings range from curiously discontent to lows of downright depression on the left end to an unexplainable, impatient irritation to full-blown rage on the right. There are times when extremely low or high A^3 triads are appropriate to get connected for doing your best. In such instances, feeling fearful, angry, agitated, or sad will be appropriate. When the 3 A's are aligned to the situation, feelings can range from extreme despair to ecstatic joy to defensive rage.

Circumstantial

The shape of the U varies depending on the circumstances.[13] For some activities it's narrow and steep with a sharp rise, an equally sharp dive, and a very narrow green band. Sprints in sports or business, fast-paced implementations of business or life plans, getting pumped up to make a deadline, hurrying everyone out of the door in the morning, keeping up with your kids on skis, and energizing yourself and your team to make a stellar presentation are all instances when the inverted-U rises sharply to guide you into the peak engagement arc. In these cases, riding over the edge might feel like a sharp plunge off a steep cliff into the depths of the o-Zone.

In other cases, the U-curve has a more rounded shape from its rise to its fall. Typically there's a broader green range at the top of the curve. Engaging with colleagues in genuine interactive dialogue in which you are seeking a mutual understanding, reading a book, taking a leisurely stroll, formulating a plan for delivering a tough performance review, or getting yourself calmed down to hear and process the honest feedback provided by a business coach or boss when it is your performance that is being reviewed—these are instances in which the curve rises and falls at a slower, steadier rate.[14] While the ride over the upper edge is less extreme, it's still important to maintain that subtle balance in the green zone.

The Tail of Disengagement

In the tail of disengagement, activation is too low for the situation. You are "asleep at the wheel," no matter where you are: behind a steering wheel, desk, stove, or computer screen. This can occur when things look too burdensome to even approach, as they did to Jim, who felt so overwhelmed by his diagnosis that he barely heard his physician tell him about the high success rate for curing his type of cancer. Or it can happen when you perceive little of interest in the current situation, so you consciously, or more often unconsciously, "check out" to another zone that frequently involves a remote control.

Now that you have read about the biological bases of *activation*, *attention*, and *attitude*, it will make sense that when you are underactivated, your attention wanders and your thinking diverges, either broadening to focus on the extraneous elements of the current situation or unproductively drifting. Unfortunately, these "time outs" don't contribute to doing well at what you are supposed to be doing at the moment. Basically, you just don't care—and it shows. Other people sit up and take note when your chin hits your chest to abruptly awaken you in the middle of an important meeting. When your energy resources are depleted and you are out of focus, confidence disappears. It can ruin a good day. As a chronic mode of operating, it can eliminate dreams of reaching personal, sports, or career goals.

At this end of the tail, your energy might be too low to step up to the table to take a leadership role like it was for Mary. When low activation is accompanied by an o-Zonal focus and a lack of confidence in your ability to confront the challenge as it was for Jim, it can be difficult to hear and deal with a difficult piece of news—a diagnosis, a personal loss, or collective trauma. Continuing to ignore the problem only makes it loom larger, which usually decimates confidence even more, spiraling the 3 A's to new lows. At this point, it is more that just a day that is ruined. Sometimes it's a lifetime.

The Tail of Enragement

At other times, the 3 A's align to plummet you into the o-Zone where mild agitation, frustration, and all-out rage are the norm. That's what happened to Tom during his days and nights.

On the downhill slide side of the curve, when *activation* levels are too high for the situation, all of your senses narrow and your thinking narrows too, which can lead to self-doubt, blame, and resentment. It's the classic narrow-mindedness of judgmental attitudes, where presumptive thinking and jumping to conclusions can disconnect you from good and bad times and lead you to charge head first into a battle of your own making.

Usually it starts with feeling mildly ill at ease. It's a subtle sensation of being under pressure, not quite up to the task, or that someone or something is threatening you. Often the causes or triggers are below the line of consciousness, especially because the mundane details of life usually dominate our thoughts. After the 3 A's have fully kicked in, you might feel under the gun, inept, tense, agitated, frustrated, or downright furious.

When you perceive a threat, conscious or unconscious, your body responds by generating a triple-A reaction that is not appropriate unless the situation is one of imminent physical danger. You go into defensive mode whether you are launching a subtle self-protection or a full-blown countermeasure attack. You're at the far-right tail of the arc, in the tail of enragement. You might not have a name for the feeling (our highly evolved brains enable us to shield ourselves from reality by denying or renaming things, including our feelings), but you can definitely feel it.

My clients who found themselves at this end of the curve were usually too agitated and angry to properly deal with their challenges, whether it was a frightening diagnosis or a tumultuous relationship at work or at home. They funneled their *activation* into other areas such as obsessive work or working out (or, in more than one case for sheetrocking entire rooms or building stone walls). They focused their anger on overblown situations largely of their own making, or they insulated themselves with alcohol. They ran away from their problems, which continued to grow. At such high levels of *activation*, people, like Tom, have trouble making deep connections with family members and others. And they struggle against enjoying the small pleasures of living.

Too much activation, just as too little, can make it difficult to relish daily routines like walking the dog, driving the kids, or the daily delights of a good meal and dinner conversation with family and friends. When we are in the arc of engagement, these simple joys are viewed as opportunities to breathe and "smell the roses," which appear a more brilliant red. When we're in the tail of enragement, however, we experience them as chest-crushing oppressions and yet another daily dozen of things to water and caretake.

There are circumstances in which it's appropriate to jack up the level of *activation* and where feeling mad is appropriate. But too many people find themselves looking for things that enrage them, and then justify their anger and their actions. *Overactivation* can erupt in angry outbursts on the roadways, in hockey rinks, at home, and at work. Chronic travel in this tail can wreak havoc with your life and with the lives of innocent bystanders.

The effects can be disastrous, even deadly. The result is a nervous system on overload. Overactivated, hypervigilant, narrow-minded, compromised by self-doubt, and reactive, your 3 A's are lined up at the wrong levels for the reality of the situation. You're ensconced in the o-Zone where accidents, poor decisions, frenzied rather than strategic actions, and "stress makes you stupid" sensations prevail. Over the long haul, this state can lead to the breakdown of the body's own defense, the immune system.

Living in the Tails Can Ruin a Day—Or Short-Circuit Your Life

When you're stuck in the tails of enragement or disengagement, you end up being captive to your physiology, resulting in a nervous system either on overload or compromised by chronic underutilization.

At both ends, natural chemical surges compromise your intellectual and emotional intelligence.[15] You find yourself dumbfounded, speechless, like your skull is numb and you've planted both feet in your mouth.

The emotions of apathy and anger are characteristic undermining interpretations of the nervous system's response to events or stimuli that you perceive as overwhelming. More frequently it is activation itself that you're aware of: Your head might ache, your back might hurt, or you might feel sick to your stomach.

In the near term, triple-A mismatches that land you in the o-Zonal tails lead to accidents, poor decisions, and inappropriate blaming of yourself or others based on jumping to conclusions. Acts of aggression as well as depression—including unbridled rage on roadways, workplaces, at home, or in schoolyards—are the sad results of the 3 A's being lined up for defensive or offensive battle.

Left unchecked, living in the low end can wreak havoc with your life through errors of omission, like sleeping through an important interview, neglecting your family, dismissing the significance of an up-and-coming competitor, or ignoring a deadly disease. Low activation can eat away at people's health and longevity, as was the case with Jim when he continued to do things as usual, instead of confronting his disease. And it can cripple or destroy entire organizations that keep their heads buried and continue to do business as usual until gobbled up by competitors they didn't see coming. These are friendly corner bookstores who neglected the influence of the Internet and designer coffee; Digital Equipment, which delighted customers with great technology geared to a central computer and chose to forego the decentralized desktop approach until others had cornered that market; and Woolworth's, where lovely wooden floors that creaked beneath your feet offered a secure feeling, but which could not compete with the low-priced specials of megamarts with linoleum flooring geared for making the dash and slide into the blue-lit specials. If you idle at the low end of the curve, when a truly dangerous situation does arise, it can be just too much effort to access the arc for engaging and dealing effectively—or it might be too late.

Chronically overactivated individuals suffer from stress-related disorders, impulsive disorders, and illnesses caused by harboring excess stress hormones. Families, teams, and organizations suffer a similar fate, spinning out of control, over budget, failing on new competitive turf for which they are inadequately prepared, compromising effectiveness due to duplicated effort, and even turning against each other in outbursts of rage.

Sustained o-Zonal extremes can be exhausting, burning you out or making you sick. Mental health might suffer also, ranging from depression to impulse-control disorders. Worse yet, when a genuinely threatening danger does present itself, a person might be too exhausted or numb to respond with the optimal levels of *activation, attention,* and *attitude* to prevail. No wonder learning to get the 3 A's under control is vital to moving beyond surviving to thriving, to stay in life for the long run and to enhance the quality of each step of the wondrous journey.

Really Do It!

What about you? Consider instances in which you've felt yourself soar over the edge of the arc into rage, or slither down to disengagement. What were the circumstances that seemingly pushed you over the edge? What are the daily events or people you encounter that seem to start o-Zonal spirals? What are your frequent personal readings of *activation, attention,* and *attitude* at the two extremes? How are they different from the markers in the arc?

It's Not One-Size-Fits-All

Just like the 3 A's, the arc of engagement is situational and personal. The morning sprint will have a curve rising sharply to high levels of activation, with a narrow arc of engagement. Soaring over the slippery edge can result in yelling at your kids or gesturing wildly at other drivers stuck in traffic. For the work and chores that demand a steady pace to complete them successfully and thoroughly, the curve rises more gradually, with a broader-banded arc of engagement. (See Figure 7-2.)

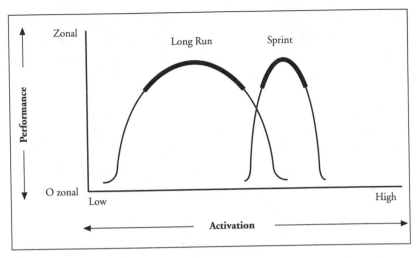

Figure 7-2 For the Long Run. The curve to the left is a good match for endurance events. The curve on the right is a good fit for sprints.

A difference is a difference. Ideal *activation, attention,* and *attitude* really are personal matters. Your partner, kids, and colleagues might each have arcs that are qualitatively different than your own, even for the same task. That doesn't mean any one of you is wrong. By learning to identify the demands of the situation, to read your own current levels of activation, attention, and attitude, and to develop personalized strategies to adjust each A, you will be able to position yourself in the arc of engagement for the various circumstances that you encounter each day—even the surprise ones.

And It's Personal

The arc of engagement is also personal, a matter of style. We each have a personal style when it comes to *activation, attention,* and *attitude.* Our personal style affects the shape of the engagement curve.

What felt like moderate levels of *activation* to Tom, the fast-forward attorney, felt like high-octane for some of his colleagues and for Jim, who prevailed over cancer at a more moderate pacing. Even for the same situation, any two people will have a unique shape to the curve. And they will have personalized marker signals that define the arc and its limits—the parameters that signal danger ahead and the indications of full-blown disaster.

When you wonder why your team members, your family, or your colleagues at work seem to be marching to a different beat or missing "the point," chances are that they are on a slower, steadier curve while you're in fast-forward, perched on a narrow arc. To enable yourself to succeed with the vast array of people and problems that you will encounter, you can learn to identify your characteristic strong suits and to be sufficiently flexible to access a variety of curves.

Even *attitude* is a personal thing. In the arc of engagement, we each use unique language and goals related to the process of building our confidence. Each tail has its own dialect of the "language of oppression" that reflects the o-Zone's *attitude* of disbelief. The disengagement tail is most frequently accompanied by subdued monotones of "I don't have it today," "I'm too tired," or "It's just too much," interspersed with long wishful "if only" sighs. A more vehement tone, frequently punctuated by foul language, pointing fingers, or hand gestures, characterizes the sound bytes of the enragement tail. It's all about beating someone or something —"Come on, let's get this going," "I'm going to let them have it," "I'm going to blow their doors off," or "I'm so pumped I could explode!" And usually that's just what happens at the enragement end of the curve, going out too fast to finish with style. The arc is personal. Yet there are a number of predictable factors that affect its shape

Getting in Shape

Time, precision, accuracy, and the demand to attend to a number of stimuli (complexity including multitasking) are among the factors that will impact the shape of the curve.

First there's the matter of time, of urgency. There are sprints in life—running for a bus, rushing to get the kids to school, racing for an appointment, dashing to finish a project. Accessing high *activation* for a short period, together with a narrow focus and an *attitude* that you can do it, will help get you to the finish line in time. For these time-limited events, the curve will rise steeply to a narrow arc of engagement characterized by high *activation*, a want and determination to really do it, and a focus on goals to get to the finish line on time. (Proactive importance versus reactive urgency works best here.) Remember though, that people will have their own personal spins on this.

Then there are longer-distance events—writing a detailed proposal, multiday strategic-planning sessions, helping your child sound out the words in a book while dinner preparations call your name from the kitchen. To effectively engage with these situations, you'll typically want a more moderate level of *activation*, enough to keep you interested and interesting but not so much that you spin into impatient judgments or slide into halfhearted disconnection. The curve will typically rise more gently, to a moderate level of *activation* with a broader band of optimal engagement, before it slips off gently into the tail of impatience.

Tom, the attorney, learned that his day presented opportunities to access a variety of engagement curves. He also concluded that he was spending too much time in the tail of enragement, whether he was driving to or from work, barking at his assistant, or ignoring his kids in their early-morning requests for lunch money or their dinnertime school tales that he dismissed as silliness.

Then there's the matter of accuracy, of doing things correctly, and of the precision that is part of fine motor tasks. For fine-motor tasks and challenges requiring attention to detail, the curve will typically ride at the lower left end of the continuum, with a narrow arc where attention to detail works best. These tasks call for a slower, more methodical approach, with a sharp focus and an attitude that recognizes or builds meaning for what you're doing, whether it's preparing your travel and expense account, analyzing a report that a novice team member prepared, explaining the directions for a math assignment to a third grader, or delegating a project to a new assistant whose will exceeds baseline skill. (See Figure 7-3.)

The curve will rest to the left as the demands of complexity and multitasking increase. As situations increase in complexity, you will want to moderate your *activation* to ensure that your *attention* aperture is adequately broad to focus in on the essential elements that cry out for your attention. When we experience multiple demands, it is also critical to proactively keep an open mind. It is often too easy to drift into reactive judgment in which we dismiss the demands as not important or to slide down to a helpless attitude where the demands

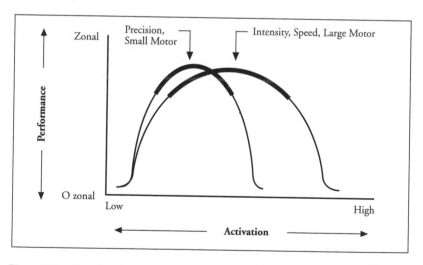

Figure 7-3 Coordination and Precision. Zonal activation will be lower with a more narrow arc for challenges calling for precision and tasks for which small motor coordination, or coordination of small groups is required for peak achievement. Large motor, or large group challenges tolerate higher levels of activation with a broader band.

feel like just too much. With increasing demands, the curve will rise more sharply and the arc will shrink. (See Figure 7-4.)

The demands to multitask hit Jim head on when he was juggling the intense time commitment of medical procedures and therapeutic processes on top of normal life demands. The subtle balance for staying in the arc and not retreating or getting angry and resentful of the extra commitments was critical to healing. The process was enhanced when Jim agreed to spend time reevaluating assumptions about how he should be handling the diagnoses and managing commitments. This enabled him to reprioritize what was important and to then align the 3 A's to engage with life's important things, including the people.

Timing, precision, complexity, which can include the styles of other people—these are just a few of the factors that influence the arc of engagement. Knowing yourself—specifically knowing your current and characteristic levels of the three A's provides the key to leverage your strengths and the strengths of others to do your best at the right thing.

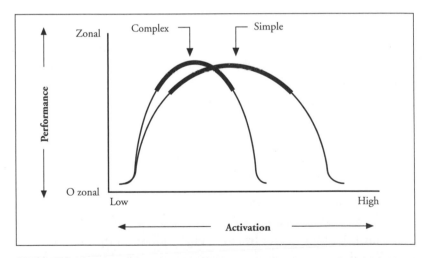

Figure 7-4 Complexity. For simple challenges, higher activation with a broader band will get us into the zone. As the challenge becomes more complex, zonal activation must be adjusted down, and the range of optimal activation will be more narrow.

Really Do It!

What about you? What are the events of your life where precision and some amount of speed are required to get the job done? Describe each of the 3 A's when you are in the arc and when you are in the tails.

Which daily events offer a respite, a time to kick back with lower *activation* and a broader focus, confident that you won't get blindsided? Consider the 3 A's for these activities.

Is there a good balance? Do you schedule "R&D" time to realign your nervous system and make sure that you will be ready to power up for the sprints?

When could you add one breather to your day? Think manageable—a five-minute block of time even if it means listening to music while you brush your teeth or taking the scenic route home accompanied by your favorite tunes?

With *The Winner's Way* you can take back control—so you won't feel compelled to fight, run, freeze, hide, or overeat when you perceive pressure. You can *willfully* engage with challenges so that you can start living in the arc of engagement—on purpose.

Postoperative Debriefing

- The Zone is not a discrete band.
- There is a personalized curve, shaped like a bell or an upside-down U, that ranges from 0-Zonal listlessness through the Zonal "arc of engagement" and over the edge into the 0-Zonal tail of enragement.

- Certain factors have a characteristic effect on the shape of the curve—such as time, urgency, need for precision and accuracy, complexity that includes multitasking. Still the arc of engagement is personal and situational.
- Living in the extremes or "tails" of the curve, in the o-Zone of disengagement or enragement, wreaks short-term losses and long-lasting disastrous effects, which include health problems, emotional impairment, aggressive behaviors, and neglecting to do things, resulting in missed opportunities.
- Living in chronic high alert or in low-level apathy impairs your ability to rally when real danger or extraordinary opportunity does present itself.
- With *The Winner's Way*, you can learn to access the arc of engagement for the challenges that life presents you— those that send you running for cover and those that pump you up to defend your turf.

Chapter 8

Basic Training—"Mad Dog" Goes to Court

GAME PLAN

Your heartbeat picks up steam while your breath becomes shallow and picks up the pace to match. Fluttering butterflies fill your gut. Your palms, with your fingernails digging imprints into them, will sweat so much that you will wonder if you have created pools beneath you. Your feet lose the battle with their own perspiration problem and turn cold and wet. Your muscles tighten up so much that your whole body throbs. The voice that squeaks out from your constricted throat will sound a lot like Donald Duck or Miss Piggy. You are out of synch and out of sorts, playing defensively in a box in a courtroom. How do you get out? It takes three smaller A's—awareness, assess, adjust—to turn the other three around.

Even before I had identified the 3 A's, I understood their power. I picked them up on the roads. I developed the basic strategies, adapting psychological techniques to user-friendly formats, when I knew that I was losing matches in the Courts—not the ones for sports.

The Competitive Court—Not for Tennis

At 5 foot 3 inches and just over 100 pounds, I was not an intimidating physical force when it came to competing in the courtroom, which is where I spent a lot of time as a younger woman. No, I'm not an attorney. And I wasn't there as a defendant. But I felt like my life was on the line. I was in the hot seat, testifying as a therapist representing my clients—abused and traumatized children and teens. It was a high-pressure adversarial situation. I wanted to win.

My opponents, the attorneys who represented the "alleged" abusers of my clients, wanted to win too. They engaged in guerilla tactics like getting right in my face, trying to distract and frazzle me while they shouted questions at me as if I was the person accused. Their techniques were robust and, before I understood my power to *willfully* align the 3 A's to engage in battle, these scare tactics worked more often than I liked.

Sitting in that witness box, I was a self-proclaimed "Scaredy Cat." I was overactivated. I could feel it in the physical muscle tensions from the top of my head to the bottoms of my feet, which poured out so much sweat that they made an audible swishing noise as I approached the witness stand. By the time I sat down, my soaking feet were icy cold, my palms were dripping profusely, and my heart beat so violently that I was convinced that everyone could see it pumping wildly through my suit jacket. But I was too scared to look down. Actually, I don't think I could have tilted my head because my shoulders had caressed my ears in a vise grip and my squared jaw felt like it was cast in stone. I was holding on for dear life with my fingers clenched into fists that shot pains through my arms. My toes were embedded in my loafers in what I affectionately called "the death grip." Though I did not have a name for it, beyond misery, this was o-Zonal activation at its worst.

My activation took my attention along for the ride. Literally scared out of my wits, I could feel the stress chemicals surging through my body, narrowing my attention and turning my skull numb. Holding my breath didn't help. Depriving my brain of oxygen, I couldn't see or think clearly. Instead of tuning in to the words being shouted at me, I retreated inward to the privacy of my thought balloon. (Let's face it; we all talk to ourselves.) Feeling trapped and cornered in the witness box, the primitive fight-or-flight instincts of survival took over as I contemplated escape routes. This zone for planning my getaway was mutually exclusive from the zone for providing stellar testimony.

My attention had created intense uncertainty, knocking my attitude down to o-Zonal lows. My thought balloon hovering over my head felt heavy, like a huge black trash bag weighted down by endless self-doubting messages. Acting as my own jury, I launched a compelling legal argument, convincing myself that I couldn't make it through this trying ordeal: "You've blown it now. How could you ever think you could stand up against this bulldog attorney? Who do you think you are? What are you doing here?" My tenacity, confidence, and assertiveness dissolved under my own self-scrutiny. I wanted to cry. Hyperfocused internally recycling, self-flagellating criticism, I didn't even hear the questions shouted at me by the attorney whose nose was within inches of my own. Looking as discombobulated and confused as I felt, with sweat beading on my forehead, I would stare with the frightened deer-in-headlights gaze while I plaintively beseeched my opponent to please repeat the question. When I heard the timid, quivering voice that spoke, I couldn't tell if it was mine.

The hoarse, high-pitched sound that squeaked out from my dry constricted throat was unrecognizable to me. Clearing my throat, releasing the lock from my jaw, and relying on the "ummm" to reclaim my voice and reformulate my thoughts, I was the poster child for over-activation, pinpointed attention, and abysmal attitude at their worst. At this point, my opponent would inevitably smile as he queried me again, knowing that the advantage was his. While he was totally engaged for battle, I was disenchanted and disconnected from the real deal, which was to simply report what I knew in an attempt to help my clients. Instead I was focused on the outcome—the escape hatch. So I missed the serve and could not return the ball. I couldn't even see the ball. All I could see was my opponent's nose.

Sitting in the courtroom with the opposing attorney's face pressed close to mine, I knew I wasn't in that Zone that I wanted to access. Unfocused, out of synch, debilitated by self-doubt, ruled by raging stress hormones and a nervous system gone awry, my A's were working together. But they were working against me! Choking, I knew that I was in some out-of-this-world unsavory state even before I had named it the "o-Zone." I wanted out.

If I was going to prevail, I understood that I had to learn how to purposefully and consistently create and sustain the same concentration, confidence, and physiologically controlled state that I experienced when running on the roads. Actually I realized that I had better do this to simply survive.

I built meaning for why I wanted to engage and do well. Devoted to doing a good job for my clients, I committed myself to finding a systematic method to move myself from the o-Zone to that other mental state of engagement where focus, relaxed shoulders, breathing, a rhythmic heartbeat, warm dry feet, and clear thinking ruled. I wanted to *willfully* get my nervous system under control. I wanted to feel the power of confidence based on connecting and doing my best even when the attorney across from me was up close and personal. So I went back to the streets where I had run thousands of miles to search for the significant factors that had powered me through. And I went back to the books to distill psychology techniques that had withstood the trial of time into a simpler system.[1]

I taught myself how to systematically get into the Zone of engagement in court. I trashed "Scaredy Cat," who sweat bullets, and replaced her with "Mad Dog," who competed confidently in the courtroom. Remarkably, it was as simple as the number three—activation, attention, and attitude. And learning to turn my 3 A's around was as simple as three smaller a's—awareness, assess, align. They work for all of life's trials.

The Smaller A's with Big Impact

Lining the 3 A's up in the Zone to connect with the moment at hand or the bigger scenes that compose your life is like a road trip. You have a starting point—your baseline activation, attention, attitude. You want markers of what your destination looks like—personal descriptors of how you experience activation and attention and attitude when you are totally committed and engaged with the current situation. Then you need a route to close the gap between where you are and where you want to be. It's a three-step process to turn your 3 A's around:

- **Awareness** to determine the current level of each A. Awareness enables you to really tune in to what is gong on within you to determine whether each of the 3 A's is well matched for genuinely connecting to the moment. When you know your characteristic style and how you experience activation, attention, and attitude when you are connected and disconnected, you cast a candid look at yourself without the filters. With practice, you will be tuned into these three elements almost unconsciously. You will also be able to detect the early warning signs, your personalized cues, of activation, attention, and attitude as they migrate toward the upper or lower limits of your personal Zone. With the third step, you will be able to head them off.

- **Assess** to identify the optimal level of each A. To make an accurate assessment, you have to open your eyes and mind to accurately assess the situation. You can do this using recall or, for new situations, you can draw on your own similar experiences or the personal bests of others, including role models, mentors, or people you observe.
- **Adjust** to align the A's with *Winner's Way* strategies that you can personalize for turning the 3 A's around. You will learn to *TRASH* the energy, focus, and assumptions that you don't want for the journey and *PACK* the ones that you want to carry on.

Taking It to the Streets

Crawling out from underneath cozy covers on cold, dark, rainy New England mornings to pound the pavement wasn't something that always appealed to me. The mile-long hills could easily fatigue me and the dark winter mornings could discourage anyone from venturing outside. Adapting principles from mind-body healing, cognitive psychology, and the psychology of manipulating attention to manage stress—determining where you look and what you want to see—I had taught myself how to get and stay optimally energized, focused, and psyched up for distance running in unforgiving New England.

Running provided me with a refueling respite from the pressures of work that were part of the job. And the horrific history of fatal heart illness on my father's side of the tree convinced me that there was a purpose to this beyond investing in Shoe-goo to resurrect my soles. So I developed my own strategies for turning my head around. Now it was time to articulate them so I could take them off the roads and into the courts.

Getting my head and my body into the game for running was a three-step process. First I made a conscious choice—"do you want to do this?" When I had to face myself in this truth-or-dare exercise, I took accountability for the decision to crawl out from under the covers. It also meant that once I was out on the roads, I had no one to blame but myself. And it gave me the power to decide if I wanted to turn around early on in the run. "You don't have to do this. It's only if you want to." This element of control reinforced my power to make the experience whatever I wanted it to be. Almost every morning, I accepted my own challenge. And just like the gambler in Kenny Rogers' song, I knew that I could always fold or walk away, or I could run.

Next, I determined where I was at—in terms of my 3 A's that is. I tuned in to my energy, my focus, and my attitude to determine if they were on-line or if they needed some tweaking. Because I normally ran early in the morning, I usually needed some adjustments to get going. And on some mornings, I acknowledged that my level of stress or fatigue required resetting the expectations. I would choose to run but I would scale my goals back. On some mornings, it felt like people were pulling the scenery past me as I crawled along in slow motion. But it was the experience I was after, and I was engaged and happy to be there.

Next, I developed a framework for where I wanted my activation, attention, and attitude to be for getting out of the door with joy and gratitude. I *assessed the situation* and determined the ideal range of activation, attention, and attitude for the day, for the weather, and for my level of fatigue. I used these as my personal *markers* and distilled them to shorthand cues that I called *"propellers"* because I wanted them to propel me into the Zone.

The attitude piece was easy. My father's ghastly family history of heart disease supplied the key. To build meaning, I pictured a healthy heart on the other side of the run. Even when I was running, I felt powered by a mission and a vision—I wasn't working out. I was training my heart for strength and endurance, putting in miles to keep it pumping for the long run. My thought balloon was filled with a strong, beating heart and images of hiking with my grandchildren in the Swiss Alps—and I wasn't married, had no kids, and had never even been to Europe. This mindset wasn't exhausting. It was exhilarating and inspiring.

Rhythmic breathing, flexing and releasing the physical tensions from my shoulders, head, legs, and feet, and blowing off sensations and images of pain and fatigue as I stretched to tunes of Springsteen were my propelling activation cues for getting my blood and heart up to speed for bolting out the door. On the road, music helped me set the pace and stay upbeat even before the days of portable tape players that walk with you. I simply brought my own music in my head in the virtual music box that we all carry around with us. Rather than complain about not being able to get a song out of my head, I chose my songs to keep my heart and my breathing at the right beat for different terrain.

I climbed hills with Springsteen, cruised the flats with Bonnie Raitt, and kept my stride in check so I wouldn't burn out my shins on the downhills with Miles Davis's smooth jazz. These tunes set my pace. They focused me on the present moment better than any mantra I could think of, and they kept my attitude upbeat even on mile four of six when it was easy to wonder to myself "are we there yet?" Breathing was vital to maintaining my beat. Four footsteps on the intake and four on the exhale kept my feet spinning even on the steepest of hills, which were never longer than 20 feet, at least not from my vantage point.

For each type of terrain, I identified a particular focus that kept my feet fleet. Without articulating it, I had developed a habit of looking only 20 feet ahead when it came to the steeps. No matter how long the hill that loomed in front of me, I was running a 20-footer. Even on those days when I ran with friends who complained and sighed as we approached a steep one-mile uphill stretch, I would tune them out with Bruce and travel the 20-foot segments until I saw the ground break away 20 feet ahead. There the earth dropped off to a cruising jazz beat and my line of sight expanded to take in the glorious scenery well beyond my 20-foot-uphill gaze. My companions who complained the most about each hill seemed to be carting a heavy backpack with them. Of course, it was really only their thought balloons overloaded with o-Zonal trash. When I stayed my A-driven course, I had to lift only my own weight. Now I had my personalized road signs of the Zone, one for each A. Still, knowing how susceptible the human mind can be, and not wanting to risk mentally highjacking myself from this glorious state of engagement, I wanted to know what signs to look for when danger was rearing its ugly head.

Next, I reviewed my previous running experiences in which I had knocked myself out of the Zone. I wanted to quantify and qualify my personal markers of the o-Zone so that I could head them off when I recognized their approach. Because these markers triggered plunges to o-Zonal disaster, I called them my "*plungers,*" an image to be avoided at all costs.

Getting out of the door wasn't the only obstacle. The 3 A's could launch impressive attacks on the road. Attention could be a powerful foe, leading me to perceive the same run that had felt exhilarating as oppressive. Sometimes it was as simple as looking too far ahead to the horizon to take in the full distance of the mile-long steep hill that loomed in front of me. At other times, my attention would wander to focus on the pain in my small toe. The sight of the hill, or convincing myself that a blister was brewing, could be enough to slow my pace and take me out of the running experience into some other reality full of pessimistic ruminations.

In other moments, I was my worst enemy, pummeling myself with random thoughts that took me away from the moment. It could be something as simple as wondering if I had turned the coffee pot off or as worrisome as fretting over the intense lineup of my day, especially on my intimidating days in court. And at other times, it was the burden of beliefs. When self-talk brought me down—"I hate this hill," or "I should have waited until after work so I could run with my friends," it was a short spin downhill to the o-Zone even when my feet were climbing up! On days that I let it happen, it could be all three.

I can remember one day vividly, during the days before online banking, the days before online anything. I had balanced my checkbook the night before only to find that I had neglected to record a check, a large check that I had written to pay a bill. That meant that my most recent car payment had bounced. I was in shock. While I had not lived at home for more than 10 years, I pictured the disapproval of my dad, a banker. That simple image sent my 3 A's soaring. Panicked, I barely slept and crawled out of bed for what felt like an obligatory run, going only because the bank wasn't open. There was nothing I could do about the bounced check until the opening bell at 9:00.

Still, even with that reassurance, the horrifying image of a bouncing check and my repossessed car haunted me, weighing down my thought balloon, for all but a few of the steps of the full six miles. Preoccupied with visions of my car being towed away, I had near misses with potholes that seemed determined to trip me up. Telling myself again and again that I was irresponsible, my mantra didn't allow me to enjoy any part of the run, not even the downhills or the scenery. Punishing myself for being so stupid, I refused to insert the Springsteen music into my thought balloon. There was no room for music at such a dark moment, only self-doubt. With the heavy weight of the stress chemicals that accompanied me that day, I assured myself that I was doing more damage to my heart than anything else. I had worked myself into the o-Zone of misery, all over one bounced check—or so I thought.

Relieved to see my car still in the driveway, I hurried through the morning ritual. Under the influence of stress chemicals and traveling at race pace, I lost my accuracy. It took even more time to redo my mascara and to find my keys, out of sight in my mono-vision though they rested in the basket that was their home. Shaking and jittery, just getting the key into the lock of my soon-to-be-repossessed car was a trial. When activation is high, precision falls apart. With my activation riding high and my attention narrowed in, I was determined to stay in the worry zone and missed the scenery between my apartment and the bank, zoomed in with a single-lens monocle on getting to that bank.

When I did arrive, I was an o-Zonal disaster. The customer service person must have recognized the wild-eyed look of panic in my eyes and the sweat on my forehead. She calmed me enough so that I could read her lips and hear her words. What she said shocked me. I had neglected to record a large deposit that exceeded any check I had written. The car was still mine, and I had money in the bank to boot. With the power of the 3 A's working against me, I had created a terrible scene that ruined my morning run and wreaked havoc on my heart. I had fabricated my personal reality and, totally bonded with that, I disconnected from the real deal. Plus I felt really foolish—really foolish.

As I reviewed the lessons of the road to transfer them to court, I realized that the contents of my thought balloon held the key to the quality of my experiences and the wisdom that I could bring to bear on the challenges that I faced. The power of my will was in my inner spirit to consciously commit to getting a full picture of my experiences so I could choose to engage or disconnect. The choice to get into it or get out of it was in my mind and my heart. And it was time to take control, to ditch the *plungers* and fuel the *propellers.*

Really Do It!

Can you recall an instance in the past week where you focused on limited data, blew it out of proportion, jumped to conclusions, and then reacted with your activation, attention, and attitude lined up for this personalized view that was a poor match for the real deal? I lost out on a great run. What did you miss out on?

Take the Trash Out and Pack Your Bags for the Ride

First things first—we all talk to ourselves. Just like Charlie Brown and his tormentor, Lucy, there is always a thought balloon hovering over your shoulders that carries information related to activation, attention, and attitude. The good news is that it's normal. The bad news is that most of what we carry is excess, negative, and weighty. It plunges us into the o-Zone. Social anthropologists have hypothesized that this negative perspective and skepticism is a holdover from our primitive ancestors who needed to be on the constant outlook for danger. Even if that is true, it doesn't do a lot for us during those moments when we could be enjoying the scenery.

I identified two major themes to the content of my thought balloons. One connected me to the actual situation. The other connected me to something else. When the balloon that hovered over my head was weighted down with the signs of the o-Zone, it felt like a dark cloud, a very heavy black cloud resembling a huge trash bag full of rancid, decaying garbage that I did not want or need. The stuff consisted of unsavory activation, attention, and attitude signs. And I wanted to trash it. The second variation was the balloon that represented my ideal activation, attention, and attitude for the terrain I was treading. Those were the triple-A markers I wanted to hold tight. I pictured this balloon as a suitcase, a small carry-on because I wanted to travel light. It was filled with the propelling cues that represented engagement.

Propellers are the shorthand words, images, and sensations that represent the triple-A *markers* of the Zone. With the *assess* process, I had identified the markers for early morning runs and the fine-tuning nuances for different turf and weather. Then I distilled them into my personalized "propellers." My four-count breathing, the 20-foot rule, and Springsteen worked on the uphills. Other variations on breathing, gaze, and music propelled me on the flats and the downhills. Now I wanted a systematic way to hold onto the images and words that I wanted and to ditch the others. *TRASHIT* and *PACKIT* were born.

Adapting and synthesizing strategies from cognitive psychology for ridding oneself of negative and unrealistic thoughts, I developed *TRASHIT!* As soon as I spotted a marker that signaled a disconnect-in-the-making, I consciously and vehemently thrust it into the bag.

Then I actively cast it aside, hurling it into the sky where, believe me, nobody else ever picked it up. I realized that one moment's trash could be another moment's treasure. Even the things that would be in my *PACKIT* balloon later that day could be cast aside in the *TRASH* by the roadside. I proactively took charge to ditch the outdated or inappropriate A's. Then I proactively replaced them with what I wanted for my road trips. (See Figures 8-1 and 8-2.)

TRASHIT and *PACKIT* are derived from the field of cognitive psychology. Cognitive psychology has provided powerful research and case study support for the power of assumptions to generate thoughts and feelings. Based on this premise, the pioneers in this field have developed an arsenal of techniques for reasoning your way out of your perceptions of and explanations for life's predicaments and for changing your mind.[2] However, many of their strategies, designed to help people change their thoughts, take the tenacity of a lawyer. It is like launching a full-court legal defense against yourself. It takes a lot of time and a lot of thought and removes you from the roads you are traversing. I wanted something quicker.

Awareness was key. While I ran, I tuned in to my activation, attention, and attitude. I pictured an imaginary internal meter that read all three. I called it *the zone-o-meter*. It worked the same way as the expensive and cumbersome biofeedback machinery that I had used with clients, but without the price or weight. As I pumped my arms and legs and breathed rhythmically, I used *awareness of each of the 3 A's* to tune into my meter. When I detected readings that were approaching the limits of my Zonal range, or worse yet, readings that were characteristic of disconnection, I threw them into the thought balloon that hovered over my head. Whether it was fatigue, a pain in my small toe,

Figure 8-1   *TRASHIT*™. For getting rid of dysfunctional levels of activation, attention or attitude, throw the *plunger cues* into your *TRASHIT*™ can.

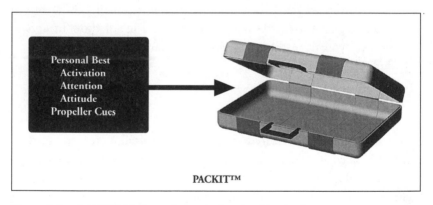

Figure 8-2   *PACKIT*™. For replacing dysfunctional levels of activation, attention or attitude with your personal best, pack your *propeller cues* into your *PACKIT*™ bag.

my lungs that burned, or a focus on irrelevant things like mythical bounced checks or self-talk that made my heart and feet heavy, I stuffed it in that balloon. And while I was running, I would gleefully hurl those o-Zonal markers, the *plungers* that I didn't want, into the air. I *TRASHed* it, and in doing so, I felt like a weighty burden had been lifted from my head. My steps got lighter and faster and the distance remaining to my destination always seemed a lot shorter after getting rid of that trash. So I named my strategy *"TRASHIT!"*

The first few times I was delighted. But it didn't take too many steps before my thought balloon could fill up again with other trash. Sometimes it was an attitude piece of trash that took over the bag, self-talk like "I'm too tired." At other times, I became preoccupied with getting back and out the door to work. And my little toe could exert its own forces on the days that it screamed so loudly that I took heed and didn't take advantage of the scenery. Needless to say, they all worked together to quickly drag me down. So one after another, I would trash them. But the same thing kept happening. More trash kept inserting itself into my thought balloon. Then it dawned on me. It was my human psyche taking over and I wanted to take back control.

I realized that I was going to have to choose the items for my road trips that I carted with me in my thought balloon or they would choose themselves. Wanting to travel light meant choosing shorthand cues— words, images, phrases, or actions that distilled the ideal activation, focus, and attitude for whatever terrain I was traversing from the hills to the muddy trails where roots could catch your feet and send you sprawling. Just like the climate determines what you pack for a trip, the triple-A markers I packed would depend on the situation. *PACKIT* was born.

Once you have determined where you want each of your 3 A's to be, *aligning* and realigning them is a two-step process. First, you get rid of the stuff you don't want, the trash. You *TRASHIT!*

> Then you choose the levels of activation, attention, and attitude
> that you want. You *PACKIT!* It does indeed sound simple. Some-
> times simple strategies are the most reliable and timely, especially
> when you are in the midst of the brouhaha.

Maintaining momentum at mile four of six even when I was depleted or in pain was easy. I literally ditched the fatigue and pain—I
TRASHed them—and I replaced them with images and sensations of
strength, of building my heart and enjoying the sensation of moving
myself through the crisp air. The rhythmic beat, the inspiring words
of the tunes I chose, and focusing on my breathing provided activation propellers. The 20-foot rule was my visual focus while rhythmic
breathing lined up activation for hills. Both kept me in the process,
leading me to my outcome. The picture of a healthy heart, hiking in
my personalized version of the Alps, and running until age 70, when
I would begin marathoning, turned my attitude around to one of confidence. I knew that what I was doing was right for me. I had made
the commitment to engage with my heart, my body, and my mind.
Just thinking about it is enough to line my A's up for a smile and a
fulfilling deep breath. That's where I wanted to be in Court. So I transferred the strategies from the roads to the Courts.

"Mad Dog's" Day in Court

First, I committed to connecting to do my best. While it seemed that
I really didn't have a choice about this activity (after all, it was part of
my job), I saw it differently. In my mind's eye, I could willfully determine if I was going to testify or not. I could find another job. Or I
could change my specialization area to work with adults or I could
limit my practice to people suffering from medical conditions. By

proactively committing to do the courtroom work and get good at courtroom competition, I made the commitment to engage willfully. It must have worked because I outlasted the average burnout rate in the field and improved my performance in the courtroom.

I prepared. First I developed a routine to get ready to testify—a *preparation ritual* geared specifically to getting my A's together. In the privacy of my old VW, I flexed my fingers and toes and shrugged my shoulders up and down while breathing in and out at a moderate pace to the beat of "my song," a Van Morrison classic, playing on the state-of-the-art 8-track. My routine provided a surefire way to burn off the excess energy that I didn't need. The words and images built meaning for the work I was doing, bolstering my confidence.

I wanted to ditch the sweaty hands and cold feet. In the witness seat, activation was seriously compromised. I wanted a system to adjust my physical and physiological response—my muscle tensions, breathing, heartbeat, and excess perspiring. Breathing and flexing my hands to relax the tensions had always worked on the road to trash tension and pack strength. But in the courtroom, flexing fingers looked a lot like I was making a fist and getting ready to punch the attorney who was invading my personal space. So I learned to flex my toes in my loafers. Wiggling my toes provided a propelling strategy for re-connecting fully. It pulled me back into the moment, prohibiting my stress chemicals from sweeping me away.

Breathing was another key. When I sensed that the air in my lungs was picking up the pace, I would take a deep breath in, and, on the exhale, I would release the trash that contained the fast-paced breathing. Breathing rhythmically to the beat of "my song" kept my heart ticking at an ideal rate even under the most grueling eye-to-eye grilling by attorneys. Miles Davis could slow me down, while the always reliable Springsteen could power me up from a downhill spiral. Now I could think clearly and formulate responses that addressed the questions. My own voice reemerged without the squeaky "umms." My feet and hands stopped sweating, my heart beat rhythmically. I was even able to peel my shoulders down from caressing my earlobes. I was activated in the zone. The rhythmic breathing kept me connected to the moment, focused on the questions. More importantly, it took my focus off of my opponent's nose, which I learned to trash.

I learned to tune out the faces of the attorneys who stood so close that I could feel their breathing and to tune in instead to their words. When I felt my focus wander to the attorney's hot breath or my own internal monologue, I trashed these hindrances and packed a personal cue—"zoom." My personal "propeller" focused me back on the essentials. I wanted to attend externally to the questions at hand rather than wallowing internally on my self-chatter and the things that seemed beyond my control—like my breathing. I needed to tune out the extraneous and get focused only on the essentials. In the courtroom I needed to move my focus off of my opponent's face and shouting, away from my own internal self-criticism, back to the questions. A question-at-a-time seemed close to a 20-foot stretch for bounding up hills.

Then there was my mindset, my beliefs, and my assumptions. It was all about attitude. In the highly competitive courtroom, I had to learn to adjust my own attitude to build confidence. I had to change my self-talk just as I had on those mornings when I convinced myself that I wasn't too tired to run. I wanted an attitude adjustment strategy in order to build my own meaning, my personal purpose that would inspire me to get moving forward.

To counter self-doubt, I relied on my personal mission of helping my clients. Instead of focusing inwardly on my signs of overactivation, I pictured my vision of helping the child for whom I was testifying. Using the one-step-at-a-time goals that had hauled me through long stretches on the road, I crafted motivating goals that pulled me through one question at a time. These *SMART goals* (specific and stretch, measurable, accepted and accountable, record and reward, timely and time-limited) affected all three ingredients. They got me energized and focused and bolstered my confidence.

I even started to enjoy court work.

My confidence grew—"Mad Dog" was born. I relished the powerful effects of my zonal self-composure and focus in and of themselves. And I enjoyed seeing their effects. While my feet remained warm and my palms dry, I could see the sweat on the forehead of the attorneys who continued to plant their faces up close and personal. The sound of water slogging in their wing-tipped shoes as they approached the witness stand was music to my ears and put a smile on my face that pushed my opponents' activation even further over the edge. I swear I could see their beating hearts under their suit jackets, and I could certainly see it in the bulging red veins in their eyeballs. On more than one occasion, an attorney retaliated, accusing me of being a "hostile witness." The judge, who now looked friendly rather than intimidating to me, always responded in the same way. "She's not being hostile. She's just not answering the questions the way you want her to." Activated, focused, and confident, I knew I had willfully accessed the zone for representing my clients with pride to ensure that their best interests were implemented. Still, I wanted to get better.

Understanding the power of practice, I trained in my dreams. I adapted the relaxation and visualization techniques that I had used with my clients to quell their fears and phobias. But this was no standard relaxation and visualization. And it wasn't a blue-sky version where you picture everything going perfectly and languish in easy victory. There was a focus to my virtual training. It was the 3 A's.

I used my virtual training sessions to practice aligning my activation, attention, and attitude under rigorous conditions. I previewed adversity, visualizing testifying in upcoming hearings in the face of angry attorneys, all the time focusing on reading and adjusting my activation, focus, and attitudes to stay connected and build confidence. In the process, I realized another remarkable thing about these three magical elements—they were interchangeable. When breathing just wasn't enough to keep my shoulders from migrating north, I shifted my focus to the words coming from the attorney's lips. Or in my thought balloon, I could picture the kids who were my clients. That was often the key for getting me back in the game. I even started to enjoy these visualizations, especially the part where I would *TRASH* the attorney's up close and personal nose.

To take advantage of lessons learned, I developed a review technique that, due to my work with physicians, I called a *postoperative debriefing*. Except this process was not full of scathing reviews. Designed to provide a forum to learn from my mistakes and from the things that I had done well, I adapted the same virtual technique to review less than stellar courtroom challenges. I wanted to create proactive images in my debriefing and to not use the word "don't" because I already knew that that word always drew my attention to the words that followed it. In these review sessions, I used a formula—"What I did well was… and … and … Next time, I will… and …, and …" Oftentimes my recommendations centered on accessing the optimal levels of activation, focus, and attitude that I needed to function more effectively. This prepared me for future situations and it built my confidence by replacing a negative view with a better memory.

With improved awareness of my activation, attention, and attitude, I learned how to read the 3 A's in any situation. I realized that this place, this yet unnamed Zone where I brought my whole self to the experience, extended beyond the roads and beyond Court. It applied to every aspect of life, and I could access it on purpose using only three processes. I realized that at any given moment I was either in the Zone or I was not. And, with my strategies, I knew at any moment where I was—whether it was the o-Zone, the Zone, or the ascent or descent toward the upper or lower limits of the Zone. Most importantly, I knew how to turn my mind and body around to get and stay in the Zone. With fine-tuning, I learned to see the signs of "danger ahead" when the descent into the o-Zone was imminent. I taught myself how to turn my mind and body around to regroup and reclaim the Zone.

I ditched "Scaredy Cat" and "Mad Dog" and simply became myself. The 3 A's and *The Winner's Way* had moved beyond the roads and sports to the really grueling distance events of life. You can put them to work for you too. It's as straightforward as those three smaller a's.

Awareness, assess, adjust is the three-step process for tuning into and turning around your activation, attention, and attitude to align them for the real deal. With these three processes, you can adjust your view to match a more commonly held view of reality. *TRASHIT* and *PACKIT* is the two-step process for replacing dysfunctional markers of activation, attention, or attitude with optimal levels for true engagement. You can choose to dismiss the activation levels, attentional perspectives, and assumptions that have generated a view of reality that is removed from the actual situation. Then you can choose to embrace the energy, focus, and beliefs that will generate a view of the situation in which you can engage and be successful. The power to choose to engage rests in the power of your will to align the 3 A's.

Postoperative Debriefing

- Closing the gap between your point of origin—the baseline levels of activation, attention, and attitude—and your destination—the optimal activation, attention, and attitude for connecting to the moment—is a three-step process.
- Awareness, assess, adjust—with these three smaller A's, you can connect to match points in a variety of life's courts.

Chapter 9

Get with It—Activation Strategies

GAME PLAN

With *The Winner's Way*, you can identify your natural activation style and learn to match your activation to the situation's requirements to get in the Zone for anything—healing, dealing, marking time, moving on, or racing to the finish line.

Identifying your standard speed and learning to read cues that alert you to your own activation and that of others will provide you with the methodology to purposefully turn up the heat or chill down to match a variety of situations and people.

Your Own Activation—It's a Personal Thing

How do you know when your activation is on target? If it's not, how can you change it?

First things first—each of us has a personal activation level at which we function at our best. It's easy to engage with situations that match

161

our natural style. Some of us are wired at an early Elvis Presley rock-and-roll pace. Sprinting events come easy. Time-outs for breathers are more of a struggle. They are often enforced by illness or disaster. Others negotiate life at a smooth and easy Tony Bennett tempo. Naturals at longer-distance life events, it takes more effort to get pumped up for the fast and furious moments of living.

When you identify your activation style, where you characteristically carry activation and how Zonal and o-Zonal activation feel to you, you cast a candid look at yourself without the filters. Just like any honest insight, it can be surprising to see yourself the way other people do. Sometimes it is even a shock.

Many clients were incredulous once they saw their activation through the eyes of others—and even more amazed when they connected their signs of chronically low or high activation with how they felt and how they performed. Rachel, who managed a sales team, was stunned to learn that she walked around in a chronic state of overactivation that easily erupted into rage. Once she tuned in to how it felt and how it looked, she realized why subordinates, and even her kids, disappeared when she approached with a pulsating jaw and elevated shoulders. Rachel's honest 180-degree self-assessment set a base for adapting her activation so that she could engage with others, and so they wanted to connect with her.

The optimal range and level of activation is dependent in part on your basic nature reflected in your temperament and your general level of energy. Even so, these factors will be affected by your general health and level of rest. Diversity is the norm—a difference is a difference—and nothing more. Everyone has the capability to adapt their activation to match a variety of scenes. What's your style?

Who Are You?

Is your baseline velocity faster than a speeding bullet like Superman's? Or are you more naturally mellow like Superman's alter ego,

Clark Kent? To assess your characteristic activation level, try this quick assessment.

This a forced-choice design—for each pair of statements, select the one that best describes you. As you respond, think of your "generic" self.

---

1. People often tell me to slow down, to hold my horses.   Y   N
2. Steady and calm is the name of my game.   Y   N

1. I'm more at ease pushing for deadlines in a fast-forward mode than in the arduous planning phase of a project.   Y   N
2. Planning a project from start to finish and proceeding along the planned steps assures my success and gives me satisfaction.   Y   N

1. The mere thought of smelling the roses can stress me out and send my blood pressure skyrocketing.   Y   N
2. I enjoy making time to reflect on my day and mentally prepare for tomorrow.   Y   N

1. At work, I travel at high speed, talking in bullets and sound bytes.   Y   N
2. I enjoy making the time to get to know colleagues and subordinates.   Y   N

1. I go for the end—and the straightest line route there—finishing projects in record time.   Y   N
2. I frequently get so involved in work processes that I lose sight of the outcome.   Y   N

1. My style is direct, cut-to-the-chase, high-powered.   Y   N
2. My approach is indirect, thorough, and low key.   Y   N

1. It's essential to have time deadlines that stress urgency.   Y   N
2. Time deadlines frazzle me and push me over the edge.   Y   N

1. I often feel like I'm on caffeine overload. And I like it.   Y   N
2. I am proud to be the poster child for calming
   medications even without ingesting them.   Y   N

1. People think of me as a fast-paced Springsteen rock
   tune.   Y   N
2. Being with me evokes smooth and easy Kenny G.
   melodies.   Y   N

1. The hyperventilating, wild-eyed Weimaraner
   puppy is who I am.   Y   N
2. I'm the mature Golden Retriever, content with big
   sighs.   Y   N

Scoring:

Add Yes responses for all #1 items. Total #1 Yes responses:_____
Add Yes responses for all #2 items. Total #2 Yes responses:_____

Subtract for your Difference Score: +/– _____

Interpretation:

If the difference is 0, you are a middle-of-the-road activator.
If the difference is +10, you're clearly a fast-forward activator.
If the difference is –10, you're a hands-down steady activator.
. Plot your difference score on the line below.

–10_____0_____+10
Steady Moderately steady Moderate Moderately fast Fast-forward
                              Flexible

Make a mental note of where you land to get a reading of your characteristic activation level. If you land on either extreme, you'll want to exert more effort when it comes time to adjust activation to get connected to challenges that don't fit your natural activation style.

Consider your score especially if it lies midrange. Are you truly a moderate-speed person? Or are you very flexible? Or do you vacillate wildly between the two extremes—especially on the golf course, the driving range, or driving in your car?

Which point on the continuum is the most difficult connection for you? Take a moment to visualize frequent challenges and people in your life. Which are a good, natural fit? Which situations or people require an activation style that is dramatically different from your normal tempo if you want to genuinely connect? Picture replacing poorly matched activation with a good fit in those situations. How would this shift affect how you do and how you feel?

So How *Do* I Know When It's Just Right?

For most of us, it's easier to identify when activation is not right—especially when it is a poor match for our natural style. Usually we have a treasure trove of vivid recollections of when activation was off, stuck in either of the tails, but not where we'd like it to be. As far as knowing when your activation is not quite right, you already know it. Consider this: When a challenge renders you bored, lethargic, unmotivated, or apathetic, you know that something doesn't feel right. It isn't. You're underactivated for the task at hand.

When we are too activated, we generally feel a burning desire to run away from what we "must" (versus "want to") do or to lash out or shout unpleasantries at ourselves or at people around us. You might even want to throw inanimate objects. Things don't feel so good here either. The agitation definitely doesn't do wonders for your performance, your driving, or for your relationships.

When it comes to activation in the Zone, people remember the sensation and the satisfaction of bringing their full force to the experience. Paradoxically intense and effortless, it's a total immersion of body, mind, and spirit. This holds true whether they're describing situations when they were immersed in fast-paced or slow-and-steady challenges in the workplace, at sports arenas, during daily tasks, or for life-threatening challenges.

Your own optimal activation might be high, low, or moderate, depending on the situation facing you and your personal style. For the clear thinking it takes to draft a strategic business initiative with your team, more moderate levels will assure success. Most likely you'll want to ramp activation up for the next stage to consistently communicate the strategy throughout the organization in a manner that engages other people's hearts, minds, and activation. Then you'll probably activate up even higher if it's a fast-paced implementation with a quick turnaround. A slower pace will most likely put you at ease for relaxing with friends and family at the end of a long workweek. But it's personal.

Tom, the attorney, cranked his activation up for courtroom battle. For him that was the ideal range. For other attorneys with whom I have worked, that would be much too high to allow them to focus and think straight.

"Really Do It!"—How Zonal Activation Feels

Each of us has a unique way of describing Zonal activation whether it's at very high, very low, or moderate levels. That's because we each experience activation in our own unique way. (And that is also why we run into trouble when we interpret someone else's activation without checking in and checking it out.) Here are some of the descriptions that clients and seminar participants have reported to me to describe activation at its best:

Activation in the Zone

Low	Moderate	High
Smooth	Clicking	Intense
Slow and steady	Middle of the road	Fast forward
Endurance, holding my ground	For the long run	Sprinting
Centered	Centered	Centered
Automatic	Cruise control	Autopilot
Effortless	Effortless	Effortless
Recharging	Charged	Charged up, charging
Right on, just right	Right on, just right	Right on, just right
Breathing easy	Breathing strong, even, and deep	Breathing hard
Barely breathing	Breathing just right	Exhilarated
Recouping energy	Energized	Expending huge energy
Battened down	Pumped up	Pumped up
Loose, easy grip	Strong grip	Holding tight
Wiggling my toes	Standing strong	Feet firmly planted
Chin at ease	Firm jaw	Jaw squared
Sitting back	Sitting forward	On the edge of the seat

Now for Something Completely Different— How O-Zonal Activation Feels

Just like the porridge that was too hot or too cold for the trespassing Goldilocks, the tails of disengagement and enragement of the o-Zone are entirely different activation stories. Whether it's too high, too low, or too middle-of-the-road, o-Zonal activation feels out of synch. You can almost feel the experience slipping from your hands while you see your performance decline in front of your eyes. It can become the gift that keeps on giving, spreading to anyone within a short radius.

My clients and seminar participants have revealed their personal unsavory descriptions of experiences when they were disconnected out in left field, with their activation off-kilter. Here is a small sampling of markers that alerted them that they were plunging into the tails of disconnection, the *plunger* cues, which they learned to use as signals to *TRASH*.

Read through the left-hand column. Make a mental note or circle the terms that most typically describe you when you are underactivated and disengaged. Then read the right-hand column, this time noting or circling the phrases that paint the picture of when your activation has spun over the top to the frenzy of agitation, or even rage. Add your own.

Activation in the O-Zone

Activation too low	Activation too high
Slow heart—"I didn't have a pulse." "Heavy heart"	Racing heart—"I thought I was having a heart attack. "throbbing in my legs," "pulsating cheek" "veins in my neck bulging"
"couldn't get it going"	"couldn't keep it under control"
"zombielike," "disoriented"	"zombielike," "out of it"
"out of synch"	"out of sorts"
"asleep"	"wide awake," "agitated"
"nodding off"	"on alert"
"needing toothpicks to keep my eyes open"	"eyes wide open," "wild eyed"
"dry throat," "cotton mouth," and other indicators of inadequate salivation	"sweating bullets," "cold feet," and other indicators of involuntary sweating

Activation too low	Activation too high
"barely breathing," "long pauses"	"hyperventilating"
"big sigh," "constricted breathing"	"not breathing—holding my breath"
"shallow breathing"	"oxygen-deprived"
"Lack of muscle tone"—general and specific	"Extreme muscle tension"—general and specific
"head nodding off"	"tight jaw," "clenched teeth"
"mouth hanging open"	"shoulders glued to my earlobes"
"couldn't keep my head up"	"lower back pain," "pain in the
"chin hitting my chest"	butt," "leg and foot spasms," "Char-
"couldn't move my limbs"	lie horses," "the fist thing"—"a
"heaviness in my fingers and feet"	grip so tight on my ski poles/hockey
"felt like I was hit by a Mack truck"	stick/lucky pen/child's hand that I
"This time it really had to be mono..."	had to pry my fingers off"
"My stick fell right out of my glove."	"the toe grip," "I felt like I was hold-
"My fingers couldn't do the walking—on my keyboard or phone dial."	ing on for dear life."
	"white-knuckled"
	"My fingernails were making im- prints on the palms of my hands."
	twitches—eyes, cheek, back

Now it's time for an honest look in the metaphorical mirror. Is there one side of the activation curve that you gravitate toward more than the other? Do you slide down to underactivated lethargy, or do you surge over the top to highly charged levels when you feel pressured or when you disconnect from the people and things that make up your life?

Consider how excessively low and high activation have impacted your engagement with, and your disconnection from, interpersonal communications (meetings, conversations, conflict resolution, negotiations) and other experiences on any of your life's fields. What effects has each side had on your attitudes, including your belief in yourself and in others? How has each side affected how you acted, how you felt, your performance, your self-image, your mood, and the results you have achieved?

Where Activation Resides

Now you have an understanding of your activation style—whether it's a raucous Robin Williams roar or a more subdued Vice President Cheney saunter. You have also identified some of your "markers" of activation when it is too high, too low, or just right for different situations.

We each have personal spots where we harbor activation in our bodies. A heavy chest alerts some people that their breathing is on hold, while rapid-fire hyperventilation is the marker for others. Feet so wet that they feel chilled and hands drenched in perspiration are common havens. Backaches and pains in other body parts are the characteristic signs of high activation for others. For many individuals, it's all about the head—a tightening migraine band holds tight to excess activation; feeling unable to think straight or to hold your head up signals activation that is too low; and a centered "heads up" stance means things are just right.

The shoulders are another common harbor for activation. Slumping and slacking provide telltale signs of low levels. Shoulder creep is a giveaway to activation on the rise. Taken to its extreme, you might have that awkward sensation that your head is being vice-gripped by your shoulders in that "shoulders caressing earlobes" posturing. This constricts peripheral vision and restricts the movement of your arms, whether you are swinging a golf club, tennis racket, a laser pointer, or holding tight to the steering wheel. With your shoulders strong and centered, you know you're ready to engage.

The area between the elbow and fingertips is a frequent-flyer area for carting activation. Who hasn't experienced the overactivated, white-knuckled grip that can tighten around whatever object is within reach? With your fingers gnarled into fists, your fingernails drill a semipermanent imprint into the skin of your palms. For those with long hair, or with any hair, spinning little ringlets offers a release from the elbow to fingertip tension. Others report a burning desire to pull all of their hair out even when they don't have any growing on their heads! Underactivated, you feel things literally slipping through your fingers. A sensation of dropping the ball alerts you to activate up. When things are clicking, you feel the strength of your hands and lower arms holding on firmly or hanging strong at your sides.

There is another characteristic area where excess activation is held— your jaw. A tight jaw coupled with a chronic desire to chomp down and chew, or to chew others out, are common signs of excess activation trying to find a release.

Fat-Free Baker's Dozen: Release Your Overactivation

Try this the next time you are getting sidetracked from your current activity by the thought of food when you know you aren't hungry. Give it a practice run right now.

Open your mouth slightly to release your jaw. Take twelve plus one deep breaths in and out through your mouth, pausing for a second or two after each exhale. Notice the effect on the pace of your thoughts and the beating of your heart as well as the sensations in your gut and jaw.

Now leave your jaw hanging relaxed and your mouth slightly open as you return to your reading.

How about you? Where do you characteristically harbor activation? *Awareness* is key. Remember the Oracle at Delphi. Knowing yourself is key. By identifying where you harbor activation, you will be able to detect the early warning signs of rising or falling activation. And, when you want to, you'll be able to turn them around.

Really Do It! Activation at Its Best

Find a pen or other writing instrument. For this exercise, you are going to recall three common situations that you encounter.

In the first, low levels of activation are what it takes to get connected.

In the second, it's high activation that engages your body, mind, and heart.

The third scene will be a challenge in which moderate activation produces a personal best and leaves you feeling good.

The goal is to identify where you typically carry your activation, where you are most aware of it when you are connected. Then you can see if there is a pattern—a particular area of your body that you can use as an early-warning system.

Drop your jaw slightly and take three slow deep breaths. Picture yourself in a common daily or weekly situation where low activation is what it takes to engage. Watching a movie, reading a book to yourself or with a child, engaging in deep conversation with a friend, reviewing a project that you just completed, planning your priorities for the day or the next week, thoughtfully considering your next personal or career steps, lifting weights, doing yoga or stretching, or brushing your teeth could all qualify here. Breathe.

Watch yourself as if you are viewing a video—this is an *external perspective for visualizing.* Then change to an *internal perspective* and experience yourself going through the motions. Get a picture of yourself from the outside and inside—your stance, pacing, the slant of your shoulders, the grip of your fingers and the grope of your toes. Read your internal cues—your heartbeat, respiration, and perspiration. Enjoy the sensation of total immersion and doing your best and the satisfaction that it brings. Take thorough readings of where you are most aware of activation when it rides at low levels that are a good fit.

Grab the pen and go to the drawing of the human figure in Figure 9-1. On the lines to the left that lie just below the full-bodied diagram, record the five spots in your body—physical or physiological sensations—that provide reliable markers of low levels of activation. Work from the top of your head to the soles of your feet. Be specific. "Relaxed jaw with mouth slightly open, light breathing, arms hanging loose and strong, hands open, wiggling toes" are clear markers that you will recognize.

Now shift gears up to take a reading on where you typically feel activation when you are in a situation where fast-forward high activation (I am not talking overdrive here) is what it takes to engage. Consider challenges where it would be easy to tailspin over the edge. But when you can keep it together, high levels of activation do the job.

> Relax your shoulders and jaw and take three deep breaths. Plant yourself in the scene you've chosen with activation at high velocity. Read your internal sensations and picture your external manifestations that proclaim to you and to others that activation is cranked up and that you are fully engaged. Scan from head to toes. Where do you feel it most intensely?

Use the pen to record your most common signs of high activation on the lines just below and to the right of the figure. Make your descriptions vivid. "Jaw set firmly, head nodding, squared shoulders, leaning forward, back straight, hands extended with palms down, fingers wrapped tight and just-right firm, feet flattened out like paddles with a slight curve to the toes" will provide you with cues as to where you most often feel high activation when it is at its best.

Now let's go to the third scenario where moderate activation is the best fit. Take yourself for a pleasant ride—a visualization of an experience where you are frequently fully connected to an activity with your activation somewhere in the middle of the two extremes. It could be a great conversation or it could be total immersion in a productive team meeting. It could even be as simple as folding laundry to the tunes of your favorite music.

> Start with the three deep breaths and relaxed jaw. Make this visualization vibrant. See it from an internal and external perspective. Give yourself the time to assess and enjoy the sensations of moderate activation when you are fully immersed in the moment.

In the lines above the body diagram, record descriptions of Zonal activation for each of the areas where you most frequently feel it when you are cruising at moderate levels. Identify your personal telltale signs to make this most effective. (See Figure 9-1.)

Compare your three lists. What are the top three areas that are consistent indicators of your current activation level? Most people have one strongest suit. Which one is your dead-on giveaway?

Now you're tuning in to your activation. Remember that awareness is a constant thing. At every moment, you are activated. Awareness, enhanced by your internal *zone-o-meter*, enlightens you about how high or how low your activation is riding and whether your current level is the right one for giving your all to the situation at hand, or whether it has you playing to beat others out or playing-not-to-lose from the sidelines.

REALLY Do It! Aware, Assess, Adjust

Once you start working with the 3 A's, your awareness of activation as well as attention and attitude will become automatic. For now, though, use this body scan technique to enhance your activation awareness.

Activation at Its Best

The Challenge: ______________________________

Moderate Activation

____
____
____
____

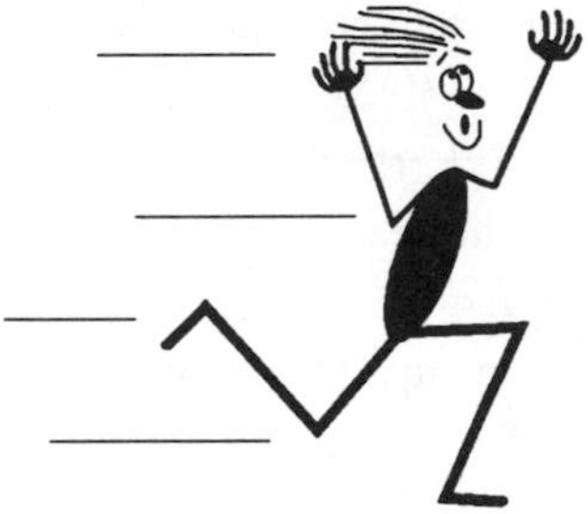

The Challenge: ______________ The Challenge: ______________

Low Activation

____
____
____

High Activation

____
____
____

Figure 9-1 Activation at Its Best

Take three deep breaths and relax your jaw. Using your *zone-o-meter*, tune in to your activation. Be especially sensitive to the areas that you just identified where you typically carry extra and where you let it all hang out. Starting at the top of your head, scan your body for signs of excess or inadequate activation and to signals that alert you that activation is just right.

Return to and focus in on the one area in which you are most aware of activation, especially when it is running overboard. Tense that area gently—firmly enough to feel the tension. Hold to a count of three. Breathe in. And as you breathe out, release the tension. Picture sending it into the air above you, into the real ozone—*TRASHIT!* Breathing deep and strong, consciously adjust the tension to a moderate level. Whether it is your jaw or your hands, your shoulders or your feet, feel the strength. *PACKIT!*

Sit up with your shoulders squared strong, take three deep breaths, and tune back in.

You can do this body scan any place at any time. Commit to doing it at least five times a day for the next week to make it automatic. You're probably already aware of activation. It's just that your awareness kicks in after you've crossed the boundaries to the o-Zone. Awareness of the 3 A's gives you an early-warning system and the opportunity to tune in to those instances when things feel just right so you can learn to recreate them effortlessly.

With practice and observation, you will start to notice the more subtle signs of excess or inadequate activation in yourself and in others too. One middle-level manager told me that she realized that her jaw was constantly tight. Simply opening her mouth slightly made all the difference in her day.

Activation—The "Walk"

Walk-the-Talk and Read the Walk of Others

Reading your own activation cues, along with your attention and attitude, enables genuine engagement, which is at the heart of doing your best. Cueing in to read others' activation is another skill that ensures your survival and success on the streets and on The Street. Not tuning in, not knowing how to interpret, or choosing to ignore the activation of other people—individuals and groups—can cost you money, time, and some amount of pride.

One investment banker, Scott, described his confusion and disappointment when, after working for months with one client to find sources for start-up money for the client's high-tech breakthrough, received a call from the client alerting him that the client had closed a deal with someone else. "Just a week ago, this guy was sweating bullets. And no wonder—things were getting down to the bottom line. If he didn't close the deal soon, he was going to be out a lot of his own money and never see his dreams come to fruition. He seemed relieved when we left the meeting, but not as grateful as I had thought. And he wasn't sweating any more. When I got through to him the next day, he sounded distant and cool. I ignored it, tending to other customers who were at the top of the list after spending months on this high-tech guy. It should not have shocked me when he called a few days later, sounding like he had never sweat a bead in his life over this. He wanted to thank me for all of our work and let me know that he had signed a deal with someone else. He took the offer we had gotten for him and used it to leverage a deal that would cost him less."

With his hands curled in to fists and his shoulders squared, Scott's activation was wired tight as he related this story. To facilitate his being able to see the situation from a different angle, I asked him to uncurl his fists. Suddenly he released a huge pent-up sigh and agreed that he had missed some important data along the way when he ignored the activation signals swirling within him. With an open mind, Scott realized the value in tuning in to read his own activation cues as well as those of others, even the ones transmitted over wireless phones and email.

Really Do It! Activation Sightings—Walk-the-Talk and Read Others' Strides

Activation is a powerful source of information about what people really think or feel. It is the "walk" of walk-the-talk. And, given that it is estimated that well over 75 percent of our communication is nonverbal, activation is a more accurate reading of what someone means and their hidden agendas than any words they might throw on the table. Yours is up for interpretation too. "Walking-the-talk" means making activation consistent with your words. Walk-the-talk and watch how others walk while keeping an eye on your own footsteps.

For the next day, tune in to the activation of those around you. Try listening and looking for activation signals that might tell a story that is different from the words that someone mouths or writes in sound-byte emails or leaves on your voicemail. Then, instead of jumping to your own overactivated conclusions or sliding down to underactivation, where you dismiss the signs as "nothing," check in and check them out. Signs of activation are all around you. When you ignore them—your own or others'— you put yourself at a disadvantage.

Remember too that you are emitting activation signals all the time as well. Make your message consistent with what you want to say and how you want others to perceive you. Walk your talk.

Assess!

It's time to put that inverted-U to work to assess the requirements for activation to determine your ideal green engagement range at the top of the arc. For each situation that we face, there's an upside-down U representing the activation curve.

The shape of the U is a personal thing. Still, there are some general principles that apply. The slope of the inverted-U and the breadth of the green Zonal arc are affected by three major factors:

- Time, duration—is this a short sprint or a long-distance endurance event?
- Accuracy, including precision and fine coordination—does the task require the total body or groups of large muscles? Or do fine motor skills ensure precision?
- Complexity—do you have to simultaneously attend to many things for intense multitasking, or can you focus on only one or two factors? Is this a decision with multiple good (or bad) choices or a hands-down favorite?

In general, the curve will have a sharper rise and fall and a narrower optimal green zone for situations that require short bursts of energy—the sprints of life. The curve will also have a sharper rise and fall for those tasks that require precision, are more complex, or require that you focus on multiple things.

Assessing the Arc and the Tails

Identifying the shape of the arc, and your personal markers that alert you to activation that is too low, too high, or just right for common personal challenges, is the jumpstart for accessing the correct level of activation. This exercise will introduce you to the thinking process that you can work through in a matter of seconds in real time. Think of a situation that is common, one in which you have spanned the range of activation from the back-slide to activation levels that were too low to plowing over the edge of the arc to levels that were just too high. Conjure up a challenge where you have spanned the entire activation curve, from the tail of disconnection to the tail where agitation took you out of the running.

It could be a meeting situation. Making a sale—whether it is to get buy-in on an idea, a product, a new way of doing things, or to enlist your kids in cleaning their rooms—is another common situation that can send people over either edge. And there is always the performance review—giving feedback in a constructive manner to enlist hearts and minds of others—whether it is to a colleague, a boss, your partner, kids, or your best canine buddy. Record the experience you have chosen on the line above the axes in Figure 9-2.

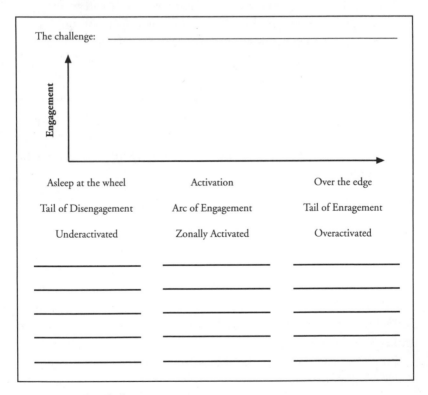

Figure 9-2   The Challenge

Drop your jaw slightly and take three deep breaths. Let your arms hang loosely. If you can, uncross your legs and sit comfortably with your feet flattened out like paddles. Wiggle your toes to really get those relaxing sensations going and to pull you into the moment.

We're going to start with the underactivated version. Picture yourself in the situation you have chosen when you were underactivated. You know the type of circumstance I'm talking about, the kind where you roll your eyes, wondering how you'll ever get it together or why you have to. Get a picture of yourself from the outside—your stance, pacing, the slant of your shoulders, the tension in your hands. Read your internal cues—your heartbeat, respiration, and perspiration. Scan your body from the top of your head to the bottom of your soles for signs of activation on the wane. Be sure to tune in to your primary harbors for activation. Get a clear picture, from the outside and inside, of how you look and feel when activation is too low for a good connection. Make a note of how such low levels of activation affect your attention, including your ability to screen out distracting factors, the internal and external ones.

Take a deep breath and move yourself up the curve into the arc. Be aware of the signs when you pass from too little to just the right amount of activation to engage and feel centered. Visualize yourself in the situation you have chosen. You're in the Zone, totally immersed in the process, confident, and activated to just the right level that works for you. Use your internal meter to read your activation—where you feel it, how it feels. Watch from an internal and external perspective. Observe your posturing, stance, the slant of your shoulders. Feel your breathing, heartbeat, pacing. Read your markers, especially the cues from those frequent harbors of activation. Notice the effects on attention, including your ability to screen out distractions and shift your focus flexibly. Tune in to the impact of ideal activation on your attitude, including your confidence.

Picture yourself wandering back toward the lower limit of optimal activation. Get a clear reading of where and how that feels and how it affects your experience, including attention and attitude.

Now move back to the center of the arc. Picture yourself moving toward the upper edge of the arc, not quite into an overactivated tumble, but pretty close. Get a reading. How broad is your green band and how steep is the slippery slope down and out of the curve?

Take yourself over the edge the same way it happens in real life. Plant yourself in the scene you've chosen with activation spinning out of control. Read your internal sensations and picture your external manifestations that proclaim to you and to others that activation is off the charts. Where does it first raise its unsavory presence? Where do you feel it most intensely? Get a solid reading of excess activation in your most frequent activation harbor. Notice how excess activation affects your focus, particularly the width of your attention. How does excess activation affect your attitude, including your confidence? What effect does it have on the speed and quality of your thinking?

Now it's time to move yourself back into the arc. Picture loading the signs of excess activation into your thought balloon, the one shaped like a trash bag. Take a breath in and *TRASHIT*—hurl the trash into the air. Picture yourself with the optimal activation that you identified when you were engaged in the arc and things were clicking—*PACKIT!* Watch yourself in this engaged state and notice the difference in your attention and attitude. Relish the confidence in your ability to choose your energy level.

Relax your shoulders and jaw; wiggle your toes. Clench and relax your fingers. And take three deep breaths.

Grab a writing instrument. If you have one, a red pen works well for recording *plungers*, those unsavory markers of the tails. Green works well for the arc.

Start with the arc. In the lines in the center that represent the *arc of engagement*, use the green pen to record descriptions of activation in the areas of your body where you most frequently feel it—those frequent-flyer harbors that you identified earlier. These are your personal markers that you are going to distill into *propellers*, cues that you can use to propel you into the Zone and back again.

Grab the red pen or writing instrument of your choice. Record your most frequent descriptions of underactivation on the lines to the left, moving from the top of your head to your toes. "Chin hitting chest, barely breathing, eyelids drooping, slack jaw" are clear markers that you'll recognize. Include internal physiological markers as well, whether it is a big sigh, holding your breath, or the slow blips of your beating heart.

Record your most common signs of overactivation on the lines to the right. Make your descriptions accurate and vivid. "Teeth clenched tight, pain in the backside, gnarled toes, and raging calf pain" are powerful plungers that you will recognize early on and that you can head off at the pass.

Return to the graph and draw the shape of your inverted-U for this challenge—is it a fast-rise/fast-fall curve with a narrow spiked center, or is it a more rounded ride? Highlight the optimal range in green; make the tails red. Mark lines to indicate the upper and lower Zonal limits and record your descriptors of the limits next to these markers.

Activation works in conjunction with attention and attitude. Together they determine how you feel and how you behave, which affect the quality of your experience and your performance. To begin to see the circular interrelationships, take a minute to consider your attention and attitude at each tail of the U-curve as well as how you feel and the actions you take. Contrast this with your focus, attitude, feelings, and actions as well as the quality of your experience and your performance when your activation is aligned at ideal levels at the top of the green curve. Record notes to yourself on the lines below the green part of the curve to describe your personal readings of attention and attitude when you were soaring in the arc for this challenge.

You just assessed the situational demands for activation using the inverted-U. You've determined your green arc zone and its cues that alert you to optimal activation. You have your signs of impending slips into the o-Zone. And you've got your red tail zones, the full-blown indicators of the o-Zone.

You can use the same assessment process in real life. Except you won't need the pens, paper, or a Palmpilot. And it takes a mere nanosecond. You'll make mental notes instead. When you're in the midst of a situation or preparing for the next challenge, consider how much activation will be ideal for you. Picture the inverted-U in full color. Then make mental notes of the words that describe activation of the green zone, its limits, and the dreaded red o-zonal tails. You can continue to revise the curve and the signs as you get more experience with it. After all, learning to live in the Zone is a process of adaptation and growth.

You Can Assess Even if You've Never Been There

What about challenges that are new or situations that always send you to o-Zonal highs or lows? How do you estimate the shape of the U and your markers? You can still assess the situational requirements for activation as well as attention and attitudinal beliefs with a few techniques.

First, consider other challenges that you think have similar activation requirements. Draw on your personal bests and worsts to estimate the shape of the inverted U and to put words to the green and red zones.

You can also draw on the experiences of others—coaches, mentors, bosses, even parents. Ask them about their best and worst experiences in this or similar challenges to learn about their 3 A's. (As a side note, I want you to remember that you can use this method to teach other people to get in the Zone by teaching them about your Zonal and o-Zonal triple-A markers.)

If you don't have access to someone you can talk to, use the power of observation. Watch videos, observe people you admire who seem to have mastered this challenge, or read about them. Movies and stories of fictional characters can work too. Tune in to signs of activation working for and against the people you study.

You can use relaxation and visualization to imagine yourself in the o-Zone and Zone to get a picture of the U-curve. This works on its own and is a great adjunct to the techniques I just outlined. It's your virtual practice field. As you develop real experience with a challenging situation, you can use visualization to fine-tune the curve and refine your personal markers of the activation Zone and o-Zone.

Now you have a picture of your activation destination. To bridge the gap between where you are and where you want to be, you're going to learn activation adjustment strategies to replace o-Zonal activation with an alternative desirable response. It's time to *TRASHIT* and *PACKIT!*

Adjust

Distilling the markers of the arc and tails to simple cues, personal activation *plungers* to *TRASH* and *propellers* that you'll *PACK,* will make your journey to the Zone much easier.

Go back to the inverted-U that you drew. Review the red o-Zone cues. You're going to pare them down to personalized shorthand cues—words, images, and sensations that vividly portray o-Zonal activation. Come up with one or two o-Zonal cues that represent underactivation and two that alert you to overactivation. Generally, the most effective *plunging cue* will be from the area of your body that frequently harbors too much activation. For me, the dead giveaway is my feet and my shoulders. (So it did not surprise me when I developed a growth in my foot after decades of thinking and running on them.) Record your personal cues in the *TRASHIT* balloon in Figure 9-3. List one signal of subzonal activation on the bottom and one signal representing excess activation on the top.

The human mind has a way of replacing the "trash" that you don't want with similar items. That is unless, of course, you circumvent the autopilot replacements. *TRASHIT* on its own is just not enough. *PACKIT* provides you with the tool to proactively insert the activa-

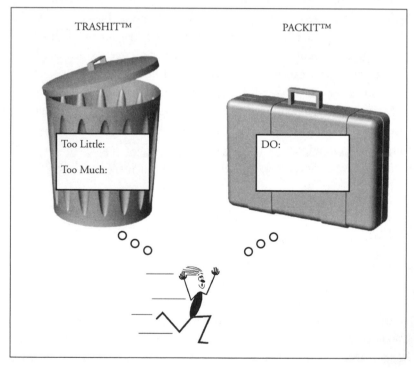

Figure 9-3 Activation *TRASHIT*™ and *PACKIT*™

tion, attention, and attitudes that you want to pack and carry on. The concepts really are one—*TRASHIT and PACKIT!*

Next you will want *propellers*, personal cues to move you swiftly into the arc of engagement. Refer back to your inverted-U. Review the cues that alerted you to engagement, the green zone *propellers*. Choose one, okay you can choose two, that represent the whole *PACK*age for you. Distill each one to one to three words or to an image that vividly portrays activation at its best fit.

Propellers are most powerful when they are active—action words or images that tell you what to do. Make them proactive. Don't use don't. "Don't think about ice cream." Did you picture a cone or a dish with sprinkles? Remember that research supports what you probably already know. We humans are visual. That's why advising ourselves or others about what to not do—"don't do this, don't do that"—creates the very image of what we want to avoid.

Turn your propeller cues into actions—alternate responses that are mutually exclusive from your o-Zonal plungers. These are your personalized propellers that you'll insert in your carryon thought balloon. Write your activation *propellers* in your *PACKIT* balloon that appears in the box above.

Wiggling your toes in your wingtips, a deep inspiring breath before you walk up to the podium, clenching and releasing your jaw, singing at the top of your lungs in the privacy of your thought balloon—these are all adjustment propellers that have been put to the test by people confronting daily and daunting challenges. They can work for you too. Certain *propellers* have steeled people through the ages. Many are research-supported. They work by adjusting the biochemical brain bath that sets your prefrontal free. Personalize any of these: Release tension with a toe wiggle or a fist release for a new grip; change your pacing or stance; act "as if" you feel confident;[1] breathe; shout a rallying credo;[2] shift the beat of your soundtrack; sing,[3] laugh,[4] cry to burn off some steam. Watch inspiring movies; read great books; listen to motivating music; move—walk, jog, skip, swing your arm; write; eat right, sleep tight. *Willfully* put these propellers to work.

Remember that awareness is still key. You want to be able to read your own activation at any moment to know if it's time for an adjustment up or down. Awareness of your cues that alert you that you are nearing the limits of the green range can keep you from spinning into an overactivated choking frenzy or sliding down to an underactivated slump. Reading and realigning your frequent harbors of activation can also tune your attention back in and open your mind. By taking back control, you will also build your confidence.

Rhythm and Breathing

There is a reason that I have mentioned music and breathing so often in this journey. Breathing and music are powerful propelling cues that can reconnect you to the moment. The right tune or breathing pattern can cool overagitation, broaden perspective, and stop rigid fast-forward thinking in its tracks. Another tune or breathing pattern can get you energized, focused, and back on track.

I know I have restricted you to one or two propellers. Still, I would encourage you to consider *PACKing* a breathing pattern and a rhythm to fall back on to jack activation up or chill it back down. Bruce, as in Springsteen, and Van, as in Morrison, and their modern-day equivalents—in Jennifer Lopez's upbeat and Dave Matthews calming meditations—are some of my standbys that have worked for others. What works for you?

REALLY Do It!—TRASHIT and PACKIT!

Moving yourself from the o-Zone to the Zone is an active process. You're going to use virtual A^3 practice to *TRASH* your *plungers* and

PACK your *propellers* to move yourself from the o-Zone to the Zone and back again.

Refer back to the challenge you identified for the inverted-U exercise. Take some deep breaths and flex-release the tension from your favorite pick areas to hold excess tension. Picture yourself in the same situation. Start in the Zone. Get a clear image of yourself optimally activated, functioning at your best. Visualize yourself moving toward the upper limit of activation. Tune in. As soon as you experience the cues of looming overactivation, stuff your o-Zonal *plungers* into your *TRASHIT* balloon. Take a deep breath in. Slowly breathe out and hurl the *TRASHIT* balloon into space, releasing your excess activation.

Breathe in deeply while you picture yourself purposefully filling your *PACKIT* balloon with your propelling cues, including your breath pattern and rhythm, of the arc for engagement. Plant it firmly on top of your head. Visualize yourself realigned and back in the arch-shaped Zone. Relish your personal power to determine and control your physical experience of the moment. Breathe deeply. Next picture yourself moving toward the lower limits of activation. Tune in to those signals of danger looming ahead. *TRASHIT and PACKIT.* Feel your personal power and breathe. Complete the exercise with a picture of yourself optimally activated in the Zone.

A^3-Visualization

If you want to get maximum mileage from this strategy, visualize yourself fully entrenched in the o-Zone. This is a real world A^3-visualization with all of the obstacles that you might encounter, the self-imposed internal and external ones. Visualizing only technique or visualizing just the good times will not provide the same training advantage as visioning rough times that you turn around by manipulating your 3 A's.

Practice wandering from the arc where things are clicking into either tail, then use your A^3 propelling cues to move yourself back into the arc.

Practice avoiding tailspins, taking yourself right up to those upper and lower limits and pulling yourself back to center again with your personalized A^3 propellers.

Use this virtual training to fine-tune your propellers and the plungers that alert you to o-Zonal tailspins that loom ahead. Take note of how you can use any one of the 3 A's to realign the other two. Play around with that idea, using attention propellers to realign activation, confidence-building language to realign attention or activation.

Use *TRASHIT and PACKIT* to power yourself back into the Zone. Always finish with an image of yourself strong and centered in the Zone.

This is a powerful technique that you can use to review and preview life challenges. Try it out on situations that have not gone as well as you would like. By reviewing them with a positive A^3 spin, you reprogram your memory and train yourself for correct A^3 responses the next time you encounter the same or a similar situation. When the actual situation does appear or recur, you will be prepared to engage and do your best. And you will have well-practiced strategies to deal with the worst. Put it to work to get activated for your next meeting, sales call, or family dinner. Use it to prepare for new challenges as well.

When you take these activation adjustment strategies to the streets, you will soon find that the signs of excess and inadequate activation cross experiences. The same triggers and propellers that work in one situation will serve you well in many different instances. Getting connected to your experiences by adjusting your activation will become quicker and easier even for the extreme challenges that you might have never predicted. When the real challenge presents itself, you'll be ready. Optimally activated, it will feel like a deja vu, a "been there, done that" experience that you already mastered and enjoyed.

Postoperative Debriefing

For matching your activation to the situation, remember these points:

- Know yourself—awareness is key. Use your Zone-o-meter. Where do you typically experience the signs of overactivation, underactivation, and activation that is just right? Identify how activation feels to you when it's in the Zone and at disconnected o-Zonal highs and lows.
- What's your natural pacing? Understand this so you can get activated to connect to people and circumstances that are more of a reach for you.
- Assess the situation to know what it will take. Use the inverted-U to delineate your green engagement Zone, the signs of danger ahead, and the full-blown crimson o-Zones.
- Distill your signs of the arc and tails to shorthand cues, *TRASHIT* plungers and *PACKIT* propellers.
- Make your propellers proactive, alternate responses that tell you what to do and are mutually exclusive from the cues that plunge you into the o-Zonal tails of disconnection.

Chapter 10

Get into It—Attention Strategies

GAME PLAN

Attention, always selective, can be directed inward or out, toward the big picture or the microscopic details. Understanding the dimensions of attention and the elements of style will enable you to *willfully* tune in to understand the points of view of others, to ferret out the essential elements for doing your best in a variety of circumstances, and to connect genuinely with a variety of situations and people whose style is different from your own—all those "difficult" people who are really just different. Leveraging difference is the key to building strong team cultures where diversity reigns.

Pay attention! Listen up! Open your eyes! Despite the jeers from the sidelines of life encouraging us to open our eyes and our ears, the truth is that we are always attending to something. It's just that sometimes we're tuned in to the wrong things. When athletes and corporate leaders describe their best or worst performances, they can always recall those items on which they were focused. It is not a lack of focus that spirals people into tailspins into the o-Zone. It is, instead, a focus on the wrong things. And it's a focus on the right ingredients, the bare essentials, that can position us for connection in the Zone. A focus on anything else, whether it's related to the current circumstances or not, lands you in the world of disconnect.

Attention, in its simplest form, includes those elements of the external and internal worlds that we select out from the bigger picture. Our focal points are in the forefront of our attention while everything else in our minds, in our hearts, and in the environment, slips away to a dull murmur.

Most of the advice that we get or give about paying attention and tuning in, even when we are acting as our own trusted advisor, offers generic cues and nothing more. Rarely do such tips meet with the desired response. Instead we get more distracted, focusing some of our valuable and limited attention on the voices themselves, even when they are in our own heads. More often than not, the volume gets turned up, creating even more distractions. I have heard athletes, corporate warriors, and young kids tell me that the admonitions from coaches, bosses, and parents were useless because, after all, they had been paying attention. It isn't enough to order attention and focus around. Proactively determining where you want your attention to be and on what you want to be focused will provide you with the keys to connect with the situations and people that you face each day. Flexibly adapting your attention for a variety of circumstances and different people whose own attention style might be dramatically different from your own are life skills that enable the engagement that is characteristic of personal and organizational bests. So listen up and open your eyes—just kidding!

What You See Is What You Get—Attention Depends on Your Screen

Attention—the word itself is derived from "tendre"—to hold. We hold things in our perceptual field. It's an active process of orienting, screening, holding on, shifting, and eventually letting go.

The way we humans structure a reality out of the wide world around us has been the object of attention of philosophers and psychologists through the ages, well before the *Matrix* movie series. Perceptual psychology researchers have enlightened us on the processes of attention whereby we take mere physical objects and turn them into pictures in our brains, encoding and decoding in nanoseconds, feats that still stand up to even the best computer or palm-held brain-in-a-box.

Researchers in perceptual psychology and the neurosciences have also explored the individual differences that affect encoding and storage as well as those that lead us to choose and process different slices of the internal and external world. The consensual conclusion, as you know, is that your reality is nothing more than what you perceive. Selection style appears to be innate and subject to experience. But now you know that you can consciously shift it. You can expand it by taking control of activation and attitude as well as attention itself with strategies geared to keep that powerful prefrontal cortex in the game.

People like Tom, the attorney, see the world through a relatively narrow lens that screens out feeling and people elements while admitting tangible items like data and results, especially anything that confirms their belief in the half-empty nature of the world and dangers that loom on the roadways of life. Others, like Jim, shine a more moderate filter that lights up people and processes over data and outcomes. People like Mary shift flexibly, though sometimes reactively, from a narrow to a broad focus and back again, admitting data and people-oriented items at different times. When under perceived stress and its associated chemical potion, we all tend to fall back on our strongest preferred suit and preferred sensory mode for gathering information.

Some Selections Are Programmed and Need Countermeasures

The "orienting response" is our automatic, innate screening mechanism that alerts us to anything unusual, new, or different in our environment that could potentially threaten our safety. Originally a signal of "danger ahead" to our ancestors battling wooly mammoths, the orienting response allowed us to survive as a species by alerting us to stimuli that could jeopardize our safety and survival. During the days when those who launched hostile takeovers were considerably hairier, zooming in to difference and change was a good thing. Today it can run you into trouble.

The orienting response still works for us in settings where tuning into your gut and responding to shifts and novelty can alert you to danger or opportunity, whether you are surfing the NYSE for hot new items, assessing changes in your child's eating habits, or inquiring about the management of the company at which you are interviewing. That is, as long as you are open to running toward the situations as well as running away from them. But it gets in the way in today's world, especially in circumstances where embracing the new or different, including change, would be better than fleeing or fighting. Novel changes, new trends, and different people and processes might be the key to engaging and succeeding, from the tennis court to the Courtroom and stock market. In many instances, overriding the orienting response is imperative to ensuring the survival of individuals and of our species, particularly when embracing differences is critical to different people sharing limited world space and resources.

This is also true when it comes to tuning in to situations or people whose style of attention is different from our own. Attentional style plays a major role in determining your reality and the items of your world with which you engage.

First we select the items of our choice from the mass of internal and external stimuli that barrage us. We have the capability to latch on with all of our senses. At the same time we hold out other things from our consciousness. Even our own memories and feelings are up for grabs here.

It's a filtering process. We screen out certain stimuli and select others to which we devote our limited attention. Screening is a process that is key to success. With daily logarithmic increases in sensory stimuli, we human beings have learned to adapt by screening out and processing only those elements of our worlds that seem relevant or appealing to us at any moment. We hold on to them and perceive them as reality. The blinders can be directed inward as well as outward. With the powerful mental mechanisms of defense, we can even banish memories to such depths of unconsciousness that we cannot recall them at all. Often the selective process is unconscious and reactive. We find ourselves connected or disengaged almost by accident.

When we proactively and consciously select and choose the elements on which we will focus, we set ourselves up to engage with the real deal—or at least as real as our brain's ability to process information and our personal lenses will allow. Just as with activation, it starts with knowing yourself.

A Shifting Reality

Because the stimuli that bombard us are constantly changing, whether they are generated internally or externally, our focal points are a work in progress. Attending flexibly depends on your selective abilities and on your ability to shift attention to the important stimuli as the demands of the task change. And, as you remember from your physiology lesson, high levels of activation interfere with the ability to move attention flexibly from one thing to another.

There are guidelines for matching attention to a particular type of situation that are more helpful than the standby "pay attention" mantras. Each person has a strong suit, an attentional style that makes it easier to engage with certain activities and types of people than others. Identifying your primary attention suit will give you a head start on fine-tuning your *awareness* of your focus at any moment and learning to change it—just as the manual shifting of a sports car gives you the ultimate control of your gears. With the slightest maneuver of the stick-shift and clutch, you can shift to *adjust* attention gears, moving your focus from one aspect of a situation to another, shifting width and depth as well.

Attention, just like its other two companions, demands attention itself in the form of *awareness*. The 3 A's remain the standard—*aware, assess, adjust*. With *Winner's Way* strategies, you can learn how to purposefully determine and focus on what's most important to engage with the challenge at hand.

Being able to determine, initiate, sustain and shift focus, and to refocus after those lapses that everyone has, are the hallmarks of total engagement in sport and all arenas of life. This includes balancing a budget, performing surgery, practicing law, cooking a gourmet meal (or, for some of us, making macaroni and cheese from a box), or connecting with a customer or friend in a stellar interaction. For any activity, we each have an optimal focus of attention. Whether it is people or things, our focus might be internal, external, narrow or broad. It might include a single element or many stimuli. Knowing what is optimal for you and learning to proactively choose and focus yourself on the essential elements can immerse you in the moment—in the Zone of engagement. Shifting attention is a proactive process requiring an active prefrontal cortex. A brain and body flooded with a rush of natural chemicals that is too strong for the moment will have a negative impact on your ability to shift attention just as it will on your ability to shift your car.

Attention à la Mode

Attention is multimodal. It includes what we see, hear, touch, smell, taste, and even more. We attend with all of our senses and our intuitive gut as well as both sides of the brain. Attention can be visual—what you see in your environment or the internal movies you play in your mind's lens. And it can be auditory—what you hear, including self-talk or your rhythm as you saunter down the street. The sensations from your nose can also captivate attention, like those days when you're trying to concentrate on your computer screen and the aroma of freshly brewed coffee calls your name. Touch, including temperature, provides another attention-grabbing force, as does the sensation of moving when you run to make a plane connection or to get out the door to pick up your child from lacrosse practice. Your gut gives you another reading on attention—the intuitive sensations that you get when something doesn't feel quite right. On the other end, your brain plays a role in what you perceive. A left-brained focus is associated with data, details, bottom-line results while a right-brain-mediated focus is associated with emotional, people-oriented elements of the world.

When it comes to our senses, we all have personal strengths and areas to develop. (Note that I do not refer to "weak" areas. Instead, I am using a cognitive psychological technique for refocusing attention to the half-full and thereby adjusting attitude. You will learn about this later. With "framing" and "reframing" you can turn weaknesses into areas to work on and develop, potential opportunities for growth and sources of satisfaction.)

Understanding that different people tune in with different senses will open your mind to the reasons underlying so many points of view and the misunderstandings that can drive people apart. Learning to access your world through a broader array of avenues will ensure that you can take in the crucial elements for engaging with a variety of challenges. And it will open your eyes (or your ears or your gut or whichever is your dominant suit) to a bright new world that has been under the surface all along.

Losing Your Mind to Come to Your Senses— Awareness

What about you? Consider your stronger suit for tuning in to the world around you. Do you take things in through your ears or your eyes? Or are you more of a hands-on kinesthetic learner? What about the other senses that have become second-string players in our current world but which were vital to survival of our ancestors? Do you shudder with the sensation of certain fabrics against your skin or those pesky sock seams, or are they below the water line of awareness? Can you enjoy the sensation of the sun warming or the wind brushing your skin? Are you the first to smell the roses on a walk with family or friends? When it comes to a choice between your gut and your brain, is it food for thought or a hearty meal that attracts you? Learning to identify your strong suit and to develop the others will enable you to tune into a broader variety of experiences, including the wonderful smell of those roses.

Really Do It! Use Your Mind to Come to Your Senses

Try this. Take three deep breaths. Now breathe in deeply and visualize smelling the aroma of freshly brewed coffee. (Though if coffee is not your thing, inhale the fumes of your favorite beverage, whether it is tea, lemonade, or rich hot chocolate.) Savor the sensation. Notice your gut's response to something that provides comfort. Now picture yourself taking a sip or gulp of that favorite beverage. Feel the kinesthetic sensation of moving the cup or glass up to your lips, the touch of the surface to your lips, and the sensation of the liquid in your mouth and throat. Enjoy the taste and the warm or cool sensation in your throat. Shift to your sense of touch. Notice the warm or cold sensation of the glass against your fingers and palms. Savor one more sip.

Which sense was the most difficult for you to visualize? Which was your strongest of these often overlooked senses? You could be missing a lot of valuable information by not tuning in with a particular sense. Take this 24-hour challenge to come to your senses.

Tune in with your sense that you want (notice the reframing) to develop for the next 24 hours. Use awareness. When you hear a person telling you a problem, tune in to the visual aspects of the scene too. Then add the underutilized sense that you want to develop further. If it is touch, feel yourself solving the problem—feel the sensations of temperature on your skin or the sensation of gripping the side of your seat during a meeting or the golf club or steering wheel. Then try another sense that you would like to add to your arsenal. Use your gut to read the climate of the meeting. Smell the grass of the golf greens. The deep breath, in and of itself, is a surefire way to release some of the excess activation that can lead grown women and men to hurl loud curses on beautiful fairways. Replace things that smell fishy with aromas of your choice to calm or rev you up and get you tuned in to the essentials.

The Objects of Our Attention Run Deep and Broad

Attention has depth and breadth—internal-external, narrow-broad. This dual dimension framework has been delineated and supported in research and case studies in sports and corporate arenas by Bob Nideffer, the pioneering sports psychology researcher on attentional style, and others. [1] Nideffer's framework, adapted with his permission, is illustrated in Figure 10-1. The top lines of each quadrant synthesize the activities that are best suited for a particular breadth or depth of focus. The bottom line identifies areas that might pose problems for those who focus primarily from this stance, without the advantage of flexibility of attention that is essential for connecting in a variety of situations and with diverse people.

I have adapted and elaborated the original model, providing vivid descriptions that you can call on when it is time to put this framework to use to assess and adjust attention. Review the diagram in terms of its good-fit for certain types or segments of your activities.

Aware, Assess, Adjust

When you decide to go on a vacation, you probably do some amount of visioning about where you might want to go, even if you ultimately decide to hide out in your home with the remote powered up and the answering machine turned to silent mode. For the initial scouting phase of an activity, the top right quadrant for scanning and visioning with its external broad focus is the best fit.

Now you will want a plan. For solving problems creatively, strategizing, and goal-setting, the bottom right quadrant is ideal. Your focus will be broad here too, but this time it will be directed internally to analyze the information that you garnered from your broad-based scan by comparing it to the information stored in your memory banks. Now you can generate a creative solution and a thoughtful plan. Do you want to hide out with the remote, go to that ski camp that you have dreamed about, or travel to a tropical island and sit back with a palm-tree-topped beverage? Skiing sounds good.

It is time to check it out, to practice your moves in the privacy of your mind's eye. Moving to the bottom left quadrant for a narrow internal focus will enable you to virtually rehearse. Perhaps the logistics of a summer ski camp are just too much for your current fatigue level or your budget. On the other hand, this check-in and mental rehearsal of what needs to be done might be just right for moving you to the next phase of really doing it. Picturing yourself skiing in the summer sun is

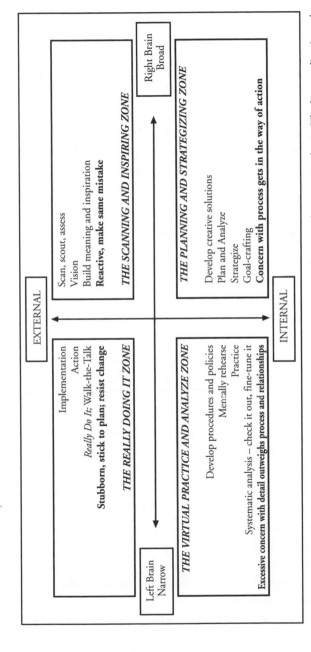

Figure 10-1 Each quadrant describes the activities that are well-suited to the particular attentional suit. The bottom line in each quadrant, highlighted in bold, describes the area that needs work. When this mode of attention is favored to the exclusion of others, engagement and performance will be negatively impacted by the patterns highlighted in bold. Adapted and expanded, with permission, from Nideffer's dimensions of attention.

just too good to pass up. In doing this, you can analyze any glitches. Of course, if you do find glitches, you will probably want to go back to the top right to rescan and reformulate your big picture vision.

Assuming no glitches and therefore no need to start it up again, you would wind down your planning with the exciting implementation of your strategic plan. Now you are in the top left quadrant, where a narrow external focus positions you to act with precision and accuracy as you implement the plan. Whether you are on the couch, on the slopes, or on the beach, you are positioned to *really* do it.

Your Minimum Daily Requirements

What about your day? Are there activities that require the big picture view and others that call for hands-on doing? On Figure 10-1, mentally write in your own daily activities, or specific segments of activities, three that fit well within each quadrant.

Is there a particular quadrant in which you spend the least amount of time? Is there another quadrant where you seem to live most of your life?

Most people live in the "doing" zone, rushing frantically from one "doing" to another. Without the thoughtful "planning" and "inspiring" zones to build meaning, even things that once seemed enjoyable can start to turn from awesome to awful in this "doing" quadrant, where activation tends to run high. Also, you will remember from our arc discussion, it is difficult to shift attention flexibly and efficiently when you are traveling in fast-forward.

Mary found herself entrenched in the "doing" zone when she decided to do the work herself rather than risk doing a poor job at people management. Her "doing" focus, accompanied by high energy and a belief in the ineptitude of herself and others, left Mary with no real option other than to play-not-to-lose and to just barely hold on. Mary was positioned to survive rather than thrive. Fortunately, Mary recognized her heavy burden of spending all of her time in the "doing" zone. And she recognized the value of the other three quadrants for facilitating her leadership abilities. The quadrants provided Mary with a map. By asking herself the awareness and assessment questions of "where is my focus right now?" and "is this the place that I want to focus in order to engage with the current challenge?" Mary was able to apply this framework to tune into the important over the urgent. In learning to distribute her attention, Mary improved her leadership skills, the work got done, and she freed up time for the planning and doing of family activities.

Tom, on the other hand, spent a good deal of his time planning. Or so he asserted. Although his work was planning work, he was actually doing the planning, which placed him mostly in the "doing" zone, pursuing the win. Tom had rarely considered strategically planning or setting goals. After all, at his high levels of activation with his attention narrowed in, he wanted to win. The thought of trying to build a motivating meaning for why he was doing the work had never crossed his mind until he realized that he really was heading for a heart attack if he stayed on the same track. Tom took time out to work on his vision for himself as a lawyer, business partner, boss, life partner, and father. By keeping his vision and mission in his mind, he refocused. He began to see the world through a different set of eyes and an open mind.

Many people are just like Mary and Tom, spending most of their time "doing" and little time "building meaning or planning." The most frequently neglected zone is the top right "scan and inspire" zone. After giving morning pep talks to your partner and kids and the pets who are left at home, few people think to use the commuting time to plan their own days, to develop visions and images that could draw them into their activities, images that are appealing and meaningful enough to activate them and turn their attitudes around.

The "planning" zone is another quadrant that is often neglected. How often have you thought to yourself that it would just take too long to plan something out, to actually record or scream aloud your goals? In the long run, you could have saved time and avoided errors, and duplication, by developing a strategic plan for getting your work and your fun things done.

Often we imagine that crafting such things as visions and goals and taking the time to carefully review a performance or a virtual dry run are too time-consuming. In reality, this use of time could save your life and your job and family. That is why you will have the opportunity, later in this chapter, to design a vision for small challenges as well as a lifetime vision. And it will take no longer than a five-minute commute.

Assess—People, Data, Big Picture, Details

Both direction and breadth of attention provide a framework for understanding the dimensions of attention and the importance of shifting between the quadrants for genuine connection and performing at your top level. But what about the content of attention? Some activities call for a focus on people; others invite a focus on things. Even within those categories, the focus can be narrow or broad.

Then there is the matter of personal style. Some of us naturally gravitate toward people-oriented information. Others prefer to stick to data, whether it is a bottom-line result or an accurate, detailed analysis. Your personal style of attention will determine which situations feel like the right-fitting shoe and which feel ill-fitting and uncomfortable.

A difference is a difference. There is no one style of attention that is superior to another. Anyone can be a good fit or a poor match. Identifying your style, and learning to adapt flexibly and refocus when you start to stray, can set the stage for *willful* connection. What about you? What is your strong suit when it comes to attention?

Know Yourself with The Winner's Way— What's Your Attentional Style?

Just like activation, aligning your attention starts with knowing yourself, your characteristic style. Try this quick assessment to determine which quadrant draws you in naturally and which is most difficult for you.[2]

From each group of four statements, choose the one that best describes you.

1. I'm a big-picture person who thrives on dreaming up strategies, especially long-range ones.
2. I thrive on details and data.
3. I'm results-oriented without regard to how it will affect other people.
4. I'm genuinely concerned with how people are feeling and how they are doing.

1. Leave the scouting to me. Leave the doing to them.
2. I'll do the analysis and then I'll do it again just to make sure.
3. Let's just do it—now before the window of opportunity closes.
4. I'll make sure that everyone is okay and on board for this plan.

1. Details? What details?
2. Give me data and make sure it's accurate and give me enough time to check it out for myself.
3. What's the bottom line?
4. How will this impact the team dynamics?

1. Why is everyone giving me that look? Was I supposed to check something?
2. I stayed up all night double and triple checking it, and I loved it.
3. Check it out for me and report back to me tomorrow at 2:00.
4. Let's check in with the team to see how it's progressing.

1. How am I? I'm glad you asked. Let me tell you about my day.
2. How am I? Don't waste our time with such a silly question. OR Exactly what do you mean by that?

3. How am I? Great. Now let's get down to business.
4. How am I? More importantly, how are you? And the kids? Your parents?

1. Go! Go! Go! Where exactly are we going? Who cares!
2. On your mark, get set, check that mark again to make sure it is accurate, go.
3. Mark-set-go fast—all the way to the finish line.
4. Everyone take your mark, get set now—is everyone okay—are you sure we're all ready? Let's go together.

1. I'd love to follow through on all the commitments I make—if only I could remember them.
2. I completed my part of the plan early so I formulated a detailed implementation plan for the rest of you. Responsibilities and due dates appear in the cells.
3. Here's my part of the project—delivered on time and under budget.
4. This deadline is too short for me. I'll need a little more time, and I think you all might need more time too or you'll stress yourselves out.

1. What do you mean I forgot the meeting? I wrote it in my *Filofax* and *Palmpilot.* They're here in this office somewhere, buried under one of the piles.
2. The meeting was supposed to start at 1:00. I've been here since 12:45. Doesn't anyone know the word "prompt" around here?
3. Sorry I'm a few minutes late. I had a meeting across town at noon and thought I could make it here in five minutes. Let's get started because I've got a 2:15 after this wraps up.
4. It is great to be back together. How was everyone's week?

1. Oops. My intentions were good—they really were. I meant to bring the report, but I couldn't find it. (OR Oh, the report, let me call my assistant and she'll run it up here. That is, if she can find it in my office.)
2. I brought the final revision of my report plus the three original versions and all of the supporting data.
3. Here's the report. Let's go directly to the conclusions and recommendations to move this forward. They're in bullets on the first page.
4. I've brought a copy of my report for each of you. The process and methodology took account of the many people that this impacted. Let's start there.

1. I might not have the answer, but I've got a great story about it.
2. What good are answers without the backup data?
3. What's the bottom line?
4. There is no one right answer because of the different perspectives we each bring.

1. Recognition? I love it—can't get enough! And I love to give it. It baffles me when people wonder if I'm genuine.
2. Recognition—if I don't need it, why do they? I focus on the details of what they did wrong so they can get it right.
3. I reward wins and point out errors so people learn to do it my way.
4. You can never give enough recognition. I make a point of sitting with each of my people for a weekly review. Plus I spend a lot of time out on the floor—management by walking around. But when it comes to reprimanding—that's where I struggle.

1. It's important to me that people get me and my jokes!
2. Getting it right and accurate is mandatory.

3. Getting it done on time and under budget is the mission of life.
4. Getting everyone through the experience feeling good is the hallmark of success.

Scoring
Add up all #1 responses (Scan & Inspire)

Total Number 1 responses ————

Add up all #2 responses (Practice & Analyze)

Total Number 2 responses ————

Add up all #3 responses (Really Do It!)

Total Number 3 responses ————

Add up all #4 responses (Plan & Strategize)

Total Number 4 responses ————

CHECK TOTAL (responses should be 12)

Total responses ————

Plot Your Attentional Style

Each of us has a strong style of attention, a quadrant in which we function most of the time, though this might vary by situation or role. Based on the scores from your assessment, you're going to plot your style in Figure 10-2.

Start in the *top right* quadrant, *The Scanning and Inspiring Zone.* Record your total of *#1* responses.

Go next to *the lower left Practice & Analyze* quadrant where you can record your *#2* responses.

Move up to the *upper left* quadrant—*The Really Do It! Zone.* Record your *#3* responses.

Drop down to the *lower right Planning and Strategizing* quadrant. Record your *#4* responses.

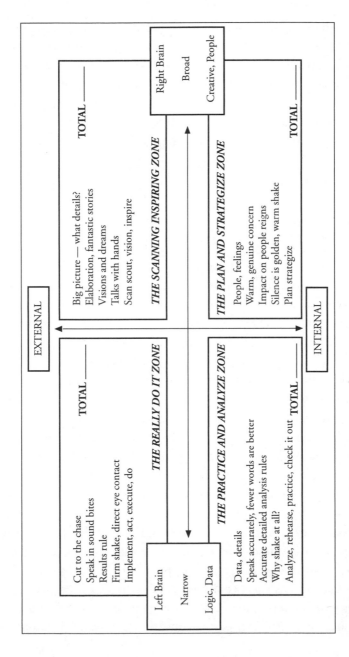

Figure 10-2 The Winner's Way™ Attention Style[3]

- Which quadrant is your strongest suit? These types of people and situations will be easiest for you to get yourself focused and engaged. (Though, in some instances, we initially react defensively with people very similar to our own style.)
- Which is the one in which you spend the least amount of time? It's there that you will want to develop flexibility for connecting with people and situations that require that type of focus.

Awareness

Attention—A Matter of Style

Running left to right in Figure 10-2, the horizontal axis depicts the breadth dimension of attention, from narrow to broad. The vertical axis depicts the direction of attention, internal or external. To the left is the left-brain, convergent and logical focus. On the right is the more creative and divergent right-brain approach to life and to problem solving. There is also a data versus people focus running left to right.

Consider this framework from two perspectives. Individuals and groups, from dynamic duos to entire organizations and cultures, have characteristic styles of attention, strongest suits. Based on that suit, they will generate their version of reality from the depth and breadth of the lens that they cast on the world and the content that most naturally captures their fancy. With such a focus, it will be easier to engage with certain activities or segments of activities and with certain people over others.

We each engage in a variety of activities during the day. By learning about each quadrant and the activities that are best suited to it, you can improve your assessment of just what the best focus is for a variety of challenges and people. You can apply this framework when it comes time to *assess* where you want your focus to be, and where you do not want it to be, particularly in interpersonal relationships.

You can also decide to develop the areas that are not your primary suits of attention.

I am going to describe each attentional style so that you can understand your own, recognize the styles of others, and learn to adapt your approach to different people and situations. In doing so, you can raise the probability that people will want to hear what you have to say. You will improve buy-in to your ideas. Perhaps more importantly, you can use your knowledge of how style of attention impacts the way other people see the world so that you can listen deeply and actually hear what they are intending to tell you. And when you do not understand, you will know how to ask for clarification.

The Scanning Inspiring Style

"Ready or not, fire, aim…" "Let's do it!" "Details—what details?" These are the rallying cries of individuals and groups who primarily rely on the broad external world as sources for the elements that become their reality. Seeing the big picture with a wide-angle lens leaves little attention for details, including time.

Individuals who score highest in this style make great visionaries, leaders, sales pros, and politicians. Scanners tune in to what others think and know who is doing, saying, and buying. And they let you know that they know. They are moved by acknowledgment and recognition.

With this style, people often digress far and wide in the wonderful stories that they relate, embellishing them with flourishes that others would never consider. Sometimes they even get lost in their own reports, wondering aloud what they had been saying to begin with. People who ride this quadrant tend to talk more than they listen. They express themselves dramatically, with big, sweeping hand movements and colorful language. Inspiration and moving others to action is characteristic of this style.

If this is your strongest suit, you probably know how to paint visions and inspire people to get going. But implementation is most likely not your favorite part. Like the lovable Spanky in *Our Gang*, these are the kids on any playground who gather large crowds of other kids around. Then they get them all fired up with whatever vision they have concocted, while they sit back and look on with pride. As adults they are often at the center of party conversations, and they are often the mavericks who start up companies and then move on to their next visionary initiative. Because they are so inspiring and uplifting, people want to follow them!

Details—what details? Enthralled with the big picture and fueled by the accolades of others, this attentional style has minimal awareness of details. Time management and organization are not high on the list, partly because they take on so much, with all of the best intentions to earn acknowledgment. In conflict mode, this style goes for the jugular in all-out attack.[4] The toughest match for a visionary type is the analytical style that is diametrically opposite on the grid.

Because they are easily distracted, when you are interacting with a broad/externally focused person, you will want to give them clear time lines. If they write the deadlines down, do yourself a favor and send them an additional email to confirm their commitments. Have frequent check-in times to ensure that they are getting to the stair-step goals that will take them to the finish line. If you want their buy-in to a team project, a new way of doing things, or a product, let them know who else is using this and how it will advance their standing or make them shine in the eyes of people whose acknowledgment they value. Recognition really is endless. With this style, you will get good return on your recognition investment. [5]

The Really Do It Style

"Show me that money—and the bottom line." "Just do it—my way!" "Snap out of it!" "What's your problem?" These are the commands shouted when an external, narrow focus provides the primary source of reality. Getting to the end zone to score is the primary force that motivates this style.

Cut-to-the-chase people, focused on the bottom line, these are the "doers," the people who love to take a plan and run with it whether it's to launch and complete a strategic takeover successfully, throw a fabulous party, or implement a new information management system. They are tuned in to the "what" over the "who," to facts over feelings, as the means to the bottom-line results that move them to action. The need to achieve sets them into action. Bottom-line results, whether it is the game score or profit margin, exceed the value of any acknowledgment that they could receive.

People who rely on this lens of attention tend to only see one way— their own. And they are happy to tell you about it in a blunt manner that can border on challenging. Usually better talkers than listeners, those who live in this quadrant speak in emphatic bullets, sometimes even pointing their fingers to drive a point home. Fast movers, they take a strong physical stance that mirrors their mental stance toward the world. While their body language is controlled, their handshakes could break your hand. And they can challenge the best with their steady eye contact that can, at times, feel territorial.

Getting things done and making sure that others follow through takes precedence here. If you use this frame most often, you probably know how you are doing at any moment, whether it is a game score or your return on investment. Because of your tendency to see your way as the right way, patience often eludes you. Tending to be a bit authoritarian, developing an understanding of what is important, and what moves others could assist you to reach the finish line with the team remaining intact. Still, when push comes to shove in a project, people will seek you out to get things moving forward.

Organized and good at managing time, people who live primarily with this "doing" outlook will get even more from people by learning to delegate effectively. (Have clear expectations about what you want, when, how it should look and why and, when necessary, how you want it done.) Also, value recognition, celebration, and fun at work and on the home front.

Easily angered and frustrated by others, this style becomes authoritarian, sometimes even dictatorial, in conflict mode. When you are interacting with this type of person, you will get best results if you give them choices, even when they are only illusions of choices. Driven by the need to achieve, and with a strong desire for control, honoring those factors produces the highest probability of getting their buy in. Once they are convinced, they will go to the mat to make sure that the endgame is achieved on time and under budget.

The Planner-Strategizer

"Are you all ready? Let's make sure we're really ready before we aim." "Let's do it for the gipper." "Is everyone on board?" The "planning and strategizing" style makes sure that everyone has, and knows, the plan and has a clear line-of-sight between what they are expected to do and how it fits with the desired results. For those who prefer a broad internal focus, thorough planning, consensus building, and empathizing are strengths. People in this quadrant are as concerned with the impact on people as they are on the bottom line, sometimes more so. Acceptance and pleasing others is a driving force of those who focus with the narrow internal people lens.

Easy listening, relaxed, warm, and sincere, people in this quadrant really want to know how you are when they ask. They ask more than they tell. Then they really listen in a genuine, thoughtful manner that can drive some "doers," their exact opposites, up the wall. During their thoughtful pauses, they are actually processing what others said, prior to planning a thoughtful response. Natural mediators, they will sacrifice the bottom line or getting to the finish first if that means that everyone will get there together. With subtle body language and tone and a tendency to acquiesce in conflict, they can be perceived as pushovers if they do not take a firm stand. And their own points of view can get garbled up by the perspectives of others.

In this quadrant, attention is ideally suited for solving problems using both creative and strategic processes. Relying on the "we" over the "I" and the process over the outcome, this is a great approach for teamwork and effective team membership. From this perspective you will be tuned in to how people are doing, but you might struggle to complete projects when you get sidetracked by the process to the exclusion of the outcome. Keeping track of deadlines and details will buffer your strength. Learning to generate intensity for achieving results and making it to the finish in a timely manner, even if some arrive with wounded feelings, will be important to building your effectiveness.

This style is hesitant to embrace change for fear that it could upset the status quo and unsettle people's feelings. You can motivate and build a relationship with the steady planner by giving them the scoop on how a proposed change or offering will affect people, including themselves. With a strong need for affiliation, for relationships of substance and endurance, you can maximize your impact on people who rely on this style by clarifying how your proposal, service, change, or product will contribute to their welfare and security as well as that of the team. In this quadrant, attention is ideally suited for solving problems using both creative and strategic processes.

The Practice and Analyze Style

"Show me the details" "Ready, aim, fire with precision." "Do it—but only if you can do it right." "I'll believe it only when I see it or when you prove it or when I can prove it myself." These are the rallying cries of individuals and groups who primarily rely on the narrow internal world as sources for the elements that become their reality. The worldview might be narrow, but it is accurate.

This quadrant is the domain of individuals and organizations that thrive on data and details—attorneys, accountants, engineers, and analytically oriented individuals and groups. Being accurate is the prime mover here, which is why checking and practicing to get it right is a good fit.

Attention in this quadrant is focused narrowly with few distractions. Precise and logical, people who live in this quadrant speak in sound bytes in a formal style. Task-oriented and analytical, they listen to analyze and scrutinize, to ensure that things are right. Language is clipped and silence is golden. After all, why waste words if there is no information to convey? If you can say it in e-mail, then that is a better choice than wasting time in meetings.

Do not be fooled by the quiet of people who rely on this style for deciphering the world. Getting things done precisely is key. To that end, more data is better, as long as it is accurate. And they will check for themselves to make sure that it is accurate. The checking is not intended to prove anyone else wrong; it is truly based on the desire for accuracy and precision that drives people with this focus. Without a time line, there can be a tendency to work and rework details ad nauseum, to become so focused on analysis and practicing things to perfection that paralysis or choking results.

While data over people, and details over big picture view, are the preferred areas of focus, people in this quadrant do enjoy recognition and praise for their real contributions. False praise or praise for things that seem foolish—those things that they might dismiss as simply being part of their job and not deserving of recognition—does not sit well with them. Being genuine and grounding feedback on data does. This style is an asset in leadership situations where precision is imperative.

Details are a forte here, which is why this analytical type of person has such a strong negative judgment toward the visionary type who lives diagonally across the quadrant. The nonverbal and verbal communication of the two styles is a dramatic contrast. Data-focused people tend to present with a rather stiff, closed, and formal posturing.

You won't get much from reading their faces, which typically are rather expressionless. And looking into their eyes can be a challenge because they often look away when they are in deep thought, analyzing what has been presented, which is most of the time. Nonverbal communication is restricted too. Why shake at all? "Cool" is how people often describe them. Speaking in clipped sentences or monosyllables (why waste words?) they are comfortable with the golden nature of silence. They might not ask how you are, and they might not want to tell you how they are. Such closeness is reserved for a small inner circle. But don't be fooled. While there are few signals of activation, people in this quadrant are often very tightly wired. It's just that they direct most of their activation to internal wheel-spinning in the privacy of their heads. So when it is conflict time, they head for the hills or into the privacy of their thoughts to *avoid conflict* at all costs.

Be accurate and praise their accuracy and precision to win this style over. Give them the data to mull over and work through before you present the summary at a meeting. Ask for their commentary and feedback ahead of time. Otherwise, don't be surprised if they correct any mistakes you made or any missing dotted "i's" in front of the whole team, even an external vendor or customer. To them they are just doing their job and trying to be helpful. And, in reality, who couldn't benefit from someone who can attend to the details, really grooves on it, and does it well? Every team needs a detail-oriented analyst. Most organizations rely on the CFO to play this role.

Assess Team Requirements

When we are in the zone, our focus of attention, in terms of both depth and direction, is matched to the requirements of the situation. Each of the quadrants is ideally suited for specific activities or segments of an activity. And we each, as individuals and organizations, have one or two suits that are stronger, more highly developed, than the others.

We tend to rely on our characteristic style most often and resort to this style when under pressure. Thus, even a broad lens becomes narrow when used exclusively and rigidly.

To get engaged and stay connected, especially under stress and distractions, it is crucial to understand your characteristic style and learn to counter your tendencies to retreat to o-Zonal quadrants when the going gets tough. Because that is when the chemicals storming the brain and body attempt to shut attentional flexibility down. Knowing yourself is the start to knowing the signs of o-Zonal danger ahead. Breathing helps too.

If your score on the assessment you took places you solidly within the extreme of any one quadrant, you will want to be on the lookout for signs that you are digging your heels in and limiting your focus to see the world, your current situation, and other people from this one perspective. Even though there are days when we wish that everyone could see the world the way we see it, any one of the styles, when used to exclusion, can run you into trouble.

To everything there really is a season. And there is a Zone for all seasons. There are situations in which each suit of attention will set you up to soar and situations in which you will, most likely, achieve a better connection and better results if you can move beyond your comfort zone and flex your attention. It starts with moving out of your corner of attention and opening your mind to the value-added of each style.

Adjust

Make a note of the situations that are a stretch for you—the challenges and people who are in the quadrant diagonally across from your strong suit. These are the situations and people that we typically label as "difficult" when, in reality, they are just different. When you encounter these situations, you will want to create your own buy-in for shifting your focus to connect *willfully*. Convince yourself ahead of time.

What beliefs about this style do you want to *TRASH* so that you can join in to resolve conflicts and collaborate? What is the value-added of this style, either to the team or for providing a different perspective for seeing the problem, and therefore for crafting a solution? Sketch a *TRASHIT and PACKIT* figure and record your beliefs about your own style and the other person's style and the focus you want to ditch. Write the value-added of the "different" style and the focus you want to add and adopt in your *PACKIT!* items.

Then practice in your A^3 visualizations. Just as you did in the previous chapter, take the time to generate best- and worst-case scenarios in which you are immersed in a challenging interaction. Picture yourself focused in the quadrant that is a good match for the segment of the activity or for the person or group with which you are trying to forge a connection. *PACK* the optimal focus. Practice gravitating toward the upper edge of the inverted-U where activation rises and your tendency is to narrow your focus to view things from your corner. *TRASH* that response and replant the optimal focus in your *PACKIT*.

Take a minute now to consider one person with whom you tend to lock horns. You just don't seem to see things from the same point of view. In fact, it is inevitable that you will see things from exactly opposite points of view. As one person put it—"They see big blue sky, and I'm wondering how we're going to make payroll." Get a picture of a recent interaction with this person. What quadrant of attention does this person live in? How is it different from your own? What is the value-added of his style? Consider this carefully. Usually we are most offended by the style that is diagonally opposite our own. Yet, in a group setting, we need that style to succeed. Purposefully use your *TRASHIT and PACKIT!* strategies to connect flexibly especially with those who are dramatically different. Turn "difficulties" into differences and results.

Once you start using your *will* to flexibly direct your attention, you will see the value and results of connecting with different people and situations. It will become more automatic and natural, even when you migrate to the quadrants that initially seem difficult at best. Also, by directing your own attention, you will become more aware of instances in which people, the media, market analysts, marketing and advertising, and politically-minded individuals and groups, and your teenagers may be attempting to capture your attention and spin a view of reality that confirms their own. And you will be prepared to make a conscious, proactive *willful* choice about where you want to focus or not focus your precious attention asset. Because, after all, the gift of attention is priceless.

Organizations Have Attentional Styles Too

Getting your attention aligned means determining what's important. What are the crucial elements that you *want* to attend to for this challenge or this aspect of an experience? The same approach works for groups from dynamic duos to families to teams and entire organizations. In fact, on an organizational basis, aligning attention to the phase of the task can make all the difference between achieving organizational bests or substandard also-rans. The words of the Oracle at Delphi apply here as well. Knowing your organizational style provides the *awareness* jumpstart that is key to adapting attention flexibly to a variety of challenges. In this day and age, Big Five leagues can be diminished to Final Fours. Organizational flexibility and paying attention to external and internal factors that can sideline you, including what is going on in the heads—the heads at the Board table—can be determining factors when it comes to staying in it for the long run or staying in it at all.

Consider an organization that is ramping up for acquiring a competitor. To get engaged for a successful takeover, an initial broad focus on the external environment will provide critical information. The focus might be on the global marketplace or on the projected economic trends to determine if it is the right timing to grow via acquisition. Still external and broad, a focus on the organization's own industry, including trends and competitors as well as competitive forces, will provide another source of valuable information to use in the next phase of planning and strategizing. Given the urgency of timing, rarely will any one focus be in play. There will, most likely, be combinations with one focus dominant over another during specific phases.

After the scan and vision, a good planning and strategizing in the broad internal quadrant can lead to a strong strategic plan. If the group is smart and flexible with attention, they will, of course, add a component of analysis to this with a narrow internal focus on details and information that will determine if the organization has the resources and processes to negotiate the acquisition successfully. If the verdict is still out, a second scanning—wide and externally again—might be necessary to ensure that this is the right move at the right time. With that additional information and a fine-tuning to the strategic plan, a second confirmation by the data team, and an approval and nod to move forward by all, including the Doer implementation crew, the organization will be positioned to launch an acquisition that has a far higher probability of success than it would have if only one style of attention had been employed, or if the wrong hand had been played at the wrong time.

During the implementation, the focus will be primarily, though not solely, external and narrow, on implementing the plan within the time and financial constraints. Of course, if the organization is really tuned in to generating further activation and buy-in, there will be a huge celebration to acknowledge the successful team effort and to recognize the value that all styles and roles brought to this achievement. And then it will be time to move forward to shift attention flexibly to integrate the people and processes who have become this new team culture where "a difference is a difference."

To maintain attention for scanning and assessment throughout would ground the organizations in constant assessment and planning without implementation. They'd be left with great logos, a nice brand, a spectacular visionary plan, and fantastic visions of acquiring impressive competitors, but such things would remain fantastic—as in fantasy.

While visions and values are important to an organization's success, without reality to ground them and activation to achieve them, they won't get you very far. Groups have gone under by maintaining visions without action or by operating out of one quadrant of attention at the expense of others.

Throughout the entire process, from initial idea to successful implementation, the focus will be on both the vision of how things could be better and the process for getting there. Because when we are in the Zone, our focus is on the process. It is an "if you build it, they will come" *Field of Dreams* orientation. This is the process orientation of athletes that ultimately takes them to the desired outcome, the win. Internal-external, broad-narrow, constantly shifting to the right stuff, that is attention when you are *willfully* engaged in the arc.

Really Do It!

What about your groups? Is there one primary style of attention? What is it? What is the secondary style? What is the style that is least represented and least utilized? How is that impairing your results? Your efficiency? Your processes? The morale and team culture? What could your organization *TRASH* and what could it *PACK* in terms of focus to be more effective and more enjoyable?

The Power of Vision to Adjust Attention

It isn't just great orators or leaders who have visions. We all have them. You can learn how to make your vision proactive and powerful enough to enlist your own heart and mind to activate up or down to pursue your dream with confidence and focus. The prefrontal cortex is that part of the brain that provides the power of will to choose and manipulate the 3 A's and override the chemical dosages that can take us out of the *willful* living game. One of our greatest gifts from the prefrontal cortex is the ability to hold onto a vision while maintaining a focus on the present moment, on the process. Great visions power us. They adjust our vision from the ordinary to the extraordinary, from the meaningless to the meaningful. Great visions enlist hearts and minds—your own and others. They present images of the new, of change, that are so vivid and appealing that they become a new version of reality to which people want to move and strive. With these new Kodachrome moving images embedded in their minds, people will create and move toward goals that had seemed unattainable or unimaginable just the day or hour before. You can paint images like these too. That's what Mary did for her team presentations and for herself.

Often we think—oh bother. It is just too much work to sit down and strategically plan out a vision or mission or even a credo for that matter. But think about it. We are always creating scenarios in our minds, playing and replaying them. Quite often, the images we run are reruns of old losses or doom-and-gloom predictions. Or, alternately, we turn ourselves into merciless victors. We trounce our opponent, usually with some amount of violence and vindication. The problem is that, even in this scene, we are rehearsing the wrong levels of activation, attention, and attitude. We are over the edge of the top of the curve, agitated and focused on the outcome, distracting us from putting our best effort forward. And most of the time we know that we would never really say or do those things even though we lay mental tracks that heighten our probability of doing such foolish things.

Given that most of us spend so much time creating visions anyway, why not get rid of the vindication scenes or the old loser replays and make the time productive and enjoyable? Visions show you where to go, where you want to go. They don't have to be lifelong visions, though most people think of a vision as a lifetime commitment. And I would encourage you to draft a bigger-picture version too. You are creating visions all the time, from morning to night, and, in fact, right through those nocturnal sleep hours. So you might as well take back the day–and the night—and choreograph your own scenes. Make them vivid, moving, vibrant, a reach but still within the realm of possibility if you turn your 3 A's around.

The 3 A's are critical ingredients in any vision that is worth its stuff. Visions with the highest potential to move people (yourself and others) to action are those that articulate the focus, the attitudes that will be worthy of the journey (and those that will be left behind), and the energy output desired to move people toward the dream. Any great vision without action is nothing more than a fantasy. At worst, it can become a delusion.

Now it is your turn to draft a vision. Remember this is not the vision of a lifetime. This is a vision of a challenge that you will face later today or tomorrow, a person-to-person challenge in which you often find yourself behind the eight ball, feeling disconnected and out of it because of mismatches of attention. It could be a dialogue at work or at home, with a customer service person, a sales person, your doctor, or with the cable guy. Think of the challenge that is yours.

Fast-Forward Triple-A Vision

Let's start with the three deep breaths. You know the drill—in through your nose and out through your mouth—if that works for you. Then breathe deeply as I take you through this visualization virtual practice.

Picture yourself as you are about to enter the challenging situation that you have chosen.

Take a snapshot of the setting and consider the attentional style of the other person.

Picture yourself through that internal perspective. You are looking out through your own eyes. *PACK* words that focus you back on being with this person when you sense yourself straying toward o-Zonal tail spins. Notice the interplay of attention, activation, and attitude when they are aligned in and when they move off-center of the arc.

Move through the scene with a stance of confidence that reflects your belief that you can connect genuinely to achieve your goals in this conversation. Then allow yourself a nice deep breath to really enjoy that feeling of strength.

Now get a reading on your attention. Where is your focus? Is that where you want it to be? If it is right on, then take note. If not, get out the trash bag and change it. Tune in now to your attitude. Inspired, empowered by your inner will and force, proactive, notice the effects of this attitude on how you carry yourself and on your focus.

Now it is time for a Postoperative Debriefing. In a Postoperative Debriefing, you focus on what you did well and what you will do next time.

When you have played the scene out successfully, tell yourself three things that you did well. Then tell yourself one thing you will do differently next time. It can even be as basic as "next time I will wiggle my toes before my face gets hot." Cut.

- What was your vision for how the encounter would go? What was the other person's style? How did you prepare to connect with that style?
- What are the three things that you did well?
- What will you do differently next time to engage more consistently?
- What are the *plunging attention* cues that alerted you to disconnection?
- What are the *propelling attention* cues that pulled you into the scene?

For the next few days, be on the lookout for telltale *plungers* and *propellers*. Make mental notes of them. Then, in the evening, try them out on practice runs. Take yourself on an A^3-visualization. Practice sliding into the tails and use your cues to pull yourself out. Feel the effects of your activation cues to shift attention too and vice versa.

Process Goals Engage Your Attention

Optimal engagement is characterized by a focus on the moment, on the process. Process goals versus outcome goals have been proven to be more effective for both engaging people in the moment and for moving people toward their end-zone goal and their vision.[6] A process goal is active and tells you what to do. They work best in stair-step fashion, as a series of smaller goals that build upon each other and bring you to your desired outcome. Don't use don't.

SMART goals is a common shorthand. But each person may use the shorthand differently. Make your process goals a series of stairsteps that follow these guidelines.

> Specific and Stretch
> Measurable (use common measures for teams)
> Accepted and Accountable
> Record and Reward
> Timely and Time-limited.

You can use this shorthand guideline for any situation. Before a meeting, design your process goals. They can be as straightforward as "Read the other person's A^3 style. Adapt my style to connect. Monitor my activation arc signals. Learn more about the prospective customer's business goals and needs." Then watch how such process goals can power you toward your goals. For the next round, when you have achieved this set of steps, ratchet it up to another set of process goals.

Postoperative Debriefing Explained

Have you ever watched one of the television shows about doctors? Inevitably there is one, or more, who, after a long siege with a patient, yells at the other physicians or trainees or support staff about what everyone did wrong. Well, that is how most of us conduct our after-the-fact reviews. I've learned from consultations with people in a variety of industries that most people review their challenges, big and small, with a negative spin. The problem is that this negative review leaves you with a negative imprint on your brain. Postoperative debriefings are designed to turn that around, to focus your attention on the half-full, on repairs and fix-ups instead of tear downs.

I named this strategy when I was working in a medical setting. When I presented it to clients in other industries and to athletes, I initially recommended that they review a game, work project, or a conflict resolution by first reviewing what they had done well and then what they would do next time. Notice I did not say "what you did wrong" because I am using a particular language choice to "frame" it positively.

I should have predicted my results. People consistently came up with one or two things that they had done well. Then they had reams of things that they would do next time. Their lists were the length of old-fashioned scrolls. And most of them were framed in a negative spin, with "don't." So I revised the format, and that initial revision still lives on. In order to give yourself a review that you can learn from and that will motivate rather than debilitate you, try this.

What I did well was: ....; and ....; and ....
Next time I will: ....; and ....; and ....

You get three positive acknowledgments and three things to work on. Don't use don't. The goal is to review by focusing on what you did well and what you will do next time. Then you can use the information to craft your process goals as you enter the next scenario that is the same or similar.

Postoperative Debriefing

- Attentional style can be conceptualized along two axes: narrow-broad, internal-external.
- Content includes people and data.
- There is a specific quadrant that is the most optimal match for engaging and doing your best: Scan and Inspire, Plan and Strategize, Practice and Analyze, *Really do it!*
- Each person and organization has a strong attentional suit.
- Flexibility of attention can be practiced in real life and in A^3 visualizations.
- Vision, process goals, and a Postoperative Debrief provide tools to pull yourself and others into the Zone for engaging and doing your best.

Chapter 11

Get over It!—Attitude Adjustment

GAME PLAN

Identifying the assumptions that drive you, including the characteristic way that you talk to yourself and others, is the start to turning your attitude around. A personally meaningful mission and credo can enlist your heart, mind, and activation to turn visions from dreams to accomplishments.

"You've got an attitude problem. Turn it around. Snap out of it. Get a new one." We've all heard these exhortations—shouted from the sidelines of life by frantic fans and coaches and screamed loudly to ourselves and to others in the privacy of our personal thought balloons. In truth, we always have an attitude. Getting a new one isn't quite as simple as gazing at your reflection and claiming to like yourself. But it is far less complex than 1,001 ways.

Attitude includes your assumptive, value-laden beliefs. We all have them, and we cart them with us everywhere in our thoughts. Some attitudes are more apparent to us. Some are apparent to others in our lives but remain out of our sight with the blinders that we all sport. And others remain buried in the bowels of our psyche, seemingly unconscious but with the same powerful effects on our activation, attention, and the quality of our lives as those that are in full view.

Attitude is a key element in our ability to both engage and to disconnect. When beliefs remain unexamined, they hamper our ability to realistically evaluate a person or situation to determine its realistic potential. When our attitudes are rigid and set in stone or amorphous and based in thin air, the two standpoints associated with the tails of the arc, we automatically rule out engagement. Either we believe that we are not good enough or don't stand a chance or we dismiss the situation as something that is below our worth. On the other end of the arc, we perceive a threat (this might be unconscious) and we respond defensively. Either way, we end up missing some wonderful opportunities, either standing on the threshold of life looking wistfully inside the door or running into walls in response to battlefields that we create in our mind's eye.

Assumptions that remain shielded to us by the powerful mental blinders of attention, and their distorting mental mechanisms of defense, are much like the underpinnings of an iceberg—invisible and yet the foundation for everything that appears above the waterline, including our attributions, behaviors, feelings, and thoughts. This foundation impacts the decisions that you make each day, starting with the initial choice to either spring out from underneath the comforter and take some running leaps onto rope swings or to crawl deeper into the mattress and bask in your pain.

But icebergs bob up and down in the water, displaying varying amounts of the base. Often, while we are blinded to our own beliefs and governing attitudes, they are in plain sight of the people who know us well. They see it in our 3 A's. Attitude adjustment starts with a good look in the mirror. But it has nothing to do with staring at your face in glass reflections and claiming to like yourself. It is deeper and more candid than that. And the payoff is far more real and far-reaching than putting on another coat of lipstick or a power suit to see if you like yourself better now.

Attitude adjustment is the third critical key for true engagement. Just as with the other two A's, it starts with *awareness* of your personal package of attitudes and the effects these have on your activation and attention and, therefore, on your experiences. More strenuous than the "JUST do it" footwear mantra, more self-revealing than reading books about soup with inspiring stories, and more sweeping than gazing at your own visage in the looking glass when merely catching a glimpse of yourself in the morning can be enough to send you back to bed for a week, attitude adjustment is still as systematic as the three smaller A's—*aware, assess, adjust.*[1]

You can only go as far as you believe you can go. Others can only go as far as you believe as well.[2] Learning to really like yourself when you gaze in the mirror, even first thing in the morning, takes genuinely knowing who you are—the attitudes and assumptions, the values that guide you and ground the choices you make—and that you don't make. Learning to like others when you see them in full view, or in your rearview mirror, requires the same consideration and review of your beliefs and value-ridden assumptions. Attitude adjustment is an active process of ditching obsolete beliefs and proactively adopting new beliefs that fit your real deal.[3]

The Power of Belief

Most of us would like to think of ourselves as positive, confident go-getters all the time. But that's not how it really is. For most people, confidence and realistic optimism have wide swings. Sometimes the variations are based on the situation and the beliefs you carry about how effective you are in the particular type of scenario in which you find yourself. And we are always making evaluations of how effective we can be in a certain situation. Psychologists call this "self-efficacy."[4] Self-efficacy can be high, in which case you feel confident. Or it can be low, in which case you feel riddled with self-doubt. Language reflects self-efficacy.

Proclamations like "I don't do math," "I can't deal with people in upper management," "I always fall on moguls," "I hate working out," "I can't cook," or the "I use-to's"—"I used to be fit," "I used to walk every day" reflect low self-efficacy. These are the self-limiting attitudes that can focus us on evidence that supports our beliefs and destroy any activation to approach the challenge. Or, as in Tom's case, such unrelenting self-criticism can raise activation to unhealthy and scary levels. Either way, performance and mood suffer.[5]

There's a flip side to self-efficacy. I call it "other-efficacy." Other-efficacy includes our attitudes about others—our beliefs about what they can and can't do. When we believe that other people are capable, we focus our attention to seek evidence to confirm our theory. We notice the things they do. This corroborates our hypothesis. We adjust our activation up to empower them to perform. That's what happened in Rosenthal's classic "Pygmalion" studies when a random group of students was assigned to teachers who were told that they had been specially selected to teach elite groups of gifted students.[6] However, the students were not special or unusual beyond what is true for each of us. They were just like the other classes that these teachers had taught.

Still, the teachers produced dramatically different results with their classes. They believed that the students were capable. Of course I see this in terms of those ever-present 3 A's. The teachers' attention had been directed toward what the students could do. This determined their attitudes toward the students and their activation, their commitment of resources to make sure that the students reached their potential. They focused on what the students could do. And they got themselves activated to engage fully and with enthusiasm in the teaching process. In self-fueling circular A^3 spirals, the 3 A's co-labored, fueling both the students and their leaders. I propose that it was more than positive belief that contributed to the success of the teachers and students. It was the 3 A's working together to get the teachers and the students engaged in their arcs for personal bests.

At other times, our attitude is colored by disbelief, by low other-efficacy. We fill our thought balloons with limiting beliefs about other people—"They never deliver on projects on time," "He doesn't know how to manage a team the way I do." Such other-limiting beliefs divert our attention from the things that people do well and focus us on what they don't or can't do, which intensifies the evaluative chatter that we keep to ourselves or, too often, that we release for public consumption and humiliation of others.

We pull back, deactivated and unmotivated. Continuing to search for evidence to support our theory, we end up creating the self-fulfilling and other-fulfilling beliefs, feeding our assumptions to new levels. From this, we elaborate further on our original beliefs and then go back to field-test these as well.

Recognition and celebration of small and large wins is a key to building efficacy in yourself and in others. Vision, mission, a credo, and *STRETCH* goals can focus you on what you want to do. Acknowledging each step along the way can assure you that you are doing it. And, once you open your eyes and acknowledge that you are already doing it, then surely you can do it! Postoperative debriefings crafted to motivate rather than debilitate can focus you on what you can do as well as what you have done well to build confidence that is grounded in real-world actions and achievements. Suddenly Igor, the mythical competitor of all time, isn't looking so good after all, because, in reality, Igor was really tied up in your own beliefs about yourself and all those Igors.

Celebrate Heartbreak Hill

If The Boston Marathon isn't famous enough in itself, it has its own special vertical climb along the way known as "Heartbreak

Hill." Strategically placed, between miles 20 and 21 of the 26-plus-mile course, the timing and slope of this climb offer an impressive challenge that can break hearts and extinguish dreams. Reaching the top deserves a two-arm raise over the head—at least.

Each one of us scales versions of Heartbreak Hill every day. On some days, we gain plenty of vertical, even when we would rather be horizontal ourselves. But how often do we remember to celebrate? Recognition is one of the most powerful forces for engaging hearts and minds in the workplace.[7]

No matter how steep or how long your heartbreak hills might be, proactively celebrate them. Set goals and be sure to recognize their achievement. Acknowledge steps along the way to reaching your vision and living out your mission. Use *postoperative debriefings* to recognize the positives and focus yourself—and others—on what you will do next.

When we recognize victories, we confirm our efficacy. We focus ourselves on the half-full, on what we can do. In doing so, we build a base from which we can draw when mile-long hills loom ahead. Raise your arms over your head to celebrate your peaks. A step-at-a-time, a question-at-a-time, and celebrating along the way can see you through miles of hills and miles of trials—in the courtroom and in life.

Aware—Who Are You?

Who are you? Here is a question that has captivated the attention and life force of people through the ages. Read philosophy and poetry, including the lyrics from music from any age, and the same question looms. Remember those devoted Greeks who trekked to the Oracle?

And the early 1970s rock opera *Tommy,* in which the band calling themselves The Who asked "Who are you?" to bring the question home to the baby boomer generation—who are you?

While I do not purport to have the answers, I do have some questions that might help you clarify more about who you are, what you believe, and what you stand for. These questions, and, more importantly, your personal answers, will form the basis for you to build your own meaning for the most mundane wax-on/wax-off chores and the daring and daunting challenges that pop up unexpectedly. These are, after all, the fabric of life.

Here is the initial food for thought. What are the beliefs that you carry with you everywhere—the half-full and the half-empty ones? How do these beliefs determine your actions and choices and the things that you rule out—each day and over a longer run? How does your language reflect your mental stance toward life? What motivating need drives you? Is it a need to achieve, to be accurate, to affiliate and be accepted, or to be acknowledged? What is your mission in both the daily double activities and the long run? What is the rallying cry that has motivated you in the past? What are the core values to which you aspire, and what are the values that are reflected in your behavior?

In other words, who are you? And is that who you want to be? Despite what they say, curiosity never killed any cats; old dogs can learn new tricks and new ways of being. And no matter how old you are, looking in the metaphorical mirror offers lots more room for exciting, productive change than the concrete glass mirror—especially when you get to be my age.

I am going to ask you to be candid, even painfully honest, as you work through the material that will guide you to answer these questions. Remember you need not use the book to respond. Grab a napkin, a piece of paper, or an airline ticket stub and mark your answers down. After a month of living willfully and choosing your Zones of engagement by adjusting your 3 A's, you can return to these assessments to see how you are doing in changing your own mind and how that is assisting you to change your own life. Remember that there is no right or wrong answer. The more honest you are with yourself, the more you will gain from the process.

Attitude Awareness—Talk to Me

It has been said that talk is cheap. While I believe that the "walk" of walking-the-talk is a far more accurate indicator of a person's beliefs, values, and intentions than the mere mouthing of words, there is no denying that talk is still a reflection of attitude. What you say and how you say it provide powerful clues about the attitudes that lie below the surface of your iceberg.

There are two ways to say anything and usually many more. When it comes to language that connects, it is positive, proactive, and full of opportunity. I call the language that connects people to their experiences and to other people *"the language of opportunity and desire"*—and it is dramatically different from the other dialect— *"the language of oppression and depression"* that can disconnect you from anything and anyone.

Just as acting "as if" can change your attention and attitude as well as your activation, speaking "as if" can produce equally dramatic shifts.[8] The way you talk to yourself is a key to building confidence, especially when it is augmented by a vivid vision as well as a personal mission and realistic *STRETCH* goals that can enlist your heart, mind, and body to move you to action. By choosing to replace the disconnecting *language of oppression* with the desire-building *language of opportunity*, you can live more *willfully* and with genuine engagement.

Really Do It! Attitude Awareness

On the menu below you will find the two dialects that can alter your approach to life. Read through the two columns. Check, highlight, or make a mental note of your most common language from each side.

What are the frequent-flyer phrases that send you soaring or ground you on the runway?

The Language of Belief

Move yourself beyond "I think therefore I am" to "I am what I think I am.

"In the o-Zone" Language of Oppression & Depression	**"In the Zone" Language of Opportunity & Desire**
Depression:	Desire & Passion:
I have to—beyond my control	I WANT to—within my control
Mustery[9]—must ...; must not...	Mastery—going one step at a time
I must..., you must...	I/you will...a step at a time.
Don't...; Doesn't...;	Do...; Does...; Did...
"If only..." idealization and denial	"As is" realization—this is how it is...
Self-deprecating—	Self-developing—
I'm not the kind of person who.	I've done... so I can probably do...
Self-limiting—"I can't"	Self-efficacy building[10]—"I can"
Other-limiting—"You can't"	Other-efficacy building—"You can"
That team can't...	The team can...
Self & Other-deprecating—	Self & Other-developing—
I/You're not the kind of person who...	I/You've done...so you can probably do...
They're not the team to do...	They've done... so they can do...
What I/you did wrong was...	What I/you did right was ...; and
Don't do...again	you could choose to ... next time.
Judgmental—Can't stand...	Leveraging differences
They're an inept team...	Let's put together a team with diverse
People who aren't like me are...	problem-solving styles.
Authoritarian to self and others	Partnering and trusting in self & others
Should...; Shouldn't...	Want to...
Coulda...; Couldn't...	Can...
Woulda...; Wouldn't...; Won't...	Will...

"In the o-Zone" Language of Oppression & Depression	"In the Zone" Language of Opportunity and Desire
Blaming others and self	Accountability & recognition
Helpless—learned helplessness[11]	Hopeful—carpe diem and take the night too!
Half-hearted, withholding	Open-hearted, open-ended, no holds barred
only this much, my way or...	full court press, all the way
Playing not to lose	Playing to win
Mistakes are bad	Mistakes are opportunities to learn
Reactive	Proactive
Tentative—maybe, if	Certain—when
Half-empty to totally dry	Half-full and then some

Assess—If the Word Fits...

Whenever I talk about the *language of oppression*, people start to chuckle. "Yes, yes!" they say as they nod their heads up and down. "This is me! How did you know? Were you eavesdropping on my thought balloon, or is this some kind of party line?" They turn to either side and see that the people sitting next to them are nodding and saying the same things.

Then I ask two questions that I will pose to you. "If you talked to the people you see on a regular basis the way you talk to yourself (this does not include your family or significant others), how many people would want to be around you as a friend, colleague, roommate, sales person, customer service rep, or whatever? How many people do you think you could alienate by noon each day?" This time people almost always shake their heads too. But now they move side-to-side in incredulity. I have never found anyone who really believed that the *language of oppression* was a good fit for any situation, not even, or perhaps especially not, for talking with your dog. That is, of course, if you don't want the dog to bite you.

I take it one step further. "Who are the people with whom you share this trusted *language of oppression*? Who are the confidantes to whom you talk the same way that you talk to yourself?" While it seems odd, the people who are the closest to us, the people we trust most, are often the ones with whom we share this negative, oppressive talk. We let them have it—all the advice and thumbs-down reviews that are more than they ever wanted. Often we justify our moves, citing intentions to help them, to teach them from our own errors.

When we speak in the resentful *language of oppression*, we alienate others, and we even alienate ourselves. What I mean by this is that we disconnect from our experiences. Either we stop trying, because it looks like just too much, or we try too hard, transforming everything into a turf battle or a defense of our valor. Sadly, this ends up creating the very thing we feared most. By playing-not-to-lose, we can never achieve as much as we can when we apply the full force of our 3 A's to engage and do our best. I am not talking about beating others. I'm talking about striving to create a personal or organizational best—about "doing it for the Gipper" and "the Gipper" is you! That requires the empowering dialect in the right column. Changing it is as simple as that dynamic duo of *TRASHIT and PACKIT*.

Adjust

Now it is commitment-to-change time. Talking about talking isn't enough. It takes action to *really do it!*

Really Do It!

Identify your top five language choices from the left-hand column. Write them in the *TRASHIT* balloon in Figure 11-1 or store them in the one that's perched atop your head—on the left, more rational and skeptical side of your head. Look immediately across from your reliable, oppressive favorites to the opportunity column on the right. Write the opportunity version of your top four trash items in the *PACKIT* balloon in Figure 11-1 and/or make a mental note—in the thought balloon on the *right* side of your head. Personalize it if you don't find what you want on the menu. Record your valuable carry-on language in 64-font bold all caps underlined. Use your own language to make it yours.

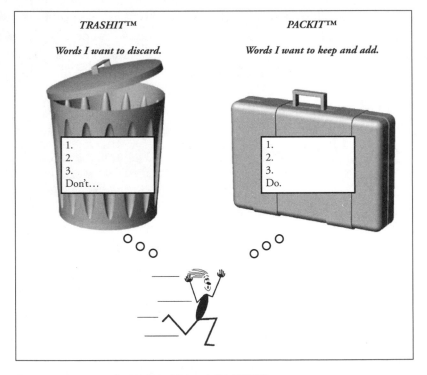

Figure 11-1   Attitude *TRASHIT*™ and *PACKIT*™.

Really Do It! Take It to the Streets

For the next 24 hours, starting now, challenge yourself to tune in with your *zone-o-meter* to the words that you choose with others and with yourself. As soon as you utter aloud (or in your virtual thought balloon) any word or phrase (or any facsimile) that you have identified as trash—*TRASHIT!* It takes a nanosecond. Simply pile the words into your thought balloon. Take a breath and quickly breathe out as you hurl it off the top of your head. Then breathe in some inspiration to *PACK* the alternate version that you identified.

As a bonus, if you did not include "Don't" on your list of top three, add it now. Whenever you hear the word "Don't…," even if it is followed by stellar counsel to yourself, replace it with "Do…." This simple reframing will paint the images for you and for others of what you want to do, how you want it done, who you want to do it, and a timeline by which you want to implement and complete your strategic plan of action. Then you will *really do it!*

Changing your language is like quitting smoking or ditching any habitual response—even finger-pointing. The first day it seems like you are always reaching for a smoke or setting up to wag that persistent pointer finger. Or, in this case, you reach for a negative frame—the words that you choose to "frame" the image—for what you are saying. With awareness, you soon find yourself looking curiously at the cigarette in your hand, the wagging finger that seems disconnected from your consciousness, or the language in your head. You wonder how you got halfway through and you realize that you can choose right now to extinguish the butt, move the pointer finger to your side, or exchange the words you want to trash for the carry-on items of your choice. Soon, you make the choice before you light up or aim your finger. With words, you choose before you open your mouth. With practice, you develop new habits. When you commit to *awareness, assessment, and adjustment* of your wordsmithery, you will find that you will frequently make the healthy choices from the right side of the menu. And, in this case, it really is the right way, because it is the method that will engage you with your life.

Jim shifted gears and language to generate momentum for engaging with grueling treatment and surgical procedures. He used the language of desire, a vision of how things would be better, and a personally crafted mission that detailed why he wanted to engage wholeheartedly in his treatments. In addition, Jim learned to visualize himself preparing for the trip to the doctor's office or hospital with his 3 A's aligned. That included self-talk that was encouraging and focused his attention on the personal mission and goals we had crafted and the vision of where he wanted to go—to a healthy state. Sometimes the goal was as basic as hanging in there for a painful procedure. By using this virtual practice that targeted the 3 A's rather than some generic visualization that denied the severity of the challenge, he felt prepared for the real deal.

Reframing extends beyond the two columns of words and is one of the most powerful tools you can choose to use to change your attitude. Reframing simply means changing the words that you use to describe something. So far you have applied it to the *language of oppression* to turn it to the *language of opportunity*. Now I want you to consider your language on a broader basis. Reframing gives you the option to build meaning and highlight the value of the things you do and the challenges cast to you. With reframing, you can engage in interactions with other people that you might have been avoiding or dreading because you saw them as difficult. With a different frame, they are merely different—and that is now a good thing.

Adjust—Reframe

"You have to go work out at the gym at the end of today's long siege of work." If someone "instant-messaged" these words to you, would you want to go to the gym? I can say that even I, an avid daily participant who has loved to play on stationary running, climbing, rowing, and cycling machines for 30-something years, would not want to go.

How does the way that message is framed—the words with which I have painted it—affect your activation in just reading it? Where do those words draw your attention—to the half-full opportunity or to the half-empty oppressive aspects of the situation? Do you want to go to the gym? Probably not in response to that message—it needs a different frame.

Reframing is intended to build an attractive image and meaning to get you moving forward. It enlists attention and attitude. With at least two ways to say or see everything, reframing puts the control back in your court, even for those nonnegotiable situations in which you sense that you do not have control: work projects, deadlines, driving your kids to and from school and the organized sports that have replaced pickup games in the neighborhood, foraging for food at the grocery store and preparing it, doing laundry, and medical tests and procedures that can send your blood pressure soaring. The list of nonnegotiables just for the activities of daily living can go on and on. Reframing gives you the choice to build meaning for them and to generate desire to do them. It provides the "why bother" along with the "what's in it for me?"

Try this frame: "You want to play on the machines with friends after work to build your bones and your heart so you can feel great and stay in it for the long run. And you will get to listen to great music or, if you prefer, you can choose to watch nightly news. Or you can catch up on the latest goings-on with a good friend."

With the simple wordsmithery of reframing, Charles Revson made lipstick the "hope in a tube" on which Revlon was launched. Stationary exercise equipment becomes user-friendly bone-building machinery. Driving your kids around looks like a mighty good opportunity to have some genuine conversation and get to know who they are becoming. Chairlift rides become opportunities to have that heart-to-heart with your life partner in a setting where they cannot leave the discussion.

Cold calls turn into opportunities for warm connections. Folding laundry is a chance to crank up the tunes to stretch and dance.

Really Do It!

Now you do it! Pick a daily activity that you often resent. It can be as wax on/wax off as emptying the dishwasher or as complex as preparing an annual report or as tedious as filling out the forms for your kids' school or camp—for the fourth year in a row. If you are truly interested in getting healthier, choose an activity like exercise or eating healthfully. In the workplace, you might consider using this exercise to reframe a difficult conversation that you really do need—let's reframe that to "want"—that you really do want to have so that you can iron out underlying tensions and work more productively with a particular person. Take a breathing minute to choose the challenge that you want to reframe.

First build meaning. You might want to empty the dishwasher to contribute to the household maintenance or let your daughter off the hook so she can get to her bus on time, or to simply surprise her! Take it from a mother of four, filling out forms each year for school can look like an incredible hassle at the end of a day. It is easy to get overactivated, wondering privately or aloud, "Why can't they use the same information? Why can't they store this on-line for a mere update?" This is a negative frame that will exhaust you and focus you on resisting rather than doing it. Or you can choose to see and frame it differently. After all, if you are away from your home often, whether it is to run your younger kids around or to take work trips, the forms ensure that your kids will have someone to call in case of an emergency and that the school can provide medical care for them if that is needed. Now the forms are looking better. They have a purpose.

Let's take it one step further and frame how you will approach the process to turn it into one of misery, mustery, or mastery. You can fill those forms out with a crummy pen that doesn't work well, and you can even yell at the pen to take the edge off of the excess activation you have generated from your o-Zonal focus and negative frame. And you can sit in the kitchen and do it solo, resenting that you don't get to see the season's finale of *Friends*. If you go down this path, you will become depleted and resentful and land yourself in a zone that is entirely mismatched for getting the forms done.

Or you can grab your favorite pen or colorful marker, and crank up your favorite music as you plunk down in a comfortable chair that is a far better perch than the wooden kitchen stool. You can even multitask and fill the forms out, surrounded by your family, while you laugh at the antics of those lovable friendly sitcom characters. The frame you choose is your choice.

Your challenge to reframe is (phrase it in the old negative way).

I don't really want to, but I have to…. In fact, I know I am going to hate it.

Now reframe it. Tell yourself what you want to do—what you get to do and why it is valuable. Give your frame meaning, passion, color.

I want to _____ because_____.
The conditions I will set up to make it pleasant include
_____. *(Remember the tunes to pump you up or chill you down.)*

This basic reframing, especially when it is strengthened by personal missions that have built purpose and meaning for home life, family roles, and work, has powered people with whom I have worked to really do things that had seemed overwhelming or wasteful of time. It has worked under conditions that many people would consider beyond belief, including the challenge of confronting a person who had inflicted harm on them.

We are always casting a frame around our experiences and the people in our lives. You might as well choose the frame that moves you to take the strategic actions that will make your life full and empower you to live *willfully,* especially in those instances when folding, walking away, or running are not on the menu. With a simple shift in words, you can shed a different light on even the most dire circumstances, and you can turn black-and-white chores into colorful fun.

Attitude Awareness

Just like activation and attention, getting your attitude aligned includes knowing your characteristic style. Try this quick assessment to determine which half—the empty or the full side—draws you in naturally and which is more of a stretch for you.

Know Yourself—What's Your Attitudinal Style?

This is a forced choice. From each pair of statements below, circle the one that better describes you.

1. I constantly barrage myself with what I should be doing when I'm driving to or from work, dashing to a meeting, or running an errand. It's a nonstop monologue.
2. For the most part, I can enjoy the journey, listening to great music or talk radio, or holding an interesting, and even

comical, monologue with myself, when I'm driving from one place to another.

1. If only people would get it together and do things my way, my life would be so much more enjoyable. But they don't, so I do it myself.
2. I hand out assignments to colleagues and the kids after telling them how to approach the task, why it's important, and when it needs to be done. Then I let it go. I recognize what they did well and tell them clearly what they could do differently next time.

1. People are generally looking for the easy way to do something.
2. I believe that people are eager to learn how to do things correctly and then to do it on their own.

1. There's a right way and there's my way. And they are both the same.
2. I continue to be amazed at how much I have learned from other people, including new young people at work and from my own kids.

1. The world has made it this far because of the "shoulds" and "musts."
2. "Shoulda, woulda, coulda"—make me want to run the other way. Tell me what I want to do and why.

1. In the face of change, I am quick to counter with a "yabut..."
2. Change is strange and strange is growth. I'm going to keep on growing.

1. I find myself wishing "if only" in response to most of what happens to me daily.
2. I want to accept things "as is" so I can say goodbye to losses and move forward.

1. I debrief myself and others by focusing on what we did wrong.
2. I focus on what we did well and what we can do next time to do even better.

1. People who need recognition bother me. If I don't need or get it, why should I give it?
2. I want to make sure to recognize what people do well—myself and others—to continue to generate more of the results that I want.

1. I want to make sure people don't make errors. So I always tell people what not to do—don't do this and don't do it that way—to make sure they do it right. It's my way of helping them out.
2. "Don't" isn't a highly motivating word when I talk to myself or to others. I turn it around to tell people what to do instead.

Scoring

Add up all #1 responses   Total #1 responses _____
Add up all #2 responses   Total #2 responses _____

- Are you tuning in to the half-full (more #2 responses) or the half-empty (more #1 responses)? Is that who you want to be?
- If you asked coworkers or people who are close to you in your personal life to answer the same questions about you, would the answers look the same?
- Is there something that they might see that you are blocking from your awareness?

Just as many people are taken aback by the activation that they reflect to others, they are also surprised by the beliefs that they carry with them each day. If your #1 responses outweigh your #2 responses, you are in good company. Most people are astonished by how easy it is to look at the half-empty and to view themselves and others from a judgmental stance. But remember, as much as we humans want to be optimistic, there might be a survival mechanism that puts our antennae up for doom-and-gloom items that could orient us to predators or threats. Also, we each cart around baggage, old memories that get awakened by aspects of a scene or a new person. These memories have the ability to initiate attitudes that set us up for a speedy flight, a fierce fight for turf, or a painful, frozen stance in which we hold back for fear of being vulnerable and getting hurt—in instances when these responses are not appropriate and get in our way of doing our best. But you need not cart this outdated material around unexamined any longer. Your power of will enables you to unearth and evaluate your beliefs to determine if they are a good fit or to dismiss them as outdated artifacts and to replace them with more appropriate, timely beliefs that will allow you to engage with all of those wonderful experiences and people you have ruled out in the past or who might be sitting right in front of your nose.

Assess

Rather than look at a specific instance in your daily endeavors, I am going to invite you to first consider your approach to life in general on the assessment you just completed.

Take some time to assess the fit of your beliefs to your life by answering the questions that follow. Putting pen to paper is not the main goal. If writing helps you to think, write it down. If thinking on its own is enough, then give yourself the gift of time to sit back and assess your life's challenges and the fit of your beliefs that you identified.

Start with three deep breaths to activate you up or down and clear any distractions, including any judgments you might have about actually completing exercises in books. *PACK* the energy, focus, and a belief in your ability to change that will enable you to get the most from this exercise. Then look yourself squarely in the metaphorical mirror with these questions.

- What are the strongest negative beliefs (either from the list or from your private stock) that drive your behaviors and that impact the choices that you make for engagement and disengagement each day?
- What are the strongest positive beliefs?
- Are the beliefs that you carry with you a good fit for most of the situations and people you encounter?
- How do they affect: Activation? Attention? The quality of your thinking, decision making, and problem solving?
- How do they impact the attributions that you make about people and things—determinations of the good, bad, ugly and utterly marvelous?
- How do they contribute to your ability to engage fully with your life? How do they interfere?
- How do they impact your behavior? What have you done, or not done, in response to the negative beliefs that you have carried in the past, that you regret and would like to change?
- Which three negative beliefs would be the easiest to ditch? Which three would be the most difficult to exchange? Do you have any theories about why this is the case?
- How do your personal half-empty attitudes impact your performance? How have they affected the performance of others around you—your life partner, kids, coworkers, boss, or those who report to you on the job?
- How do the half-empty beliefs impact your general mood and the range of feelings as well as the most common feelings that

you access each day? How do they limit your access to a good laugh even if it is at some of the buffoon-like things that we adults can do?

- How do they curtail risk-taking and what have you possibly (or probably) missed out on over the past week, month, or years because you were hauling around a lot of half-empty trash? Consider opportunities as well as relationships here. What different results could you have achieved if you had left them in your trash can and packed an alternate "play-to-win" attitude? Choose one such instance and review it, ditching the trash and replacing it with reframed attitudes in your thought balloon.

Adjust

Worst-case scenario fear-factor time—let's go back to the beliefs that you identified from the assessment tool.

- What is the worst thing that will continue to occur if you hang on to the negative beliefs? What will happen if you continue to direct your attention to what you have to lose? Can you play-to-win with this stance? Can you do your best? Can you reach your goals? Will anything change?
- On the upswing, what is the worst thing that can happen if you ditch the beliefs you have identified that get in your way of true engagement with the people and things that are your life? How can you redirect your attention to the potential gains? What are the amazing things that you could explore and change?

I would never diminish the power of change to send anyone, including myself, into a tailspin, holding tight to anything and everything, even the things we complained about the day before and the things we never much cared for. Change is unsettling. Our human nature hasn't quite caught up to the speed of change that surround-sounds us. But remember, looking for the positive aspects of even the most grueling experience is a way to direct your attention in order to embrace and latch on to change. In doing so, it becomes easier to let go of the things that you might lose.

Really Do It!

What changes in beliefs will help you to turn your mind around? Specifically, which beliefs about yourself and others do you WANT to *TRASH*? Which do you WANT to hold on to, to *PACK* in your daily and lifetime carryon of self- and other-talk?

Record your Top 3 in the thought balloons below. To weight it toward the positive, *TRASH 3 and PACK 4.*

A³ Relaxation and Visualization Review

It is time to rewrite a previous scene, inserting the triple-A characters of your choice.

Picture one situation or interpersonal encounter (a conversation, conflict, e-mail dialogue) in the past week in which you carted a half-empty or totally void attitude set. How did these negative beliefs about yourself or the other person affect the process and outcome?

Take three deep breaths.

Rewrite the scene—visualize that same experience with the new beliefs that you have packed in your thought balloon. Make your visualization real. Allow yourself to migrate toward the negative mindset. Use *TRASHIT and PACKIT* cues to identify markers of looming danger and to pull yourself back to engage with the moment. Enjoy and recall the different results and quality of the experience.

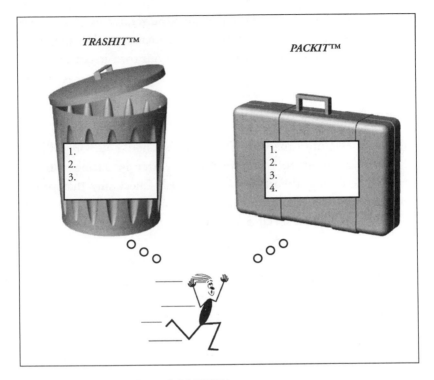

Figure 11-2   *TRASHIT*™ and *PACKIT*™.

Assumptive Behavior

Awareness

Attitude includes our mindset—our beliefs and assumptions about ourselves, others, the world, and how it should be. Assumptions lead us to create and hold onto self-limiting and other-limiting beliefs in an attributional process that is determined by where you are on the arc of engagement.

Assumptions create autopilot hooks and rules that can be conscious or unconscious. These become the road rules by which we live. When we do not take them out to examine them to see if they are a good fit for the reality at hand, we end up tripping ourselves, turning away from situations that could be the opportunity of a lifetime and turning ourselves and other people off with obstacles of our own making.

The Needs That Drive Us

Check the column marked "SELF" for the hooks in your rulebook. Add any others you have that are currently getting in the way of achieving a work or personal goal. Check any that you believe apply to others in our culture in the column marked "OTHERS." Use a specific or "generic" other.

The Belief	Self	Others
1. I am what I accomplish.	___	___
2. I get my bearings by being recognized.	___	___
3. I will go out of my way to please other people.	___	___
4. I have low to no tolerance for mistakes.	___	___
1. If I let up, I will fail.	___	___
2. I like to impress others.	___	___
3. I am not competitive. I am kind.	___	___
4. Rational, logical thinking and having the accurate data to support decisions is imperative.	___	___
1. I want to know how to get things done efficiently.	___	___
2. I want to be innovative and stand out.	___	___
3. I want to know what other people feel about things.	___	___
4. I want to know the details supporting the method.	___	___

1. I want people to see me as competent. _____ _____
2. I want people to invite me to the right
   gatherings. _____ _____
3. I want everyone to think of me as a
   good person. _____ _____
4. I want people to come to me for the
   right answers. _____ _____

1. Making a definitive decision is key to
   success. _____ _____
2. Considering all of the options is
   my forte. _____ _____
3. I am concerned with the impact of
   decisions on the emotional well-being
   of myself and others. _____ _____
4. I can not make a decision without
   considering all of the angles and details
   as well as the possible outcomes from
   A to Z. You shouldn't either. _____ _____

Scoring
   Sum of # 1 responses (Achievement) Total #1 responses _____
   Sum of # 2 responses (Acceptance/Acknowledgment)
                                              Total #2 responses _____
   Sum of # 3 responses (Affiliation)   Total #3 responses _____
   Sum of # 4 responses (Accuracy)   Total #4 responses _____

Assumptions Concerning the Final Four

Achievement/Being best and being in control.
Acceptance/Acknowledgment/Being recognized.
Affiliation/Being the harmonizer.
Accuracy/ Being right.

Each of us is driven by different needs. Philosophers and psychologists through the ages have sought to distill the needs that drive us—after the basics for food, shelter, and safety have been adequately satisfied. Four of the primary drivers that run consistently through different schools of thought in psychology include four other A's—achievement, acceptance, affiliation, and accuracy.[12] Generally we have one need that drives us more than the others. When push comes to shove, it is powerful enough to set us in action. When we do not understand the value in diversity, it is easy to assume that other people are running on the same drivers and to judge them as wrong or inferior when they do not. But success as an individual or as a contributing member to a group, whether it is to a family, team, work group, company or culture, entails all four drivers. In reality it still boils down to the "difference is a difference" framing that highlights the value of diversity and learning to embrace other motivational drivers in your own life as well.

People like Tom thrive on doing. Achievement is their prime mover. Being in control and being best are significant to them. For Mary, acceptance was the driver. Being recognized kept her going. Jim thrived with affiliation and enjoyed creating harmony amongst people with different agendas and points of view. In addition to achievement, Tom also sought accuracy, which tends to be a domain in which other attorneys, accountants, and engineers thrive.

What about you? Which of the final four is your strongest driver? Which is the second? Which is least important to you? Are there instances in which your primary need leads you to misperceive the situation and to disconnect either into overagitated or apathetic activation?

Assess the Fit

The four needs are tied in to your fear factor. Each person tends to perceive threat more easily around their most frequent need. People or situations who kick up the need become your "Igors" in life. When we perceive attack, we launch a defensive countermeasure.

When Tom felt that his sense of control was on the line, he went into high activation self-defense. Mary launched her own defense when she perceived that her former colleagues could not accept her and would not recognize her as a competent leader. When Jim thought he was losing the harmony that he had injected into his life at work and at home, he retreated.

That is indeed what happens when we fall prey to rigid beliefs and assumptions that are no longer a good fit. We create a self-fulfilling prophecy just as the teachers in the Rosenthal study did.[13] But the point in that study is that you can create positive prophecies by replacing outdated inappropriate beliefs with a more appropriate motivating set. It is called attitude adjustment.

Adjust

There is much to be learned from asking questions. Yet how often do you ask yourself questions that could lead to doing things differently? You just asked yourself one.

Return to your top belief in the questions on drivers. Consider a situation in the past week when holding on to that belief kept you from genuine engagement with the scenario that confronted you. Was this a good fit? Is that the belief that you want to pack for the next time you confront the same or a similar circumstance? Picture yourself in the same scene with the same old belief. Then visualize *TRASHing* the outmoded belief and replace it with the new predetermined better fit. *PACKIT* and watch the difference in the results you achieve and the experience you have.

Aware—Attitude Is Meaning

Our search for meaning, for a purpose to our time on earth, predates those ancient Greeks who consulted with the Oracle. And it continues today. Eventually, no matter what age in which we live, we realize that we will never find meaning. As much as it would seem like a great idea on some mornings to open your *New York Times*, or the paper of your choice, to find a full-page ad with your name in large print announcing that your meaning has been found and will be faxed to you later that morning, it is not going to happen. Even if it did, it wouldn't work. Meaning is personal. Meaning is something that you build. You generate it. And you are the only one who can create a meaning that will move you. No one can give you theirs, and you wouldn't want it anyway. While you can introduce concepts to others, they will have to latch on and create a meaning of value for themselves.

Even before Tom Cruise put his touch on impossible missions, the power of taking on a mission that seems out of reach has intrigued individuals and groups who have ventured beyond perceived limits of flat horizons. The power of mission to propel individuals to push beyond comfort levels has crossed the millennia. For the past decade, the concept has crossed into the field of business, with much written about mission as a key ingredient for a successful venture.[14] More recently, individuals and teams within businesses have started to hold each other and even the top dogs accountable for living up to those missions and the core values that allegedly ground them. The most motivating organizational mission, even when it is carved in marble on a plaque that could knock your socks off, will do nothing if individuals are not powered by their own missions and values that have some amount of alignment with the organization's mission and values to provide guidance for choosing behaviors and strategic pursuits.

Rather than simply tell you that it is important to have a mission, I am going to invite you to craft your own mission right now in the same way that I do with seminar participants and clients. A personal mission statement delineates your purpose. Consider a challenge that often gets the better of you—in other words, you end up disconnecting because it is too hard or you feel agitated. Even though you might not be aware of a conscious threat, you disengage and go over the top of the curve into frustration and enragement or you simply never hop on the curve at all, dwelling on the threshold.

Jim's mission had always centered on providing stellar customer service, communication, and development opportunities to the people who worked for him and with him, including his customers and vendors. When Jim was stricken with cancer, he forgot to honor those principles to himself. By revisiting his company's mission and translating it into personal terms that touched his new circumstances as a cancer fighter, Jim came up with this: "My personal mission is to provide informed state-of-the-art service and care, communication, and development opportunities to everyone about whom I care including myself." Jim's first goals set him on his way toward this mission when he researched and lobbied for his own care. Later this same mission served him to ground his decision to leave the business world and to become a teacher and coach.

It's your turn to write your mission, a purpose that will power you through most of your daily activities. What is your role in your family, in groups outside of the home, at work? How does that role contribute to the greater whole? You can think in terms of a specific role or more globally in terms of your mission while here on earth.

Before you forge ahead, I am going to ask you to review the accomplishments in your life that have given you the most satisfaction and pride. In light of these achievements and your vision for where you are going with your life, what is your personal mission? What is the underlying theme? Are you a teacher, a developer of people, a healer, a caretaker, an athlete extraordinaire, or a defender of those who have been victimized? Is your mission to harness your potential to achieve as a scholar and an athlete? Is your mission to provide compassion, care, nurturing and guidance to others in your role as a parent, partner, leader or mentor?

Write a life mission that builds meaning and spurs you to align your 3 A's to pursue it. Then take it down a level. In light of your mission, consider a current challenge that you would like to align to this bigger picture mission. Record the challenge and draft a mission for that specific challenge, whether it is to build a relationship or to embrace the new software for tracking materials at work that seems to be throwing everyone, including yourself, into a tizzy.

Build Meaning with the PASSION of Mission to Move Your Self beyond Limits of Belief

MISSION MAKING
Your purpose.
A personal and organizational mission grounds you. It builds meaning to provide a foundation and bearings, both of which are especially critical when the going gets tough—and it always does.
It answers the "why bother"—why something is important enough to make changes in your activation, attention, and attitude in order to change your behaviors.

My big-picture mission is

A challenging situation for which I want to build meaning is

My mission for this challenge is

Attitude Is Value—Aware

The concept of values predates current business gurus.[15] Values have been the food-for-thought of philosophers throughout the ages. By values I am referring to enduring principles that guide behavior, principles for which you are willing to go to the mat and fight, and for which you will hold yourself and others accountable. Values, along with mission, provide us with a way to gauge whether our attitudes are aligned for living with authenticity and in true engagement with the experience at hand.

Again, I am going to put you to work on this one. The actual recording of the values is not as important as taking the time to thoughtfully consider the values that you talk and the ones that you walk and to determine how you want to hold yourself accountable.

You can use this for yourself and then you can apply it with your life teams. Families, sports teams, work groups, and entire organizations have used this framework for developing awareness of their attitudes that are reflected in their core values. Then they have used the values as a measure to assess if they really were lined up for engagement with life. In holding themselves and each other accountable, they could then choose to ditch behaviors that were in conflict with the values and to replace them with behaviors that aligned with their values. And even for such a complex issue as values, the dynamic *TRASHIT- PACKIT* duo served them well for getting rid of the behaviors that they wanted to ditch and planting those that they wanted to pack for the organizational junket to excellence.

Really Do It! Values

Each person has a set of values that guide their behaviors, decisions, and attributions. Some of our values are conscious. We are proud to hold them as guiding principles. Others are below the surface. We might be proud of them or, when the behaviors that reflect such behaviors are brought to our attention, we might feel badly. Consciously delineating your values—putting words and behaviors to them—is a start to holding yourself and others accountable.

Take three deep breaths—in through the nose and out through the mouth if you can. Picture yourself in a challenging context where conflict and tension are the norms. Consider yourself in this situation. Observe your behaviors as well as what you say and how you say it. What values can you see—reflected in your behaviors and tone as well as your words—that underlie your behaviors and decisions? What would a friend see that is different from what you see? What would they see that confirms your assessment? Are the values that you observe consistent with the values with which you want to live?

Record your top five values that you want to live by. If you observed anything that is inconsistent with the way you want to live, either values or behaviors, cram them into the thought balloon over your head and *TRASHIT! PACK* an alternate response that is aligned with the values that you want to adopt.

Value	Behavior That is Consistent	Behavior That Is Inconsistent
1.		
2.		
3.		
4.		
5.		

Remember that holding yourself accountable is essential to engaging and doing your best. Opening your eyes to the truth—at least as close to reality as you can get—is a start. Here is where the walk of walking the talk comes into play. In a high-functioning individual or organization, the values that are talked about are consistent with the values that are enacted.[16] When organizations and individuals are not engaged or functioning at their top game, they don blinders that allow a disconnect between the values that they would like to believe that they hold and those that come across in language, tone, nonverbal communication channels, and behavior.

Consider your behaviors in terms of the five values you have chosen.

Jot down the behaviors that are consistent with your proclaimed value and those that are in conflict with it. The more honest you are, the more you can improve.

Turning accountability from words to action is a key step in getting yourself engaged. When you do find yourself acting in a manner that is not aligned with your core values, you will know that it is time to make a change. Yet again, reliable *TRASHIT and PACKIT* will serve as your trustworthy travel partners. Each time you find yourself sliding into one of the inconsistent behaviors, plunk the trash into your thought balloon and get rid of it. Replace it with the behaviors that you know, in your heart and mind, are consistent with the value—*PACKIT.*

When in Doubt, Shout It Out!

A rallying cry can get even the most comfortable out of the chair and off the couch. Rallying cries, or credos, provide a cue to align all three of your A's to go. Choose a rallying cry that works for you. You might have one for ratcheting up and another for cooling down. Practice in your dreams to turn things around with this simple mantra that you can use across settings. Teams that share a common credo can use that one simple phrase or word to turn every member's 3 A's around. What is your credo?

Preparation—Get Ready!

Preparation is an important part of peak performance in sport and life. Watch any athlete just prior to an event or the big tee-off swing. You can almost see the workings in their minds. They tune everyone else out while they tune in to the essentials which they have determined ahead of time. At the same time, they adjust activation up or down, balancing it within the arc of engagement that may be broad and flat or extraordinarily narrow with the threat of a sudden catastrophic spin into the tails of the o-Zone. Simultaneously, they hold on to the assumptions that will ensure a personal best. Anything else is rejected, thrown out with the *TRASH*. Use the items that you have determined to be worthy of your travels to get yourself ready to roll. Practice your A^3 preparation routine in your relaxation and visualization dreams. Then enjoy the journey.

Postoperative Debriefing

- You don't have to know the words to join in with life, and you don't have to do it for the Gipper. Unless, of course, the Gipper is you.
- Figure out what is important to you. Draft a mission and core values that can provide bearings during dark moments.
- Change your language to change your life. Move from the *language of oppression* to *the language of opportunity*.
- Align your 3 A's in preparation routines and practice in your A^3 relaxation-and-visualization training. When the real deal does present itself, you will be ready to go.

Chapter 12

Really Do It!—
Why Bother? How to Put the 3 A's to
Work for You

GAME PLAN

Genuine engagement with life starts with the commitment to make a leap, a change. Change, no matter how good the promise on the other side, is strange and evokes resistance, including fight-flight-fright. Generating personal buy-in is the best way to ensure a high probability of success. It means making your own case for the "why bother?"

Living a rewarding life in the Zone isn't just a choice. Now it's a responsibility. No matter where you live, or your country of origin, since that fateful day in autumn of 2001, every one of us has had to connect more fully to our circumstances to manage fear, muster energy for the tasks of living, and bolster confidence that we will persevere. On top of this, we are determined to proactively seize the day and the evening hours to live with renewed vigor. Learning how to get into and stay in the engagement Zone for every circumstance is a true necessity.

Why Now?

Developing your winner's will to connect fully is more timely than ever. Every one of us wants to be prepared for the daily double and for unpredictable challenges that loom over the horizon. Plus, we want to succeed without losing sight of our guiding principles, the values of honor and the respect for human life. We long to connect in a meaningful way with the moments that compose our lives. Yet, even on a daily basis, this seems more challenging, as we each perceive ourselves to be vying for fewer resources. For the most part, this perception is accurate. The world has become more competitive throughout the lifespan, with more of us vying for the most prized spots in the workplace, in colleges, on sports teams from kids' travel teams to collegiate athletics, and even for highly-prized slots in daycare centers and kindergarten. The need to chart your course and pursue it *willfully* begins early and continues through the lifespan.

In today's world, where it often seems like dog-eat-dog competition where survival of the fittest ensures success and longevity in the marketplace, the ability to consistently engage with challenges enhances your chances of staying in the game. That means committing fully to the process so you can reach your desired outcomes. Now, more than ever, individual, team, and organizational success depends on accessing the inner power of *will* to commit fully. The results include personal and organizational bests of which you can be proud, outcomes grounded in core values and win-win visions that have the power to engage others in the Zone with you.

Why Bother?

Committing to living in the Zone means, I hate to say it, change. It entails making changes in how you approach a challenge as well as shifts in your activation, attention, and attitude.

Let's face it—change doesn't come easily to most of us. That's because we tend to perceive change as a threat, a potential loss. For many, our natural habitual response is to unleash a full-blown fight-or-flight-or-freeze release of stress chemicals. We steel ourselves to defend against the perceived threat. But this ready position is often too much for the actual circumstances, landing us in the o-Zone with our 3 A's lined up in just the wrong constellation.

Fleet of feet, we hightail it, running away from a proposed change as fast as we would from a predator in pursuit. Alternately, we let them have it in a verbal barrage that can rival any beating in terms of quality and quantity. Or we freeze, literally dead in our tracks, victimized by our own analysis-paralysis. Activation flies over the top or plummets to new lows for hiding, attention hones in on what will be lost, and we adopt an attitude of "I don't want to" or "I won't." Sometimes it's both. We have *will*, all right. And it's powerful. The power of triple-A alignment to not do something can rival its power to move us to engage in difficult endeavors.

We end up on the wrong curve! In some instances, we assume the ready-for-battle stance. We grit our teeth, narrow our eyes to glare skeptically, and we might even polish our fangs so we can hold on tight to what we might lose—a position, a process, a location, an image we have of ourselves, a lifestyle, or a way of doing things. We launch a full defense even when we weren't really fond of the anticipated lost items the day before. With our mental defenses kicking in, we forget that the roof on the house we just sold always leaked during the March thaw. Or, after being redeployed to a new project, you idealize the team and boss you left despite the fact that you had complained about them incessantly for the previous year. Other situations stimulate a burning desire to seek safety. We bury our heads in what I call the "ostrich stance" or we hide under a pile of leaves, as they say in Maine. We seek escape from changes that have the power to heal us and to make us do and feel better.

We end up in the Zone for holding on for dear life, clinging even to things that aren't the best for us and holding on to idealized memories as we sing about the way we once were. We respond to change as a threat when in reality, change is often the very thing that can move people and groups to the next level, ensuring survival and the ability to grow and thrive as individuals, teams, organizations, and cultures. Worse yet, our enmeshment in the "no-change zone" creates the very result we most feared—our unraveling. This is the opposite of the change Zone where letting go, looking forward, creating heartfelt meaning, and reaching out for a new vision can get you moving forward. Walking a step at a time and with your eyes wide open to the real deal, including all of its risks, can move you forward with courage and commitment.

The need to adapt to change and to learn to thrive with stress during these times of constant low-level alert is urgent. Now, more than ever, it is critical that we learn to connect fully with life events, to bring meaning and joy to each day, to live with integrity and a passion for human life, and to teach others to do the same. In some instances, it's the difference between living in misery and regret versus living a life of mastery, recognition, and pride. In other situations, accessing your inner resources to bring your strength of *will* to live fully, in sickness and in health, can make the difference between life and death.

If you want to engage with life, you will want to build personally meaningful desire. To convince yourself that living in the arc of engagement is worthwhile, you will do best if you make a case for yourself. Focus on what you have to gain—a vision of how things will be better and of how proud you will feel when you have connected with and mastered the current challenge—to get geared up to *"really do it."* So why bother?

First, the Bottom Line—The Results Are Superb

When we're in the arc of engagement, we create personal, team, and organizational bests. We might be immersed in dialogue, making a speech to hundreds, solving a simple problem, crafting a complex strategy, getting a flu shot, recovering from surgery, running a "Race for the Cure" 5 K in honor of a friend who has passed on to other fields, or running for our lives in a disaster.

I'm not suggesting that you will always win. But you will do your best with the resources available. Some days you will have more to bring to the table than others. It depends on your physical health, the weather, your equipment, the competitive field, and the people available for a team effort. When you're in the Zone, you direct all of your A^3 resources to gain a maximum return on your investment.

Whether it's called "the Zone," "flow," "optimal experience," "primal leadership," or "self-actualization," personal, team, and organizational bests have been reported in research and recorded in case studies and anecdotal recollections. The results cross fields from sales, manufacturing, the defense industry, law, financial services, medicine, the military, sports, leadership challenges at work and at home, where parenting can spiral even the best of us into tailspins of o-Zonal highs and lows.

The thinking, decisions, problem-solving process and solutions, products, service, sales, leadership, team membership contributions, healing, communication, and relationships that we create when we are genuinely engaged and in the Zone are a far cry from the substandard performance that we put out at other times when we're half-present, holding back, resisting, or disengaging. The great feelings and pride of the Zone are a sharp contrast to the misery and self-doubt of the o-Zone.

The descriptions that my clients and seminar participants have reported of their achievements when they've been firmly planted in the arc of engagement of the Zone are dramatically different from the results that they have endured in the disengaged tails of the o-Zone. Across the board, from competitive business situations, sporting events, negotiation tables at work or home, and dealing with painful medical treatment regimens, they have achieved superior results when their 3 A's were aligned for the challenge. Their results in the o-Zone paled in comparison, ranging from ho-hum mediocrity to disastrous calamity. The results cut across life's fields.

Results in the Zone	Results in the O-Zone
Scores improve—whether it was an increase in sales of products or services, legal cases won, improved patient care, or successful implementation of competitive strategy. Improved scores lead to improved confidence, further escalating scores.	Falling scores seen in floundering sales, cases lost, loss of preferred supplier status and other organizational quality awards, and inability to effectively execute (or even try) strategic plans that remained nothing more than dreams, further decimating confidence to turn it around.
Improved speed with accuracy. Turn-around time decreases for delivery of products, services, projects, and proposals, leading to positive partnerships with customers, vendors, contractors, bosses.	Speed slows and deadlines are not met or speed quickens and errors abound. Delivery times extend beyond projections, spiraling people into the o-Zone on other projects at work and at home, alienating customers, contractors, employers, family.
Improved accuracy whether it was for performing surgery, preparing a proposal or financial analysis, or responding to questions as an expert witness.	Errors and miscalculations abound and can spiral out of control in a variety of settings from the Operating Room, Courtroom, fields of sport, or commuter roads and rails.

Results in the Zone	Results in the O-Zone
Improved precision, especially for activities requiring fine motor coordination or precise collaboration.	Accidents abound on roadways, in the home, and at work where injuries can cost a company dearly.
Thriving during times of stress and chaos, whether it was health, family matters, or the stock market that seemed to be falling.	Barely surviving, holding on for dear life, flying by the seat of your pants, during periods of minor and significant stress, and loss.
Conflict is accurately identified and addressed, enabling a couple, family, team, or entire organization to work effectively and move on.	Conflict is avoided, simmering and draining energy as it festers, creating team dissension and compromising group effectiveness in sports, at work, and at home. OR Conflict erupts as rage in excess for the reality of the situation and is often directed at the wrong person—rage on the road, at work, at home, and on fields and sidelines of sporting events ensues. People scream at their innocent dogs or the customer service person or referee just trying to do a job.
Productivity and effectiveness are high at work and at home. People work smarter and feel better.	Inefficiencies abound as people work harder, duplicate efforts, or do the wrong things for diminishing returns.
People stay, creating a culture of team. Turnover at work, on sports teams, and on the home front is low. People want to partner with you and be on your team—as customers, vendors, and employees.	People flee and alert others to avoid you. Turnover spirals as people dash for the revolving door at work, sport, in relationships, and in families. Customers, employees, and family members leave.

Results in the Zone	Results in the O-Zone
Thinking is clear, creative, strategic, open-minded, and systems-oriented. People open their eyes and minds to "see out of the box" to "think out of the box." People think straight and see options to forge solutions that are strategic and extraordinary.	Thinking is muddled, cloudy, mundane, within the box, burdened by stupor or "stress makes you stupid" disconnects. Narrowly focused and narrow-minded thinking results in ordinary solutions that keep people in their comfort zone. It's business as usual.
Emotional intelligence soars. Awareness of your own emotions and the emotions of others around you improves and so does awareness of your impact on others. The ability to see other perspectives and to take the role of another, also known as empathy, improves.	Emotional imbecility reigns. Insulated from awareness of activation, unaware that there are other perspectives or that other perspectives might have value, and entrenched in assumptive beliefs that remain unexamined, individuals and groups are divorced from their own emotions as well as the emotional climate around them.
Individuals and groups experience the full gamut of emotions appropriately.	The range of emotions is constricted in individuals and groups, often restricted to variations on mad and sad.
Strategic proactive actions. Committed people direct the power of their A^3 wills to move themselves and others to take new goal-directed actions that move them forward. It's thoughtful—beliefs are examined rather than adopted blindly. Attention is consciously focused. Actions in pursuit of strategy are considered	Impulsive reactive actions often leading to hoof-in-mouth disorder. Beliefs are adopted with a narrow perspective and thoughtlessly acted out without consideration to the impact. At one extreme, people throw all caution to the wind and engage in "crimes of impulse." At the other, people follow lemming-like in frenzied

Results in the Zone	Results in the O-Zone
and modified to maximize positive and minimize negative impact. People walk-the-talk with commitment.	fanaticism. Or they freeze in fright. Paralyzed by analysis or fear of failure, they never harness their 3 A's to implement strategies, even those to which they have committed verbally.
People stay healthier, get injured less frequently, heal faster, and turn physical injuries, traumatic experiences, and life-threatening illness into experiences from which they learn and gain meaning to pursue life with gusto, playing to win. Organizations become strong while still principle-driven.	People get sick more often, are injured more frequently, heal more slowly and less thoroughly, and seem to never move beyond life's curve balls of illness, injury, and emotional trauma that keep them on the sidelines of life, playing not-to-lose. Organizations become weak, easy prey for competitors.
Communication is clear.	Communication is muddled and muddy.
People work through and move on from traumatic events. By connecting, they allow themselves downtime to grieve losses and feel genuine sadness. This allows the person to move on. This, in turns, can free those who have been traumatized to experience a wide range of emotions and experiences.	People dissociate from painful experiences, including diagnoses and traumatic memories. In the avoidance Zone, they are overcome with the agitation that results from holding off the 3 A's that are optimal for grieving. Some check out and others burn out from sustained agitation. Emotions are constricted. Anxiety, irritability, and displaced aggression or depression and apathy can ensue.

Results in the Zone	Results in the O-Zone
Individuals, teams, organizations, entire cultures can rise to the occasion when real danger threatens them.	Exhausted by living in the self-protective o-Zone, people see danger where none exists or exert energy to hold reality at bay. People are not ready when true danger presents itself.
Moods soar. Joy, satisfaction, pride, accountability, and self-respect abound.	Moods plummet. Sadness and despair, embarrassment and shame, anger and rage, frustration and anxiety prevail.

Sometimes the Results Move Beyond Great— They're Miraculous

People like you and me have learned to direct their 3 A's to prevail over challenges that have shaken their worlds. These have included entire organizations whose lifespans were in jeopardy due to decimating internal forces like poor management or inadequate attention to competitive forces that blindsided them, threats capable of eliminating a front-running company and wreaking lifestyle-shattering layoffs on loyal employees. The 3 A's have provided an assist to teams and organizations that learned to face lifelong competitors that were slowly gnawing away at them and industrial giants that threatened to gobble them up.

There was an opposite extreme that was the experience of those who could not get it together to face their situation. With excessively low energy, their approach to perceived threat and the feelings of inadequacy that it engendered was a downward spiral to the fright-flight-freeze zone. They buried their heads under the sand or under the covers even in response to perceived catastrophes that they had blown out of proportion. It could be a look or tone or the news of the day or market jitters that sent them into an o-Zonal spin. When it came to their real challenges, they often ran the other way, either underestimating the severity of the problem, denying that it existed at all, or convincing themselves that they had mono and would have to deal with it tomorrow. At either extreme, activation along with attention and attitude were not good matches for confronting the challenge head-on.

Turning Objects That Make Us Perspire into Objects of Desire
Connecting to the Real Deal

When the 3 A's are out of whack, we create our own sensations of threat. Our own assumptions, endless mulling of thoughts, jumping to conclusions, and responding to media-spun images of catastrophe, disaster, market crashes, and dangerous weather patterns as if they lurked outside the door can be enough to send us running for cover or ready to fight. We overinterpret other people's responses as an affront to our self-image or as attempts to steal something from us, like breathing space on the roadways of life. We perceive a look, a tone, a question as a threat to our competence as a negotiator, loyal employee, leader, parent, manager, team member, salesperson, public speaker, or friend. We interpret our kids' age-appropriate independence as an insult to our parenting. Market projections cause high-activation jitters, shortsightedness, and a play-not-to-lose stance that spur us to download stock portfolios, causing the downspin we feared. A colleague's advanced degree engenders self-doubt, so you talk about the promotion you've received that outshines his modest position. The driver in the lane next to ours endangers our ability to get to work on time. Their newest sports car, a lifelong object of your desire, sends you into the o-Zone of inadequacy and anger. Taken to its extreme, during long sieges of traffic when activation rides high, we retaliate in rage against the other drivers who are out to rob us of our lifestyle. And then we rationalize our behaviors, claiming that the other person made us do it, that they deserved it. And we really believe our personal version of the truth. Just like Tom, it's our way or the highway.

Tom, the attorney who traveled in the left lane of life, related one instance in which he got so enraged with how another commuter was driving that he missed his exit.

"I was really late for a meeting with a new prospective client. Naturally the traffic was horrible. You know the deal, everyone volleying for road space. This one guy had been tailgating me when the traffic was moving. And he was right on my rear when it turned bumper-to-bumper. He just wouldn't give up. So when he tried to pull into the left lane to pass me, I beat him out for it. I was still congratulating myself and laughing as I looked at the poor guy in my rearview mirror when I realized that I was in the wrong lane. I needed to be way over in the right to exit.

Needless to say, I didn't make it. I think some of the other drivers were out of whack with their A's too because they defended their turf tooth and nail. No one would let me in. Actually, they had probably seen my aggressive tactics and were giving me some of my own medicine. That's what I would've done. By the time I got over to the right, I was two exits down and I ended up being late, angry, sweating bullets, and way too jacked up for my meeting with the new client."

I could see Tom sweating as he retold this haunting tale. As he proceeded, I knew why. It got worse.

"Once I circled back, snagged a parking spot, and raced to the new client's office, I was soaked in sweat, breathing fast and totally out of focus. Looking back on it now, knowing what I do, I would call to say I couldn't make it. But no, I stormed in, bellowed my name out to the assistant, and paced in front of the door until it opened.

When it did, I stopped dead in my tracks. It was my worst nightmare. There in front of me, at close range, was the guy in my rearview mirror. Here he was on his own turf, smiling so slyly that it looked like a sneer. I was dumbfounded. Needless to say, I didn't land the account. That night

I had a mega cardiac arrest worrying about how I was going to tell people that I had blown it. When the truth did come out, I had a hard time living it down.

Now I know it was my own 3 A's that made me late and knocked me out of the game. Quite honestly, I think the reason that guy got me so agitated is that he was driving the sports car I've always wanted."

From Tom's perspective, his livelihood and his self-image were on the line when he was behind the wheel. When Tom learned to review the elements of his selective attention and the assumptions that he layered on top of these, he was able to see the situation differently and to align his 3 A's for driving thoughtfully. It also helped when he learned to turn on his favorite slower-paced blues in bumper-to-bumper situations, an attention-captivating rhythm that kept his activation in check. Most importantly, Tom reaffirmed his commitment to saving for his kids' college tuitions, framed as a more valuable investment than any roadster.

Just like Tom, without even realizing it, we respond to neutral situations like our lives are on the line when it's really our sense of self that's under attack. We regress to self-preservation mode where we fight, flee, freeze in fear, or feed, soothing ourselves. And most often we don't realize that many of our actions are reactions to attributions that we have made based on our baseline activation, attention, attitude, and our propensity to make certain attributions due to our characteristic A^3 style. Responding to the uncertainty of novelty, change, difference, and the unknown as if they could destroy us, we launch an unconscious defense of our valor.

Even in dire circumstances, I have seen clients turn stressors that had destroyed their desire to live into manageable challenges that affirmed their zest for living including ski accidents, potentially fatal diagnoses, child abuse that most could not imagine, financial and organizational losses. In reality the things that happen, including our own thoughts, are neutral. It's how we respond with our 3 A's to stressors that determines our evaluation of their quality and, therefore, our responses—our thoughts, feelings, and behaviors. Because the 3 A's are both cause and effect of the attributions that we make, learning to identify and adapt these three essential elements holds the power to turn life around. The power is within you—in your *Winner's Way*. And that, as you know, is as straightforward as the 3 A's.

It Feels Great—Even When It's Hard Work

No matter what the challenge, the feelings of the Zone contrast sharply with those that people have experienced when they have spiraled into the o-Zone. Functioning in the Zone feels great.

> Evidence of the positive feelings that accompany total engagement is available in the sports psychology research where confidence is the most frequently reported feeling when athletes are competing at their top level across sports. Accounts of individuals and groups who have faced extreme stress and of people who have battled rivals including sports opponents, business foes, Courtroom competitors, as well as life-altering illness and disability bring to life the positive feelings of functioning in the Zone. People fighting for their lives or pushing through grueling physical therapy or sport events might not report feelings of joy. However, they do report feeling confident, assured, connected, committed, and powerful when they are genuinely engaged in the Zone. The pride that follows this type of experience is a stark contrast to the chagrin, embarrassment, shame, or regret that we experience from a half-baked effort in a one-time event or a life half-lived.

Here are some of the words people have used to describe their experiences when they were in the Zone versus in the o-Zone. Which column sounds better to you?

Feelings "In the Zone"	Feelings "In the o-Zone"
Awesome	Awful
Mastery, masterful	Miserable
Terrific	Terrible
Self-confident	Riddled with self-doubt
Believing in my team	Doubting my team
Courageous, brave—even when they felt fear	Scared, frightened, timid Paralyzed by fear
Full steam ahead	Running on empty
No holds barred	Withholding
Passionate, inspired	Apathetic, disenchanted
Committed	Disengaged
Genuine, real	Fake, imposterlike
Pride, relish, satisfaction	Shame, regret, embarrassed, humiliated
Flying, soaring	Down in the dumps
Powerful	Weak, helpless
Proactive, meaningful, valuable	Reactive, meaningless, devalued
Appropriate sadness, grieving	Avoidant, apathetic, complacent, mad instead of sad—irritable
Appropriate anger expressed constructively at the right people in the right amount at the right time	Unbridled anger, chronically agitated, on edge, furious for no reason, explosive at the wrong time
Letting go and moving forward Thriving	Holding on for dear life Surviving

It's Contagious, So You Can Get Other People in the Zone Too

How many times have you sat in a meeting where the emotional and physical energy started to spiral—either down to doldrums level or up to frenetic frenzy? In a lemming-like phenomenon, you find yourself following the pack over the edge to a hyped-up dizziness or into a hypnotic daze right into the o-Zone. The quality of decisions falls into abysmal dullness as creative thinking slips away. The ability to reason takes a back seat as groupthink based on narrow minds and narrow vision reigns. And the beat really does go on, like the bouncing ball, touching everyone in the meeting, spreading like the plague.

The 3 A's are contagious. On good days, we catch the good Zonal vibes and on bad days, we catch the o-Zonal stuff. Group morale, moods, and emotional climate can sour or soar depending on whether people know how to match the 3 A's to the moment. Because of their highly contagious nature, the 3 A's exert an impact on decision making, creative thinking, strategic planning, individual and group motivation, and the ability to craft a meaningful vision that can move people to make strategic changes. This, of course, affects the bottom line in life. If you want to take control of a group's emotional climate, the 3 A's hold a key. You can willfully move yourself from victimized lemming to visionary leader. And you can take others along with you. The great part is that it's still as simple as 3 A's.

We witness the ill-fated power of triple-A contagion too often in the news. Unbridled rage between hockey dads where one father, over-activated in response to watching his kid's practice, narrows in on the comments and reactions of another father and lays a bed of negative assumptions on his constricted view. Interpreting the other man's words and actions as a personalized attack, he returns to the rink to pick a fight with the other father. Ultimately he kills the other father in front of the children.

In other instances we read of teenagers caught up in the activation of computer video games that get them so jacked up that they can barely see straight. Pumped up in fight-or-flight mode, they pick a battle with another young teen, also jacked up from attending to these extreme stimuli. Both of them are unable to think clearly, and they find themselves caught up in the contagion of the 3 A's run amok. Violence more extreme than most of us ever dreamed of in our high-school years ensues—school violence, Internet café murders, cheerleader murders, family violence, and sports parent homicides. Those are the 3 A's gone far astray. It's time to get in touch with and get a grip on our A's—to heal ourselves and those around us who suffer from the ill effects of the 3 A's run amok. It's time to access our *Winner's Way* to get in the Zone across the lifespan.

Really Do It! Why Bother?

To access your 3 A's, I'm asking you to commit to making changes in how you see yourself as well as the things that happen to you and how you respond.

So you tell me—what's in it for you? Why bother?

What are the experiences at home that you would like to improve by learning to connect fully with them in the Zone? Think of those times when things were not clicking, when you felt out of synch and out of sorts in the o-Zone. Picture it vividly. What are the short-term and long-term gains that you can achieve in your relationships with family and friends by genuinely connecting?

What's your vision of how things could be once you learn to live in the Zone?

How about work? Whether you work outside of or inside your home, where household maintenance along with managing kids and finances crowd your plate, what experiences would you like to turn around, challenges where you often feel out of synch? Is it communicating effectively to delegate, run meetings, call customers, or service providers, confront someone else in a constructive manner, or connect fully to inspire someone else to pursue projects or homework with passion?

What are the results and feelings you'd like to achieve and how do these differ from when you're fumbling, mumbling, or hollering in the o-Zone?

You Can Do It!—You Are Doing It!

The Winner's Way provides a simple system for learning to succeed and still be true to your virtues. With *The Winner's Way,* you can consciously choose to pursue a vision that fits your passion and principles. You can chart your course and go for it *willfully,* committing the power of your activation, attention, and attitude to create the best outcome possible. You can reap the benefits. And you can enjoy the ride.

I know that living in the Zone isn't a choice. It's a way of life.

You can live there, too.

If your attention wanders no matter how hard you try to concentrate, I want to ease your mind: You *can* refocus, and you can stay focused.

If you worry that events tend to overwhelm you and send your energy levels spiraling down or over the edge, I want to reassure you: You *can* deal with them.

If you wonder whether you hold the courage to maneuver your way through tough times, guided by your inner principles, and come out on top, I want to assure you: You *do.*

You have *The Winner's Way.* With your winner's will, you can access it and put it to use to change your life. But only if you want to. It is still as simple as those 3 strategic A's.

Postoperative Debriefing

- The results of living in the Zone impact bottom-line results and feelings and improve our ability to communicate effectively, heal optimally, and deal with stress. The results can be miraculous.
- Living in the o-Zone, on the other hand, can be disastrous, sometimes even deadly.
- Effective leadership, team membership, family relations, and teamwork are positively affected when we function in the Zone.
- At work and at home, learning to connect fully with the 3 A's in the Zone improves individual and group intelligence of intellect and emotions.
- Living in the Zone has powerful positive effects on other people—and it's contagious!
- To be in the Zone or to be in the o-Zone—the choice is yours. Make your own case for why *you want* to bother. Then set the conditions to get out there to *Really Do It*. Recognize and celebrate every step along your path. You will be living your journey in the arc of engagement. Long may you run—I hope to see you out there.

Appendix

Relaxation from Your Fingers to Your Toes

You can use this relaxation to set the stage for the exercises in the book. And you can use it for your A^3-relaxation-and-visualization training, though not, of course, if you are training while you are stuck in traffic. That would plunge your activation well below the green curve for connecting with driving, literally putting you asleep at the wheel.

As you progress through this relaxation, flex each muscle or group to the point that you feel tension. You are not striving for muscle spasms. This is not a competition. In one corporate setting, a participant who competed in bicycle races and triathlons in his spare time (when he wasn't working 70 hours a week) determined that he would be the best relaxer in the group. Determined to win, he did indeed prove himself to be the best tenser. And he demonstrated this to all of his colleagues when he tensed the muscles in his back, one of his primary spots for activation, so tight that he caused a muscle spasm. Flex to the point that you feel the tension—spasms are not the goal. Hold your breath slightly—this is not hyperventilation time. It's all about moderation and learning to take control of the muscle tensions and relaxation that can ground you to immerse you in the arc of engagement.

Take three deep breaths. If it's possible, breathe in through your nose and out through your mouth.

Curl your fingers into fists and feel the tension in your hands and in your lower arms, extending from the tips of your fingers up to your shoulders. Now bend your arms, pulling your fists up to your shoulders, flexing your biceps and lower arms. Be aware of the tension that runs throughout your arms, from your shoulders to the tips of your fingers. Picture your thought balloon shaped like a huge black trash bag hovering over your head. Fill it with the tension. It's time to *TRASHIT!* Hold on to the tension, take a deep breath in, and, as you slowly release the breath, let your arms drop gently back down to your sides and release your fingers. Breathe the tension out through your fingertips and release it into your thought balloon into the air— *TRASHIT!* Feel the strength flowing throughout your arms and hands as you breathe deeply. Insert this image of strength into your thought balloon, now shaped like your favorite carryon suitcase (make it the design and color of your own choice)—*PACKIT!* Be aware of your own power to adjust your physical energy, to control your activation with breathing, flexing, and releasing. Take three deep breaths.

Pull your shoulders up to your earlobes; scrunch your face up as if you're making a fist with your face. Notice the effect on your breathing. Take a breath in, hold on to the tension for a moment. Then load it into your *TRASHIT* balloon. As you breathe out slowly, release your face, drop your jaw slightly, lower your shoulders back to center, let your head sit strong atop your shoulders and release the *TRASHIT* balloon into space—you just *TRASHed IT!* Feel the effect on your breathing, which has become deep again. Take three deep breaths.

Move your focus down to your feet. Curl your toes under, burrowing them into the soles of your shoes. Feel the tension that shoots into your lower legs. Hold on to the tension for a count of three. Then breathe in deeply and quickly pile the tension into your trash bag. Breathe out, hurling the tension into the ozone and release your toes. Wiggle them while you flatten your feet out into paddles. Stretch your toes out as you keep your feet flat. Gently flex your calf muscles by pointing your toes toward your knees just until you feel the tension running from your knees down through your lower calves, through your soles and over the tops of your feet back up to your knees. Hold for a count of three, then breathe in deeply, hold for a moment as you load up the trash. As you breathe out, relax your legs and cast your tension off in that trash bag full of pressure. Take another three deep breaths as you enjoy your sensation of strength and relaxation.

Move the focus to your center. Take a deep breath then gently pull in on your stomach muscles. Notice the effect on your breathing. At the same time, tighten the muscles under your seat, the buttocks muscles and the upper leg muscles, just to the point where you feel the tightness. Feel the tension and your power to create and release it at will. Breathe in, hold for a quick three-count, and release the tension along with the breath. Notice the effect of releasing your center as your breath deepens. Take three slow, deep breaths and move your focus back to the central control, your shoulders and head.

Gently tip your head back and feel the tension in your neck, jaw, and skull. Clench your jaw slightly. Take a deep breath in and as you release it, release your jaw as you let your head drop to a centered, relaxed stance. Breathe deeply, releasing any tension that remains.

Feel the strength and your own power to choose and adjust your muscle tensions from your fingers to your toes. You're engaged in the arc. You're in the Zone.

Endnotes

Chapter 1—A Zone for All Seasons—And an O-Zone Too

1. R.B. Malmo, "Activation: A Neuropsychological Dimension," *Psychological Review*, 66 (1959): 367–386.
2. E.R. Kandel, J.H. Schwartz and T.M Jessel, eds., *Principles of Neural Science and Behavior*, 4th ed. (New York: McGraw-Hill, 2000).
3. M. Csikszentmihalyi and I. Csikszentmihalyi, eds., *Optimal Experience: Psychological Studies of Flow in Consciousness* (Cambridge: Cambridge University Press, 1988); G. Privette, "Peak Experience, Peak Performance, and Flow: A Comparative Analysis of Positive Human Experiences," *Journal of Personality and Social Psychology*, 45 (1983): 1361–1368.
4. Ibid.

Chapter 2—The Power of Will—It's As Simple As 3 A's

1. L. Bossolo, D. Bergantino, B. Lichtenstein, and M.Gutman, "Many Americans Still Feeling Effects of September 11th Are

Reexamining Their Priorities in Life." February 11, 2002 at *http://www.greenbergresearch.com/publications/press_releases/prstateofmin d021102.pdf*; cited in "Happiness from a Bottle—Depression on the Rise," *HR* Magazine, Society for Human Resource Management (SHRM), 5 (2002): 47.

2. C. Coffman and G. Gonzalez-Molina, *Follow This Path: How the World's Greatest Organizations Drive Growth by Unleashing Human Potential* (New York: Warner Books, 2002), 127–128.

3. G.E. Simon, C. Barber, H.G. Birnbaum, R.G. Frank, P.E. Greenberg, R.M. Rose, P. Wang, and R.C. Kessler, "Depression and Work Productivity: The Comparative Costs of Treatment Versus Nontreatment," *Journal of Occupational and Environmental Medicine*, 43 (2001): 2–9.

4. A.V. Carron, "Cohesiveness in Sport Groups: Interpretations and Considerations," *Journal of Sport Psychology*, 4 (1982):123–138; T. Pearce, *Leading Out Loud: The Authentic Speaker, the Credible Leader* (San Francisco: Jossey-Bass, 1995); Note 2.

5. R.S. Lazarus and S. Folkman, *Stress, Appraisal, and Coping*. (New York: Springer Verlag, 1984).

6. H. Selye, *Stress Without Distress* (New York: Lippincott, 1974); H. Selye, *The Stress of Life*, 2d ed. (New York: McGraw-Hill, 1978); A. Ellis, "The Revised ABCs of Rational-Emotive Therapy (RET)," *Journal of Rational-Emotive and Cognitive Behavior Therapy*, 9, no. 3 (1991): 139–172.

7. M.B. Andersen and J. M. Williams, "Psychological Risk Factors and Injury Prevention," in *Psychology of Sport Injury*, ed. J. Heil (Champaign, IL: Human Kinetics, 1993) 49–57.

8. R. Lazarus, "Universal Antecedents of the Emotions," in *The Nature of Emotion: Fundamental Questions*, ed. P.E. Ekman and R.J. Davidson (New York: Oxford, 1994), 163–175.

9. F. Ebb, B. Fosse, and J. Kander, *Chicago* (1975) based on the play *Chicago* by Maurine Dallas Watkins (1926).
10. Privette, *Journal of Personality and Social Psychology*, 45: 1361–1368; S.A. Jackson and M. Csikszentmihalyi, *Flow In Sports: The Keys to Optimal Experiences and Performances* (Champaign, Ill: Human Kinetics, 1999).
11. K. Ravizza, "Peak Experiences in Sport," *Journal of Humanistic Psychology*, 17 (1977): 35–40.

Chapter 3—Activation–Keep Breathing and Sweat the Big Stuff

1. Malmo, *Psychological Review*, 66 (See Chap. 1, note 1).
2. D.M. Landers and S.H. Boutcher, "Arousal-Performance Relationships," in *Applied Sport Psychology: Personal Growth to Peak Performance*, 2d ed., ed. J.M. Williams (Mountain View, CA: Mayfield, 1993), 170–184.
3. H. Benson, *The Relaxation Response* (New York: Morrow, 1975); R. Eliot and D. Breo, *Is It Worth Dying For?* (New York: Bantam Books, 1987).
4. C. Maslach and M. Leiter, *The Truth About Burnout: How Organizations Cause Personal Stress and What to Do About It* (San Franscisco: Jossey-Bass, 1997).

Chapter 4—Attention—What You See Is What You Get

1. R.M. Nideffer, "Test of Attentional and Interpersonal Style," *Journal of Personality and Social Psychology*, 34, no. 3 (1976): 394–404.

2. Ibid.

3. Ibid.; D.M. Landers, M.Q. Wang, and P. Courtet, "Peripheral narrowing among experienced and inexperienced rifle shooters under low- and high-stress conditions," *Research Quarterly,* 56 (1985): 57–70.

4. Note 1; A. Freud, *The Ego and the Mechanisms of Defense (The Writings of Anna Freud, Vol 2)* (New York: International Universities Press, 1971); C. Argyris, *Overcoming Organizational Defenses* (Needham, MA: Pearson Allyn & Bacon, 1990).

Chapter 5—Say It When You Believe It and Believe It When You Say It

1. M.O. Burns and M.E. Seligman, "Explanatory Style Across the Life Span: Evidence for Stability Over 52 Years," *Journal of Personality and Social Psychology,* 56, no. 3 (1989): 471–477.

2. S.B. Simon, *Values Clarification: A Handbook of Practical Strategies for Teachers and Students* (Hart Publishing Co., 1972).

3. M.E. Seligman and J.M. Weiss, "Coping Behavior: Learned Helplessness, Physiological Change, and Learned Inactivity," *Behaviour Research and Therapy,* 18, no. 5 (1980): 459–512.

4. A. Ellis and A.R. Harper, *Reason and Emotion in Psychotherapy* (Oxford, England: Lyle Stuart, 1962).

5. Ibid; A.T. Beck, "Thinking and Depression, II: Theory and Therapy," *Archives of General Psychiatry,* 10 (1964): 561–571.

6. J. Collins and J. Porras, *Built to Last: Successful habits of visionary companies* (New York: Harper Collins, 1994).

7. K. Patterson, J Grenny, R. McMillan, A. Switzler, and S.R. Covey. *Crucial Conversations: Tools for talking when stakes are high* (New York, NY: McGraw-Hill/Contemporary Books, 2002); Pearce, *Leading Out Loud* (1995).

8. J. Kouzes and B. Posner, *The Leadership Challenge: How to keep getting extraordinary things done in organizations* (San Francisco, CA: Jossey-Bass, 1995); T. Pearce and D. Pottruck, *Clicks and Mortar: Passion-driven growth in an Internet driven world* (San Francisco, CA: Jossey-Bass, 2001).
9. V. Frankl, *Man's Search for Meaning* (New York: Washington Square, 1963).
10. J. McCain and M. Salter, *Faith of My Fathers* (New York: Random House, 1999).
11. D.C. McClelland, *Human Motivation* (Cambridge, England: Cambridge University Press, 1987); W. Schutz, *FIRO: A Three-dimensional Theory of Interpersonal Behavior* (Oxford, England: Rinehart, 1958).
12. C. Peterson, M. Seligman, and G. Vaillant, "Pessimistic explanatory style as a risk factor for physical illness: a thirty-five year longitudinal study, *Journal of Personality and Social Psychology*, 55 (1988): 23–27; M. Seligman and P. Schulman, "Explanatory Style as a Predictor of Productivity," *Journal of Personality and Social Psychology*, 50, no. 4 (1986): 832–838.

Chapter 6—The Inner Circles—The Brain-Brawn Teamwork of the 3 A's

1. Lazarus and Folkman, *Stress, Appraisal, and Coping* (see Chap. 2, note 5).
2. B.S. McEwen, "Sex, Stress, and the Hippocampus: Allostasis, Allostatic Load, and the Aging Process," *Neurobiology of Aging*, 23, no. 5 (2002): 921–939.
3. Benson, *The Relaxation Response* (1975); M. Murphy and S. Donovan. *The Physical and Psychological Effects of Meditation: A Review of Contemporary Meditation Research with a Comprehensive Bibliography 1931–1988* (San Rafael: Esalen Institute, 1988).

4. R. Kipling, *"If—"* in *R. Kipling Complete Verse: Definitive Edition* (New York: Anchor Books (Reprint Edition), 1989), 578.

5. L.Cahill, R. Babinsky, and J.L. McGaugh, "The Amygdala and Emotional Memory," *Nature,* 377, no. 6547 (1995): 295–96.

6. D.T. Stuss and D.F. Benson, "Neuropsychological Studies of the Frontal Lobes," *Psychological Bulletin,* 95, no. 1 (1984): 3–28; M.S. Gazzaniga, *The Social Brain: Discovering the Networks of the Mind* (New York: Basic Books, 1985).

7. P. Vendrell, C. Junque, J. Pujol, and M.A. Jurado, et.al., "The Role of Prefrontal Regions in Stroop Task," *Neuropsychologia,* 33, no. 3 (1995): 341–352; D.G. Amen, *Healing ADD: The Breakthrough Program that Allows You to See and Heal the Six Types of ADD* (New York: Berkley Books, 2001).

8. P.W. Burgess, E. Veitch, A. DeLacy Costello, and T. Shallice, "The Cognitive and Neuroanatomical Correlates of Multitasking," *Neuropsychologia* 38, no. 6 (2000): 848–863.

9. D. Goleman, *Emotional Intelligence: Why It Can Matter More Than IQ* (New York: Bantam, 1995), 24–29.

10. K. Ravizza, "Increasing Awareness for Sport Performance," in Williams, *Applied Sport Psychology,* 2d. ed., 148-157; D. Goleman, R. Boyzatis, A. McKee *Primal Leadership: Realizing the Power of Emotional Intelligence* (Boston: Harvard Business School, 2002), 13–14, 29, 45–48.

11. C.R. Knee, C. Neighbors, and N.A. Vietor, "Self-determination Theory as a Framework for Understanding Road Rage," *Journal of Applied Social Psychology,* 31, no. 5 (2001): 889-904.

12. M.I. Posner and M.E. Raichle, *Images of Mind* (New York: Scientific American Library, 1994); D. Amen, *Healing ADD* (2001), 62–63, 101-110, 269–270.

13. D.Q. Beversdorf, J.D. Hughes, B.A. Steinberg, L.D. Lewis, and K.M. Heilman, "Noradrenergic Modulation of Cognitive Flexibility in Problem Solving," *Neuroreport,* 10, no. 13 (1999): 2763–2767.

14. Jim Henson's *Sesame Street* character.
15. S. Iversen, I. Kupfermann, and E.R. Kandel, "Emotional States and Feelings," in Kandel, Schwartz, Jessell, *Principles of Neural Science,* 4th ed., 988–993.
16. Goleman, *Emotional Intelligence,* 13–29; Goleman, Boyzatis, McKee, *Primal Leadership: Realizing the Power of Emotional Intelligence,* 13–14, 29, 45–48.
17. W.T. Gallwey and R. Kriegel, *Inner Skiing* (New York: Random House, 1977).
18. L. Cahill, R. Haier, J. Fallon, M. Alkire, C. Tang, D. Keator, J. Wu, and J.L. McGaugh, "Amygdala activity at encoding correlated with long-term, free recall of emotional information," *Proceedings of the National Academy of Sciences,* 93 (1996): 8016–8021.
19. S. Iversen, L. Iversen, and C.B. Saper, "The Autonomic Nervous System and the Hypothalamus," in Kandel, Schwartz, Jessell, *Principles of Neural Science,* 4th ed., 961–981.
20. Note 2.
21. B.S. McEwen, B.S. McEwen, and E.N. Lasley. *The End of Stress As We Know It* (Washington, D.C.: Joseph Henry Press, 2002); B.S. McEwen and T. Seeman, "Protective and Damaging Effects of Mediators of Stress: Elaborating and testing the concepts of allostasis and allostatic load," *Annals of the New York Academy of Sciences.* 896 (1999): 30–47.
22. C. Peterson and M.E. Seligman, "Causal Explanations as a Risk Factor for Depression," *Psychological Review,* 91, no. 3 (1984): 347–374; C. Peterson, S.F. Maier, M.E. Seligman, *Learned Helplessness: A Theory for the Age of Personal Control* (London: Oxford University Press, 1993).
23. Notes 2 and 21.
24. H.M. Praag, "Serotonin Disturbances and Suicide Risk," *Crisis,* 21, no. 4 (2000): 160–162.

25. C. Petibois, G. Cazorla, J-R. Poortmans, and G. Deleris, "Biochemical Aspects of Overtraining in Endurance Sports," *Sports Medicine,* 32, no. 13 (2002): 867–878.

26. Benson, *The Relaxation Response* (1975).

27. J.M. Cackowski and J.L. Nasar, "The Restorative Effects of Roadside Vegetation: Implications for Automobile Driver Anger and Frustration," *Environment and Behavior,* 35, no. 6 (2003): 736–751.

28. H. Glaubman, et. al., "The Effect of Presleep Focal Attention Load on Subsequent Sleep Patterns," *Psychophysiology,* 16, no. 5 (1979): 467–470.

29. D.B. Givens. *Love-Signals: How to attract a mate.* New York, NY: Random House (1983); D. Givens site at *http://members.aol.com/nonverbal2 /nvcom.htm*

30. H. Benson, J.F. Beary, and M.P. Carol, "The relaxation response," *Psychiatry,* 37 (1974): 37–46.

31. H. Benson, "The Relaxation Response: Its Subjective and Objective Historical Precedents and Physiology," *Trends in Neuroscience,* 6, no. 7 (1983): 281–284.

Chapter 7—All Together Now—The Arc of Engagement

1. Chapter 3, note 1; Y.L. Hanin, "A Study of Anxiety in Sports," in *Sport Psychology: An Analysis of Athlete Behavior,* ed. W. Straub (Ithaca: Mouvement, 1978), 236–256.

2. C. Hull, *Principles of behavior* (Oxford, England: Appleton-Century, 1943).

3. A. Maslow, *Motivation and Personality* (Oxford, England: 1954).

4. Anderson and Williams, in Heil, *Psychology of Sport Injury* (see Chap. 2, note 7).

5. R.M. Yerkes and J.D. Dodson, "The Relation of Strength of Stimulus to Rapidity of Habit Formation," *Journal of Comparative Neurology & Psychology,* 18 (1908) 459–482.

6. Y.L. Hanin, "Individual Zones of Optimal Functioning," in *Emotions in Sport,* ed. Y.L. Hanin (Champaign, IL: Human Kinetics, 2000), 67.

7. D.C. McClelland, *The Achieving Society* (Princeton: Van Nostrand, 1961); Note 3.

8. M. Buckingham and C. Coffman, *First Break All The Rules: What the World's Greatest Managers Do Differently* (New York: Simon & Schuster, 1999); J. Kouzes and B. Posner, *Encouraging the Heart: A leader's guide to rewarding and recognizing others* (San Franscisco: Jossey-Bass, 1999).

9. Landers and Boutcher in Williams, *Applied Sports Psychology:* 176–182; Y.L. Hanin, "Individual Zones of Optimal Functioning," in Hanin, *Emotions in Sport,* 65–89.

10. J. Fazey and L. Hardy, *The Inverted-U Hypothesis: A catastrophe for sport psychology?* BASS Monograph1 (Leeds, U.K.: White Line Press, 1988), cited in Hanin, *Emotions in Sport,* 97.

11. L. Hardy, "A Catastrophe Model of Performance in Sport," in *Stress and Performance in Sport,* ed. J.G. Jones and L. Hardy (Chichester, U.K.: Wiley): 81–106.

12. Csikszentmihalyi and Csikszentmihalyi, *Optimal Experience:* 30-32; P. Brill and D. Freigang, "Flow States in Training and Competition in Competitive Swimmers," *Journal of Applied Sport Psychology,* 8, S158, (1996).

13. Note 9.

14. Ibid.

15. Goleman, *Emotional Intelligence: Why It Can Matter More Than IQ* (1995); Note 9.

Chapter 8—Basic Training—"Mad Dog" Goes to Court

1. J.O. Prochaska, *Systems of Psychotherapy: A Transtheoretical Analysis* (Oxford, U.K.: Dorsey, 1979).
2. A.T. Beck, *Cognitive Therapy and Emotion* (International Universities Press, 1975); A. Ellis and R. Grieger, *Handbook of Rational-Emotive Therapy,* (Springer, 1977).

Chapter 9—Get with It—Activation Strategies

1. W. James, *Principles of Psychology* (New York: Holt and Company, 1890); –, *The Varieties of Religious Experience,* (New York: Modern Library; reprint edition, 1994); R.M. Suinn, "Psychology and Sport Performance: Principles and Applications," in *Psychology in Sports: Methods and Applications,* ed. R.M. Suinn (Minneapolis: Burgess, 1980), 26–36.
2. L. Beamer and K. Abraham, *Let's Roll: Ordinary people, extraordinary courage* (Tyndale House, 2003).
3. J. Leeds, *The Power of Sound: How to manage your personal soundscape for a vital productive, and healthy life* (Rochester, VT: Healing Arts Press, 2001).
4. N. Cousins, *Anatomy of an Illness* (New York: Bantam, 1983).

Chapter 10—Get into It—Attention Strategies

1. Nideffer, *Journal of Personality and Social Psychology,* 34 (see Chap. 4, note 1).
2. Ibid.; R.M. Nideffer, *The Ethics and Practice of Applied Sport Psychology* (Ithaca, NY: Mouvement Publications, 1981); R.M.

Nideffer, "Concentration and Attention Control Training," in Williams, *Applied Sport Psychology*, 2d. ed., 243–261.
3. Note 1, 396, adapted with permission of R. Nideffer.
4. Note 2.
5. Kouzes and Posner, *Encouraging the Heart.*
6. Csikszentmihalyi and Csikszentmihalyi, *Optimal Experience,* p. 32; S.A. Jackson and H.W. Marsh, "Development and Validation of a Scale to Measure Optimal Exerience: The Flow State Scale," *Journal of Sport and Exercise Psychology,* 18 (1996): 17–35.

Chapter 11—Get over It!—Attitude Adjustment

1. P. Brill, "Strength Training for the Brain: A Look into Sports Psychology: What it is and what it can do for you," *The Sports Weekly* (Hanover, NH), February 19, 1996: 1,4.
2. R. Rosenthal and L. Jacobson, *Pygmalion in the Classroom: Teacher expectations and pupils' intellectual development* (New York: Holt, Rinehart & Winston, 1968); R. Rosenthal and D.B. Rubin, "Interpersonal expectancy effects: The first 345 studies," *The Behavioral and Brain Sciences* 3 (1978): 377–415.
3. Beck, *Cognitive Therapy and Emotion;* Ellis and Grieger, *Handbook of Rational-Emotive Therapy;* (see Chap. 8, note 2).
4. A. Bandura, "Self-efficacy: Toward a unifying theory of behavioral change," *Psychological Review* 8 (1977): 191–215.
5. P. Brill and D. Freigang, "Flow States in Training and Competition in Competitive Swimmers," *Journal of Applied Sport Psychology,* 8, S158, (1996).
6. Note 2.
7. Buckingham, Coffman, *First Break;* Kouzes, Posner, *Leadership Challenge,* 269–291.
8. W.T. Gallwey and R. Kriegel, *Inner Skiing* (New York: Random House, 1977).

9. Ellis and Harper, *Reason and Emotion in Psychotherapy* (1962).
10. Note 4.
11. Seligman and Weiss, *Behaviour Research and Therapy* 18: 459–512 (see Chap. 5, note 3).
12. D.C. McClelland, "Motives in the Personality Tradition," in McClelland, *Human Motivation*, 31–67; W. Schutz, *FIRO: A Three-dimensional Theory of Interpersonal Behavior* (Oxford, England: Rinehart, 1958).
13. Note 2.
14. Kouzes and Posner, *Leadership Challenge*, 91–148.
15. Simon, *Values Clarification* (1972).
16. Ibid.; C. Argyris and D.A. Schon, *Theory in Practice* (San Franscisco: Jossey-Bass, 1974); Collins and Porras, *Built to Last*; Kouzes and Posner, *Leadership Challenge*, 209–241.

Index

About the Author

Pamela Brill, Ed.D., is the founder and President of In the Zone, Inc., a firm providing customized consultation, coaching, assessment, and educational services. She consults with organizations in diverse fields—from the offices of the U.S. Senate to corporate boardrooms to world-renowned ski schools—and has provided private sports psychology consultations to athletes and coaches. Dr. Brill teaches individuals, teams, and entire organizations how to get "in the Zone" for generating personal and organizational bests on every field of life.